# 2018

# FANTASY FOOTBALL ALMANAC

## and

## DRAFT GUIDE

### First Edition

## Prepared By
## Sean Ryan of The Functional Sportsaholic

# Contents

# Introduction

People play fantasy sports for several reasons. Chief among them are winning money, acting out the fantasy of running a professional sports franchise and/or competing and hanging with friends.

For years, I participated in a fantasy football keeper league whose prize was a rotating trophy. Much like the NHL's Stanley Cup, the winner was able to display the cup for an entire year – sharing taunting pictures of the "Walter Peyton Cup" throughout the year for good measure. My late teens and twenties were devoted to one purpose – win the cup and obtain my rightful place in fantasy football glory.

Having spent over three decades playing fantasy sports, I've found that its various publications do a fine job in setting the top tiers (the first 2-3 rounds) of a draft. From a strategic point of view, you're not going to win or lose your league championship in these rounds. Your sole goal in rounds 1 and 2 is to find two top-tier players who score consistently. Based on who you obtain (RB/WR, WR/RB, QB/WR, etc.), the key to winning your league is adapting to the draft in rounds 3 through 10 and finding players that will pop in rounds 11 and beyond.

Having participated in a deep keeper league (we kept 10 players year-to-year), my draft strategy for a decade revolved around identifying emerging talent and undervalued players ready to break out. I've created several metrics, strategies and proprietary statistical information to help identify these difference makers. Since then, these tools have evolved into the most accurate fantasy football forecasting engine (and Fantasy Football Almanac) in the marketplace.

# Why Does This Matter?

Why are we better than a fantasy football magazine you can pick up from the grocery store? The Functional Sportsaholic has spent months crunching numbers to offer you the most accurate fantasy projections in the marketplace. We have immersed ourselves to provide game-by-game scores for all players. Instead of "Green Bay gives away the 3rd most points to Wide Receivers", The Functional Sportsaholic can tell you "Green Bay gives away the 4th most points to WR3s, the 10th most points to starting TEs and the 20th most points to RB1s." Nobody else offers these crucial details.

The 2018 Fantasy Football Almanac is the Inaugural issue of the most analytical, granular fantasy football information available. Unlike the popular websites (ESPN, NFL, etc.) which focus primarily on compiling player rankings, displaying average draft position and creating projections based on what we find to be misleading statistical analysis, The Functional Sportsaholic applies proprietary statistical information with industry-recognized player grading tools to provide the most accurate ranking information in the industry.

# Definitions:

**Fantasy Opportunity Ranking**: This is a proprietary tool of measurement created by The Functional Sportsaholic. This ranking measures a player's role in an offense and is useful to forecast players playing in a new offensive system as well as identifies sleepers and undervalued players for fantasy football and Daily Fantasy.

**Position Rankings:**
- **Running Back 1:** The player who will receive the bulk of rushing attempts throughout the season.
- **Wide Receiver 1:** The player who will receive the bulk of targets in a given season.

## Sleeper Classification:

- **Popular Sleepers:** The players that most publications and websites will label as a "sleeper" or "breakout" candidate. As fantasy football players know, these widely distributed player lists vary little from publication to publication. Thus, they aren't sleepers, they are more of a recommendation to be drafted in the middle-to-late rounds.

- **Deep Sleepers:** Many publications also offer their version of "deep" sleepers, which tend to include a lot of players in new offensive systems and/or rookie skill players. We identify these sleepers as well.

- **Hibernators:** These are players so far off the regular fantasy football radar, that you are unlikely to find them in other publications. These sleepers are identified based on our increased offensive coaching play calling analysis and game-by-game matchups. We've identified several "hibernation" sleepers within this publication. They are players that can offer high caliber performance, but could be available in the last rounds of your draft or even via waivers.

  If you are a Daily Fantasy player, our hibernators could be great value plays. We update our sleeper rankings weekly on our website (www.functionalsportsaholic.com), so continue to check back as the season progresses.

# Methodology:

### Fantasy Opportunity Ranking:

There's a lot of math behind this metric. As stated in our definitions section, Fantasy Opportunity scores are a means of measuring a typical player's role in an offense to identify undervalued players to assist with your fantasy draft and in Daily Fantasy selection.

### Running Backs:

We define RB1 as the player who received the most carries in 2017 analysis or the assumed starter in 2018 (i.e. free agent acquisitions or rookies).

### Wide Receivers:

In today's NFL, determining the key play makers isn't as easy as looking at a depth chart. Defining the receiver most likely to be targeted in a given game requires analysis of target totals and weekly personnel matchups.

The Functional Sportsaholic uses total targets in games started as the primary driver of WR rankings. A perfect example of this is Minnesota. In 2017, though most analysts consider Stefon Diggs to be the top WR for the Vikings, fellow WR Adam Thielen received more targets. Therefore, we labeled Thielen as last year's WR1 from a *fantasy football* perspective.

### Draft Rankings & Strategy: We Perform the Intense Analysis and Make the Draft Easy for You

We use statistical analysis, the Fantasy Opportunity Rankings and head coach/coordinator play call analysis to determine the final rankings of players. We are a fantasy football scouting agency that backs current statistics with film study and historical analysis. There is no other fantasy football publication that goes into this level of detail or science to give you a competitive advantage.

### Why We Are the Best

Most publications think of players in terms of what round they should be drafted. While we offer that style of ranking in both Point-Per-Reception (PPR) and non-PPR leagues, our true value is our **tier ranking**.

We offer color-coded rankings by tiers to make things easy for you. Are you having trouble deciding between a WR or RB in round 2? You'll find guidance here.

Unsure if you should draft an elite TE or a QB? Our tier-level gives you insight as to which position's output is more likely to be found later in the draft.

### Win/Loss Totals

This is a proprietary rating that takes film study, personnel matchups, coaching analysis and previous performance into account. We created an algorithm that is applied to every game in the 2018 season to provide a science-based prediction of win/loss totals for each team. If you don't like our analysis for your favorite team, please do not take offense. This is <u>not</u> based on personal opinion. This is a computation made by a robot you'll never meet.

## Our Philosophy

We are the industry's first Fantasy Football Scouting Service. This almanac takes the deepest dive into performances and trends to offer unparalleled information to the Fantasy Football enthusiast. While solidly rooted in math, we won't hit you over the head with it. First and foremost, the 2018 Fantasy Football Almanac and Draft Guide is written to be informative and *entertaining*.

Included Within:

- Over half of the league has a new head coach or offensive coordinator. How does this impact fantasy potential?
  - We've updated our algorithms to include play calling tendency of coaching staffs
  - We've adjusted overall fantasy values with these tools to provide the smartest and most accurate fantasy football forecasts in the market
- Defense and Kicker analysis has been completed to identify competitive advantage at these positions, which are commonly ignored
- We've completed an easy to follow draft guide with useful tips for fantasy football rookies and fantasy football experts alike
- Detailed analysis of offseason player movement
- Team-by-team 2017 reports, 2018 offseason analysis and 2018 performance forecasts
- Overall player "tiers" definition (which is more useful for draft strategy when playing in leagues with multiple team counts)
  - Over 40 Sleepers Categorized by Grades (undervalued players, sleepers everyone will know about by draft day, deep sleepers which aren't as obvious, and finally, hibernators that you'll be able to either draft or add to your initial waiver watch list)
- Fantasy Rankings for different league types: Points-per-Reception (PPR), Standard/non-PPR and Rookies (for Dynasty Leagues)
- Fantasy Draft Tracking Worksheets

AFC EAST

# AFC East
## Buffalo Bills
### 2017 Fantasy Opportunity Summary (Offensive Positions):

| Position | Player | PPR Opportunity Rank vs Position | Standard Opportunity Rank vs Position |
|---|---|---|---|
| Quarterback | Tyrod Taylor | 23 | 23 |
| Running Back | LeSean McCoy | 6 | 9 |
| Running Back 2 | Mike Tolbert | 26 | 24 |
| Wide Receiver 1 | Zay Jones/Kelvin Benjamin | 32 | 24 |
| Wide Receiver 2 | Zay Jones/Jordan Matthews | 29 | 32 |
| Wide Receiver 3 | Deonte Thompson | 24 | 26 |
| Tight End | Charles Clay | 16 | 23 |

**Fantasy Opportunity Analysis by Position (Offense Only):**
**Quarterback:**

Though Buffalo quarterback Tyrod Taylor measured well in efficiency metrics, the truth is that he wasn't a viable fantasy starter. As you can see in the wide receiver position rankings, pushing the ball downfield to their WR group was an issue for the entire season.

Buffalo ranked dead last in adjust targets and adjust receptions and 31st in adjusted team yards. Taylor's saving grace was his ability to hit Charles Clay or LeSean McCoy out of the backfield. He also accounted for roughly 17% of Buffalo's running game – one of the largest percentages of a quarterback.

**Running Back:**

McCoy was a beast. He ranked in the top 3 in rushing attempts and receptions across the NFL and asserted his status as a tier-1 fantasy running back throughout the season. Though Buffalo changed their offensive coordinator (more on this later), LeSean McCoy is one of very few bell cow running backs. He's a 3-down player who gives very little to his RB2.

As you can see in the RB2 ranking, relative to his peers, Mike Tolbert was in the bottom fourth of the league. In terms of drafting a running back in the early rounds of your fantasy draft, having a poorly-ranked RB2 is good news for your RB1.

**Wide Receiver:**

Overall, the adjusted stats are jarring. The WR1 and WR2 positions were ranked 30th and 32nd in targets. Only WR3 Deonte Thompson ranked inside the top 25 (#23) against his peers.

There's no sugar coating this: Buffalo's wide receiving group was one to avoid in 2017. I'd sooner start Randy Moss from his network analyst desk than Zay Jones or Deonte Thompson. The addition of Kelvin

Benjamin helped, but not much. I do see potential for a leap forward in 2018 (more on this later), but proceed with caution.

**Tight End:**

TE Charles Clay made the most of his opportunities, but he was in and out of the lineup. He has the ability to break out in 2018 if he has a QB that can get him the ball in intermediate routes.

**2018 Offseason Analysis**

**Transactions**

| Key Losses | | | Key Additions | | |
|---|---|---|---|---|---|
| Pos | Player | New Team | Pos | Player | Old Team |
| MLB | Preston Brown | Cincinnati | DT | Star Lotulelei | Carolina |
| CB | E.J. Gaines | Cleveland | QB | AJ McCarron | Cincinnati |
| OT | Cordy Glenn | Cincinnati | LB | Trent Murphy | Washington |
| OT | Seantrel Henderson | Houston | RB | Chris Ivory | Jacksonville |
| WR | Jordan Matthews | New England | CB | Phillip Gaines | Kansas City |
| WR | Deonte Thompson | Dallas | CB | Vontae Davis | Indianapolis |
| CB | Shareece Wright | Oakland | DB | Rafael Bush | New Orleans |
| OT | Cordy Glenn | Cincinnati | C | Russell Bodine | Bengals |
| QB | Tyrod Taylor | Cleveland | OT | Marshall Newhouse | Oakland |
| OG | *Richie Ingognito* | *Retired* | WR | Kaelin Clay | Carolina |
| C | *Eric Wood* | *Retired* | WR | Jeremy Kerley | NY Jets |

**Draft Summary**

| Round | Overall | Position | Player | College |
|---|---|---|---|---|
| 1 | 7 | QB | Josh Allen | Wyoming |
| 1 | 16 | ILB | Tremaine Edmunds | Virginia Tech |
| 3 | 96 | DT | Harrison Phillips | Stanford |
| 4 | 121 | DB | Taron Johnson | Weber St |
| 5 | 154 | S | Siran Neal | Jacksonville St |
| 5 | 166 | G | Wyatt Teller | Virginia Tech |
| 6 | 187 | WR | Ray-ray Mccloud | Clemson |
| 7 | 255 | WR | Austin Proehl | North Carolina |

**Coaching Changes**
**Offensive Coordinator, Brian Daboll**

Brian Daboll's most recent position was offensive coordinator and quarterbacks coach of the Alabama Crimson Tide, but he is far from a "college coach". Daboll has a long list of NFL jobs on his resume and has resided comfortably in the Bill Belichick coaching tree.

Like the Patriot offenses, Daboll has shown a balanced attack and distributes the football. Interestingly, he has a trademark of favoring play calls to one receiver. In Miami, it was Brandon Marshall. Kansas City featured Dwayne Bowe. I anticipate Kelvin Benjamin being the beneficiary of additional targets in 2018.

The Functional Sportsaholic team analyzed Buffalo's current personnel and compared the team to Brian Daboll's coaching experience. For 2018 rankings, I am likening the play calling structure to the 2011 Miami Dolphins team, with a slight decrease in overall WR1 potential and a corresponding increase in TE1 potential.

## 2018 Fantasy Outlook

### Projected Position Rankings

| Position | Player | PPR Rank vs Position | PPR Overall rank | Standard Rank vs Position | Standard Overall Rank |
|---|---|---|---|---|---|
| Quarterback | A.J. McCarron | 29 | 183 | 29 | 185 |
| Running Back 1 | LeSean McCoy | 10 | 21 | 11 | 21 |
| Running Back 2 | Chris Ivory | 28 | 240 | 28 | 234 |
| Wide Receiver 1 | Kelvin Benjamin | 29 | 122 | 29 | 97 |
| Wide Receiver 2 | Jeremy Kerley | 28 | 192 | 27 | 204 |
| Wide Receiver 3 | Zay Jones | 18 | 217 | 16 | 214 |
| Tight End 1 | Charles Clay | 7 | 81 | 7 | 107 |
| Kicker | Stephen Hauschka | 23rd Against Kickers | | | |
| Defense/ST | Bills | 22nd (tied) Against Defense/ST | | | |

**Position Commentary:**

**Quarterback:**

I'm assuming Buffalo will begin the year with AJ McCarron at quarterback. The best look we've had of him was the 2015 season where he started 7 games in backup duty for Andy Dalton. He completed 66.4% of his passes with a 3:1 TD to INT rate. His QB rating was 97.1. To put that in context, that stretch was more impressive than the 2014 season of spot duty for Kirk Cousins (61.8% completion rate, 1:1 INT rate and 86.4% rating).

McCarron should exceed Taylor's TD and INT totals from 2017. However, he will have less overall rushing yards and could be pulled in favor of rookie Josh Allen at the first sign of trouble. I suggest avoiding the Buffalo QB situation in the draft.

**Running Back:**

LeSean McCoy is a standout fantasy running back. The greatest danger where he is concerned is whether or not new offensive coordinator Brian Daboll will give him more rest (thereby cutting his snap count). McCoy has been a 3-down back his entire career, but the addition of Chris Ivory is concerning. McCoy's opportunity score drops as a result.

**Wide Receiver:**

I see an improvement across the board among Bills receivers *if* A.J. McCarron is a full-season starter. Daboll has shown a history of favoring his number 1 receiver, which leads us to believe Kelvin Benjamin has blue skies ahead. The danger for fantasy GMs is that the name of Kelvin Benjamin might hold a little more value than his output. I see him as a solid WR2 or premium WR3/Flex performer.

The addition of WR Jeremy Kerley could be an interesting pickup. He was the darling of Daily Fantasy last season, putting up consistent numbers while being priced at bargain value. I will put him as a possible low-tier flex option on my draft board or high-priority watch list during the waiver period.

**Tight End:**

Charles Clay has been a player that has popped on film. He reminds me a bit of Delaine Walker before Walker broke out in Tennessee. Daboll will have plays dialed up for the TE position.

I see Clay performing well regardless of who is starting at quarterback. If McCarron is playing, I think he'll catch fewer passes, but have a higher yards-per-reception average. If Buffalo starts Allen, I think deeper passes will be fewer and further between, but they will dial up more short and intermediate routes to ease his transition. The Functional Sportsaholic Opportunity Ranking for Clay is in the top-10 in both PPR and non-PPR leagues. He could be a mid-to-late round steal.

**Kicker:**

I don't project Buffalo to get enough field goal attempts or yards to make the kicking position draftable. Strategically speaking, it would be wiser to pick an extra position player and hold until the start of the season rather than fill out the K roster spot.

**Defense/Special Teams:**

As a fantasy unit, I expect Buffalo to be in the middle or back half of the league. They were in the middle of the league in opponent points scored and opponents yards per play last season. The sack and turnover totals weren't anything to write home about.

If Star Lotulelei can return to his previous form when he last played under head coach Sean McDermott and if Trent Murphy can avoid suspension and stay on the field, perhaps those measurables can improve this year. I suspect a similar 2018 campaign.

**Sleeper Watch**
***Popular Sleeper: TE, Charles Clay***

*Projected Stats: 60 receptions, 840 yards, 5 TDs*

***Deep Sleeper: WR, Zay Jones***

*He received over 70 targets last year, but caught under 30 passes.  He has play making potential, but the Bills weren't able to hit him deep last season.  I expect that to change in 2018 regardless of who is lined up at QB.  Projected Stats: 51 receptions, 537 yards, 3 TDs*

**Hibernators: N/A**

## Miami Dolphins
### 2017 Fantasy Opportunity Summary (Offensive Positions):

| Position | Player | PPR Rank vs Position | PPR Overall Rank |
|---|---|---|---|
| Quarterback | Jay Cutler | 25 | 25 |
| Running Back | Jay Ajayi/Kenyan Drake | 15 | 16 |
| Running Back 2 | Damien Williams | 13 | 25 |
| Wide Receiver 1 | Jarvis Landry | 8 | 14 |
| Wide Receiver 2 | Kenny Stills | 7 | 7 |
| Wide Receiver 3 | DeVante Parker | 2 | 3 |
| Tight End | Julius Thomas | 23 | 23 |

**Fantasy Opportunity Analysis by Position (Offense Only):**
**Quarterback:**

The 2017 season started with a season-ending injury to Ryan Tannehill and a week-1 game cancelled by hurricane. The Dolphins never recovered. Though Jay Cutler had familiarity with the Gase offensive system, he was unable to recreate the success the two had together in Chicago. 19 TDs and 14 INTs might have worked in the 1950s, but not today.

**Running Back:**

The emergence of Kenyan Drake afforded Miami the luxury of trading previous starter Jay Ajayi. Though Drake popped in his short time as a starter, the truth is that he did so because Damien Williams was not available in the back half of the year.

The disparity in the RB2 ratings displays his pass catching boost in PPR leagues. This is a sign that Miami likes to pair a 2-down back (Ajayi/Drake) with a 3rd down specialist for pass catching and pass blocking duties (Williams).

**Wide Receiver:**

Like Buffalo, Miami's quarterbacks did not score well. Unlike Buffalo, the Miami receivers were viable starts. Landry amassed 161 targets during the year – good for 5th best. Though they were only 17th in the league in total passing yards, the targets largely went to the top-3 in the depth chart.

**Tight End:**

There wasn't much here in 2017 to be excited about. When Julius Thomas reunited with Adam Gates, I thought the offensive design could bring him back to his glory days in Denver. Unfortunately, Peyton Manning's quarterback play seems to have more impact on Thomas' output than the system.

**2018 Offseason Analysis**

**Transactions**

| Key Losses | | | Key Additions | | |
|---|---|---|---|---|---|
| Pos | Player | New Team | Pos | Player | Old Team |
| OG | Jermon Bushrod | New Orleans | WR | Danny Amendola | New England |
| LB | Neville Hewitt | NY Jets | RB | Frank Gore | Indianapolis |
| WR | Jarvis Landry | Cleveland | C | Daniel Kilgore | San Francisco |
| K | Cody Parkey | Chicago | QB | Brock Osweiler | Denver |
| C | Mike Pouncey | LA Chargers | LB | Robert Quinn | LA Rams |
| DT | Ndamukong Suh | LA Rams | OG | Josh Sitton | Chicago |
| SS | Michael Thomas | NY Giants | DT | Akeem Spence | Miami |
| RB | Damien Williams | Kansas City | WR | Albert Wilson | Kansas City |
| QB | Jay Cutler | NA | | | |

**Draft Summary**

| Round | Overall | Position | Player | College |
|---|---|---|---|---|
| 1 | 11 | S | Minkah Fitzpatrick | Alabama |
| 2 | 42 | TE | Mike Gesicki | Penn St |
| 3 | 73 | OLB | Jerome Baker | Ohio St |
| 4 | 123 | TE | Durham Smythe | Notre Dame |
| 4 | 131 | RB | Kalen Ballage | Arizona St |
| 6 | 209 | DB | Cornell Armstrong | Southern Miss |
| 7 | 227 | LB | Quentin Poling | Ohio |
| 7 | 229 | K | Jason Sanders | New Mexico |

**Coaching Changes**

No relevant coaching changes have taken place.  The key changes to the Miami Dolphins in 2018 will be the return of QB, Ryan Tannehill and the departure of WR Jarvis Landry.

# 2018 Fantasy Outlook

## Projected Position Rankings

| Position | Player | PPR Rank vs Position | PPR Overall rank | Standard Rank vs Position | Standard Overall Rank |
|---|---|---|---|---|---|
| Quarterback | Ryan Tannehill | 18 | 179 | 18 | 181 |
| Running Back 1 | Kenyan Drake | 18 | 50 | 18 | 47 |
| Running Back 2 | Frank Gore | 24 | 227 | 25 | 179 |
| Wide Receiver 1 | Danny Amendola | 13 | 47 | 18 | 55 |
| Wide Receiver 2 | DeVante Parker | 21 | 120 | 22 | 114 |
| Wide Receiver 3 | Kenny Stills | 3 | 123 | 3 | 112 |
| Tight End 1 | Mike Gesicki | 30 | 232 | 30 | 226 |
| Kicker | TBD | 28th (tied) Against Kickers | | | |
| Defense/ST | Dolphins | 27th Against Defense/ST | | | |

## Position Commentary:

### Quarterback:

Tannehill coming off of injury provides an interesting option for fantasy GMs. He played well in 2016, but is coming off a season-ending injury in 2017. Our fantasy Opportunity Ranking has him ranked as the 18th-best quarterback. He's worth a roster spot as a backup quarterback, but my concern is that the Dolphins lost their most targeted receiver.

### Running Back:

People are going to be very high on Kenyan Drake. I had him on a roster last season and he was an important player to have, but buyer beware. The Dolphins have played a committee for years. Damien Williams has had a lock on passing downs and has historically taken goal line snaps away from the "lead" back.

Drake scored well at the end of the year, but this came at a time when Williams wasn't playing. You can expect excellent production when he gets snaps, but I don't expect him to play much on passing downs. The addition of RB, Frank Gore, could eat into goal line carries as well. For this reason, I think his opportunity ranks 18th against his RB1 peers. This means that he'll be a solid Flex or second RB option, but there are many WRs and RBs that should be drafted in front of him.

### Wide Receiver:

The departure of Jarvis Landry hurts, but also provides fantasy opportunity. Landry saw 161 targets and 112 receptions in 2017. The Functional Sportsaholic assumes that new receiver, Danny Amendola will pick up a lot of those targets, but not all of them. Albert Wilson, previously of Kansas City, has yet to meet expectations.

**Tight End:**

The tight end position has not produced in Miami. I expected Julius Thomas to pop last season, but he never seemed to get off the ground. I have the Dolphins TE1 position rated as a do-not-draft. I'd rather use the draft pick on a D/ST or K differentiator.

**Kicker:**

Miami's offense hasn't provided enough scoring opportunities to make a Dolphin kicker worthy of draft position. 2018 projects to be no different.

**Defense/Special Teams:**

Love him or hate him, the loss of Ndamukong Suh hurts the defense. This team already finished 22nd in yards per play last season and 29th in points against. Take them off your draft board.

**Sleeper Watch**

*Popular Sleeper: WR, Danny Amendola*

*Note: Amendola isn't a real "sleeper", but he will be in line for a lot of targets and is likely to be undervalued on draft day.*

*Deep Sleepers: N/A*

*Hibernators: N/A*

# New England Patriots

**2017 Fantasy Opportunity Summary (Offensive Positions):**

| Position | Player | PPR Rank vs Position | PPR Overall Rank |
|---|---|---|---|
| Quarterback | Tom Brady | 6 | 6 |
| Running Back | Dion Lewis/Mike Gillislee | 20 | 17 |
| Running Back 2 | James White | 10 | 10 |
| Wide Receiver 1 | Brandin Cooks | 19 | 12 |
| Wide Receiver 2 | Danny Amendola | 15 | 19 |
| Wide Receiver 3 | Chris Hogan | 3 | 2 |
| Tight End | Rob Gronkowski | 3 | 1 |

**Fantasy Opportunity Analysis by Position (Offense Only):**
**Quarterback:**

Some say Tom Brady is showing the first signs of aging. His play in the back half of the year hasn't quite measured up to his own ridiculous standard. Let's be honest though, as a fantasy quarterback, he was a top pick in 2017 and will be in 2018.

**Running Back:**

The Patriots hold a weekly running back lottery. Week to week, the position group scores well, but they've traditionally been "impossible" to predict. This past season, I took a dive into the game-by-game numbers and a few things stuck out:

1) If a Patriots RB fumbles and does not return to the game, you may as well trade them. Mike Gilleslee disappeared from the backfield almost overnight.
2) James White is essentially a wide receiver. It's to the point where we should probably give him a new position name: backfield receiver. He had 43 rushing attempts compared to 72 targets and 56 receptions. To put that in context, he'd score in the back half of the WR2 rankings without taking his carries into effect. If you're looking for consistent points in your lineup from a Patriots RB, he's your man.
3) Rex Burkhead was utilized mostly when Gronk was out with injury. Rather than move down the depth chart to their 2nd tight end (Dwayne Allen), the routes and targets went Burkhead's way. That's a handy tip for Daily Fantasy and emergency start weeks.

**Wide Receiver:**

The loss of Julian Edelman prior to the season hurt, but the Patriots have a "next man up" philosophy and do a better job of implementing that approach that most of the league. Brandin Cooks led the team with 114 targets. Danny Amendola was targeted a solid 86 times. Overall, this group underperformed and the passing attack was primarily routed through running backs and tight ends. Beware Patriot Receivers in 2018, but the offense is healthy nonetheless.

**Tight End:**

The days of Gronkowski being a step above everybody are gone. However, when healthy, he's still a tier-1 tight end. With the quarterback change in Kansas City, I expect Kelce's numbers to dip and Gronk to still be the number 1 guy overall.

**2018 Offseason Analysis**

**Transactions**

| Key Losses | | | Key Additions | | |
|---|---|---|---|---|---|
| Pos | Player | New Team | Pos | Player | Old Team |
| WR | WR, Danny Amendola | Miami | OG | Trent Brown | San Francisco |
| CB | CB, Johnson Bademosi | Houston | DE | DE, Adrian Clayborn | Atlanta |
| CB | CB, Malcom Butler | Tennessee | RB | RB, Jeremy Hill | Cincinnati |
| WR | Brandin Cooks | LA Rams | WR | WR, Jordan Matthews | Buffalo |
| OT | OT, Cameron Fleming | Dallas | CB | CB, Jason McCourty | Cleveland |
| RB | RB, Dion Lewis | Tennessee | WR | Cordarrelle Patterson | New England |
| OT | OT, Nate Solder | NY Giants | NT | Danny Shelton | Cleveland |
| OLB | James Harrison | Retired | OT | Matt Tobin | Seattle |

**Draft Summary**

| Round | Overall | Position | Player | College |
|---|---|---|---|---|
| 1 | 23 | T | Isaiah Wynn | Georgia |
| 1 | 31 | RB | Sony Michael | Georgia |
| 2 | 56 | CB | Duke Dawson | Florida |
| 5 | 143 | ILB | Ja'whaun Bentley | Purdue |
| 6 | 178 | ILB | Christian Sam | Arizona St |
| 6 | 210 | WR | Braxton Berrios | Miami |
| 7 | 219 | QB | Danny Etling | LSU |
| 7 | 243 | DB | Keion Crossen | Western Carolina |
| 7 | 250 | TE | Ryan Izzo | Florida St |

**Coaching Changes**

Defensive coordinator Matt Patricia left to take the head coaching position with the Detroit Lions. With Belichick's focus, personnel upgrades and healthy 2018 team, the defensive unit is likely to improve slightly.

## 2018 Fantasy Outlook

### Projected Position Rankings

| Position | Player | PPR Rank vs Position | PPR Overall rank | Standard Rank vs Position | Standard Overall Rank |
|---|---|---|---|---|---|
| Quarterback | Tom Brady | 10 | 59 | 10 | 61 |
| Running Back 1 | Sony Michel | 24 | 98 | 24 | 67 |
| Running Back 2 | James White | 12 | 101 | 12 | 100 |
| Wide Receiver 1 | Julian Edelman | 26 | 67 | 23 | 78 |
| Wide Receiver 2 | Jordan Matthews | 24 | 154 | 25 | 155 |
| Wide Receiver 3 | Chris Hogan | 6 | 205 | 5 | 203 |
| Tight End 1 | Rob Gronkowski | 1 | 13 | 1 | 22 |
| Kicker | Stephen Gostkowski | 3rd Against Kickers | | | |
| Defense/ST | Patriots | 21st Against Defense/ST | | | |

**Position Commentary:**

**Quarterback:**

Tom Brady is starting to degrade, but barely. He's still an elite fantasy quarterback and should be drafted early. Our fantasy opportunity scores have him listed at 10, but don't forget his extreme efficiency (which is considered in our rankings below). He's a tier-1 QB and worth dropping a pick on when the run on quarterbacks takes place between rounds 3 and 5.

**Running Back:**

I've already seen the articles discussing Sony Michel. Although I don't doubt his talent or his effectiveness when he gets snaps, you have to remember that a) he won't get the snaps of a typical round-1 RB and b) there are a lot of mouths to feed on that offense.

The last time New England drafted a running back in round 1, he saw 175 rushing attempts and just under 940 all-purpose yards. The moral of the story is do not be seduced by Michel's draft position or what you saw in college. He'll be a solid mid-round pick, but steer clear until at least until round 4 or round 5.

**Wide Receiver:**

On any other team, I'd be concerned about Amendola and Cooks leaving. They were the top two WR targets (114 and 86, respectively). But this is the Patriots. They've had a revolving door at WR for most of the Brady/Belichick era.

Julian Edelman should return to form this season and will be a great PPR play. I would have projected him at over 100 receptions this season, but the PED suspension will hurt. I've had to downgrade his ranking as a result.

Jordan Matthews could be a very sneaky play at WR2. The Patriots like to spread their targets and attack opposing defenses based on personnel matchups. Matthews won't be an elite player every week, but like his fellow WR Chris Hogan, he'll be an elite WR for 3-4 weeks per year. Keep an eye out for our weekly matchup rankings if you're in need of a desperation WR play or a Daily Fantasy sleeper.

**Tight End:**

When Gronk is healthy, he's a tier-1 tight end. When he's injured, his targets will be distributed between James White and Rex Burkhead.

**Kicker:**

Stephen Gostkowski is a perennially draftable kicker. I'd argue that his consistency is such that he could even be drafted before the last two rounds. Your issue won't be the Patriots' ability to put him into kickable positions, but rather, the Patriots offense is too good. They score a lot of touchdowns and also go for it on 4th down quite a bit. Both push his total field goal attempts down, hurting his overall scoring number. That's why I have him ranked #3 in Fantasy Opportunity among kickers.

**Defense/Special Teams:**

I see the Patriots defense improving for two key reasons. 1) Bill Belichick will be assuming complete control of the unit due to the departure of Matt Patricia to Detroit and 2) their personnel will improve thanks to an offseason of healing and an influx of new talent. The addition of Clayborn could be a boon for sack numbers – a key contributor to the D/ST ranking.

2017's yards-per-play ranking was paltry (31st), but their opponent points-per-game ranking was 7th. This was a bend-don't-break unit last year. If they can make minimal improvements in the yards-per-play area, this could be a top-10 defense. I don't think you'll want to draft them early (as evidenced by the Opportunity Ranking), but they will be an option if you're looking for a defense in the last round or during the waiver period.

**Sleeper Watch**

*Popular Sleeper: Jordan Matthews, WR*

*Matthews had a couple of good years in Philadelphia under Chip Kelley in another high-volume offense. If he can pick up the playbook, he could see 50-60 catches and 6-700 yards. TDs are also going to be available with Tom Brady behind center.*

*Deep Sleeper: James White, RB (PPR only)*

*I'm including him here because the Sony Michel hype train will be out of control by draft day.*

*Hibernators: N/A*

## New York Jets
### 2017 Fantasy Opportunity Summary (Offensive Positions):

| Position | Player | PPR Rank vs Position | PPR Overall Rank |
|----------|--------|----------------------|------------------|
| Quarterback | Josh McCown | 22 | 22 |
| Running Back | Bilal Powell/Matt Forte | 28 | 26 |
| Running Back 2 | Elijah McGuire | 9 | 9 |
| Wide Receiver 1 | Robby Anderson | 16 | 13 |
| Wide Receiver 2 | Jermaine Kearse | 6 | 8 |
| Wide Receiver 3 | Jeremy Kerley | 23 | 25 |
| Tight End | Austin Seferian-Jenkins | 17 | 22 |

**Fantasy Opportunity Analysis by Position (Offense Only):**

**Quarterback:**

Many experts thought the Jets would finish with the worst record in the league. Josh McCown does not instill confidence in NFL circles, but he quietly had a completion rate of over 67% and a 2:1 TD-to INT ratio. He was surprisingly startable and The Functional Sportsaholic team happily played him in our Daily Fantasy lineups in what was a week-after-week bargain.

**Running Back:**

Frustratingly, this team stuck with a three-headed monster attack for much of the season. Matt Forte, now retired, showed his age. Bilal Powell was a viable play when either Forte or McGuire were inactive. As you can see by the 28th overall rank among running back 1s, the three musketeers approach was a constant stomach punch to fantasy owners.

Elijah McGuire showed promise in his limited time as a rookie last year. He was valuable in spot starts and in Daily Fantasy.

**Wide Receiver:**

I mentioned the Josh McCown blue light special for Daily Fantasy players. Robby Anderson is another example of bargain shopping. 114 targets, 63 receptions, 941 yards and 7 TDs last year. He's a solid WR 1 and is entering his third year in 2018.

**Tight End:**

Austin Sefarian-Jenkins wasn't graded particularly well in football circles, but he produced well in his time with the Jets.

## 2018 Offseason Analysis

**Transactions**

| Key Losses | | | Key Additions | | |
|---|---|---|---|---|---|
| Pos | Player | New Team | Pos | Player | Old Team |
| K | Chandler Catanzaro | | QB | Teddy Bridgewater | Minnesota |
| ILB | Demario Davis | | DE | Brandon Copeland | Detroit |
| DE | Kony Ealy | | RB | Isiah Crowell | Cleveland |
| QB | Christian Hackenberg | Oakland | LB | Neville Hewitt | Miami |
| C | Wesley Johnson | | CB | Trumaine Johnson | LA Chargers |
| TE | Austin Sefarian-Jenkins | | C | Spencer Long | NY Jets |
| DE | Muhammad Wilkerson | | WR | Terrelle Pryor | Washington |
| C | *Nick Mangold* | *Retired* | RB | Thomas Rawls | Seattle |
| RB | *Matt Forte* | *Retired* | K | Cairo Santos | Chicago |
| | | | C | Travis Swanson | NY Jets |
| | | | ILB | Avery Williamson | Tennessee |
| | | | DT | Henry Anderson | Indianapolis |

**Draft Summary**

| Round | Overall | Position | Player | College |
|---|---|---|---|---|
| 1 | 3 | QB | Sam Darnold | USC |
| 3 | 72 | DT | Nathan Shepherd | Fort Hays St |
| 4 | 107 | TE | Chris Herndon | Miami |
| 6 | 179 | CB | Parry Nickerson | Tulane |
| 6 | 180 | DT | Foley Fatukasi | Connecticut |
| 6 | 204 | RB | Trenton Canon | Virginia St |

**Coaching Changes**

2017 Offensive coordinator John Morton was fired and replaced in-house with previous quarterbacks coach, Jeremy Bates. Bates has lived the life of an NFL assistant, having bounced around the league for years. His lone experience as an offensive coordinator came in Seattle in 2010 where they finished 23rd in points scored.

Bates was hired from within and though there will be changes to the system, I don't expect a large difference in offensive output. I compared this Jets roster to Seattle's 2010 roster, but don't see enough correlation to use the 2010 Seahawks offensive distribution as a basis for future analysis. Instead, the key change to 2018 will be Matt Forte's retirement.

## 2018 Fantasy Outlook

### Projected Position Rankings

| Position | Player | PPR Rank vs Position | PPR Overall rank | Standard Rank vs Position | Standard Overall Rank |
|---|---|---|---|---|---|
| Quarterback | Josh McCown | 27 | 110 | 27 | 124 |
| Running Back 1 | Bilal Powell | 22 | 91 | 20 | 66 |
| Running Back 2 | Elijah McGuire / Isaiah Crowell | 6 | 97 | 6 | 99 |
| Wide Receiver 1 | Robbie Anderson | 24 | 68 | 20 | 52 |
| Wide Receiver 2 | Quincy Enunwa | 12 | 187 | 12 | 111 |
| Wide Receiver 3 | Jermaine Kearse | 27 | 233 | 27 | 235 |
| Tight End 1 | Eric Tomlinson | 19 | 193 | 19 | 215 |
| Kicker | Cairo Santos | 24th Against Kickers | | | |
| Defense/ST | Jets | 26th Against Defense/ST | | | |

### Position Commentary:

### Quarterback:

Fans and Fantasy GMs alike assume that Darnold will provide an immediate boost at the quarterback position, but as I mentioned in the 2017 analysis, McCown's 67% completion percentage is nothing to sneeze at. They will want more than 18 TD passes, however.

The Jets will likely have a position battle to open training camp, which I expect McCown to win initially. The Jets staff will switch to Darnold at the earlier of two scenarios: 1) they lose three-to-four games in a row or 2) they are officially out of the playoff race.

### Running Back:

Matt Forte is out of the equation, but the Jets added Thomas Rawls and Isaiah Crowell in free agency. This leads me to believe there will be a 3-way division of running attempts once again. Bilal Powel should lead the way, but real value will come if and when one of the running backs will be deactivated.

I like the prospects of Elijah McGuire, but his value will live and die in the passing game's efficiency. He's explosive and should receive more touches, but this backfield isn't one you'll want to use early draft picks on. I'll be watching the distribution of snaps throughout the pre-season. Rawls could also get snaps. Whoever wins the starting RB position will have decent RB2 or flex value.

### Wide Receiver:

Robbie Anderson took a leap forward in production last season. I expect him to match or slightly exceed last year's numbers in 2018 if McCown is the starter. When (not if) the Jets move to Darnold as the starting QB, his numbers will likely dip for a few weeks and then climb back to his usual production. Over time, his potential will increase with Darnold's output.

Jermaine Kearse (along with departed Jeremy Kerley) was a nice spot-starter at the flex spot or a week-to-week fantasy bargain. Like Anderson, his value should remain constant regardless of the quarterback situation. There could be a slight dip in Darnold's initial starts, but it will improve over time.

The addition of Terrelle Pryor could provide a jolt in Red Zone offense. He produced well in 2016 for the Browns and has the physical makeup to be a play maker. He never meshed well in Washington. This could be his last chance to make an impact in the NFL, so he should be properly motivated.

**Tight End:**

Outside of a few starts by Austin Sefarian-Jenkins in 2017, the Jets TE position was one to avoid at all costs. Unless 4th round pick Chris Herndon can win snaps, I don't see this position group offering much in the way of fantasy value. Keep an eye out for week-to-week matchup-based starts in Daily Fantasy.

**Kicker:**

The Jets don't score enough to make a kicker draft-worthy.

**Defense/Special Teams:**

The Jets saw Kony Ealy and Muhammad Wilkerson leave in free agency. This line had lackluster sack totals in 2017. They made improvements at LB and Cornerback, but I don't see enough improvement to make an impact in fantasy scoring. Avoid them in the draft and only play them in Daily Fantasy against a weak offense.

**Sleeper Watch**

***Popular Sleepers: Robbie Anderson, WR; Elijah McGuire, RB***

*Robby Anderson saw his targets increase from 78 in his rookie season to 114 in 2017. He's entering his third year. If his QB situation was more stable, I would have boosted his rating further.*

***Deep Sleeper: N/A***

***Hibernators: Quincy Enuwa, WR***

*Enuwa missed 2017 with injury, but he caught 58 passes for 857 yards and 4 TDs in 2016.*

# AFC NORTH

# AFC North
## Baltimore Ravens

**2017 Fantasy Opportunity Summary (Offensive Positions):**

| Position | Player | PPR Rank vs Position | PPR Overall Rank |
|---|---|---|---|
| Quarterback | Joe Flacco | 32 | 32 |
| Running Back | Alex Collins | 21 | 19 |
| Running Back 2 | Javorius Allen | 6 | 7 |
| Wide Receiver 1 | Mike Wallace | 29 | 30 |
| Wide Receiver 2 | Jeremy Maclin | 25 | 28 |
| Wide Receiver 3 | Chris Moore | 25 | 27 |
| Tight End | Ben Watson | 15 | 15 |

**Fantasy Opportunity Analysis by Position (Offense Only):**
**Quarterback:**

I covered Flacco in Episode 2 of The Functional Sportsaholic podcast. Flacco is reaching a crossroads in his career. The honeymoon phase after his Super Bowl victory is a thing of the past. He hasn't shown the kind of growth the Ravens were hoping for when they extended his contract. The offense was anemic through much of the year and his QB play backs that up.

**Running Back:**

The Ravens run a true committee. Alex Collins started to take over the feature back role in the middle of the season. He's brought stability to the backfield. Look for this to continue in 2018.

Javorius Allen ranked 6th among his RB2 peers. He received goal line carries, touches in key situations and a lot of passes; he was someone you could start in a pinch.

**Wide Receiver:**

In Mike Wallace and Jeremy Maclin, Flacco had a great receiving corps…. Well, that's what I'd say if this was 2012. It's hard to get a gauge on this group. I mentioned that Baltimore's offense was putrid from a fantasy perspective last year. All receivers ranked in the bottom-fourth of the league against their peers. Was that Flacco's fault? The receivers'? The truth: likely somewhere in the middle.

**Tight End:**

Interestingly, of all pass catchers, Ben Watson ranked the highest against his peers. Unfortunately, he's now back in New Orleans.

**2018 Offseason Analysis**

**Transactions**

| Key Losses | | | Key Additions | | |
|---|---|---|---|---|---|
| Pos | Player | New Team | Pos | Player | Old Team |
| C | Ryan Jensen | Tampa Bay | WR | John Brown | Arizona |
| WR | Mike Wallace | Philadelphia | WR | Michael Crabtree | Oakland |
| WR | Griff Whalen | Oakland | | | |
| RB | *Danny Woodhead* | *Retired* | | | |

**Draft Summary**

| Round | Overall | Position | Player | College |
|---|---|---|---|---|
| 1 | 25 | TE | Hayden Hurst | South Carolina |
| 1 | 32 | QB | Lamar Jackson | Louisville |
| 3 | 83 | OT | orlando Brown | Oklahoma |
| 3 | 86 | TE | Mark andrews | Oklahoma |
| 4 | 116 | CB | Anthony Averett | Alabama |
| 4 | 122 | ILB | Kenny Young | UCLA |
| 4 | 132 | WR | jaleel Scott | New Mexico St |
| 5 | 162 | WR | Jordan Lasley | UCLA |
| 6 | 190 | S | Deshon Elliott | Texas |
| 6 | 212 | OT | Greg Senat | Wagner |
| 6 | 215 | CB | Bradley Bozeman | Alabama |
| 7 | 238 | DE | Zach Sieler | Ferris St |

**Coaching Changes**

No relevant changes were made to the offensive coaching staff. Expect a similar run/pass distribution (43.6% to 56.4%) in 2018.

Previous defensive coordinator Dean Pees retired after the 2018 season. Roughly 4 weeks later, he came out of retirement to join the Tennessee Titans. Previous linebackers coach Don Martindale has taken over the defense in Baltimore. Expect the trademark Baltimore attacking style to stay in place.

**2018 Fantasy Outlook**

## Projected Position Rankings

| Position | Player | PPR Rank vs Position | PPR Overall rank | Standard Rank vs Position | Standard Overall Rank |
|----------|--------|----------------------|------------------|---------------------------|------------------------|
| Quarterback | Joe Flacco | 32 | 186 | 32 | 189 |
| Running Back 1 | Alex Collins | 26 | 99 | 25 | 126 |
| Running Back 2 | Javorius Allen | 8 | 95 | 8 | 140 |
| Wide Receiver 1 | Michael Crabtree | 13 | 125 | 18 | 144 |
| Wide Receiver 2 | John Brown | 21 | 209 | 22 | 205 |
| Wide Receiver 3 | Willie Snead IV | 3 | 237 | 3 | 238 |
| Tight End 1 | Hayden Hurst | 20 | 170 | 20 | 166 |
| Kicker | Justin Tucker | 7th (tied) Against Kickers | | | |
| Defense/ST | Ravens | 2nd Against Defense/ST | | | |

### Position Commentary:

### Quarterback:

Flacco has had a tough couple of seasons. In Lamar Jackson, the Ravens feel they've drafted the quarterback of the future. At this point, Flacco can go one of two ways. If he feels entitled to the position given his Super Bowl over 5 years ago, then he could implode. If he can use this as motivation, he could have a campaign similar to Alex Smith's 2017 run in Kansas City.

Based on the last few seasons, I think Flacco will have another underwhelming fantasy season. Baltimore's tough play will keep them competitive for much of the year, so I doubt we see Jackson playing meaningful minutes until late in the year.

I've ranked the Ravens dead last in Fantasy Opportunity. Stay away. Far, far away.

### Running Back:

Alex Collins is firmly entrenched as the lead running back on early downs and in short yardage, but that doesn't mean a ton.

The Ravens have made a commitment to keep RB Javorius Allen involved in the offense. He receives a lot of goal line looks and pass targets. He represents the 8th-best RB2 in our Opportunity Ranking and is worthy of a roster spot. He can solidify your roster during bye weeks.

### Wide Receiver:

Is this team hungry for wide receivers or is the team hungry for a quarterback who can get WRs the ball? It's a chicken vs. egg argument. Though the Ravens lost Mike Wallace to Philadelphia and have left Jeremy Maclin unsigned, the signing of Michael Crabtree is a bright spot for the group. Crabtree was Oakland's best receiver last year (overshadowing teammate Amari Cooper). More encouraging, Crabtree also produced results with the 49ers while Colin Kaepernick was behind center. That bodes well for any struggling quarterback throwing him the ball. I have Baltimore's WR1 spot ranked 30th in opportunity, but Crabtree's influence will improve the overall ranking.

Ex-Cardinal John Brown is an interesting pickup. He put up nice numbers in 2017 on an offense that evenly distributed passes to WR2, WR3 and WR4. I don't suggest drafting him, but he's worth a waiver watch.

There's not a lot to be excited about with regard to the rest of the group. Breshad Perriman has yet to get his career going after injuries derailed him after his rookie draft. I like what Chris Moore could bring to the table. 30-50 receptions aren't out of the question, but he's such a deep sleeper that he's on hibernation status. Flag him on your waiver watch list.

### Tight End:

Of all the pass catchers, Baltimore's starting tight end could see the most fantasy production. I have them ranked 20th in our Opportunity Rankings. While unworthy of an initial roster spot, you'll want to keep an eye on the trio of Maxx Williams, Nick Boyle and rookie Hayden Hurst. The leader in snaps could end up being a lower-tier TE starter. You'll also want to pay attention in game three of the preseason. If one tight end dominates snaps with the starting group, they are likely to be an inexpensive Daily Fantasy week-1 player.

### Kicker:

Here's a great example of a dumb stat: Justin Tucker leads all kickers in opera performances. He also makes a great pick in one of the last two rounds of your fantasy draft. The Baltimore offense might not put a lot of touchdowns on the board, but they do take advantage of field goal opportunities. Tucker's accuracy and strong leg make him a guy that you'll want to draft, if available.

### Defense/Special Teams:

Baltimore's defensive reputation precedes them, and they back it up on the field. The days of Haloti Ngata, Ray Lewis and Ed Reed are long gone, but this unit remains one of the strongest in the league. I have them ranked at #2 in overall fantasy opportunity against other D/ST groupings thanks to their pass rush and ability to create turnovers.

### Sleeper Watch

*Popular Sleepers: N/A*

*Deep Sleeper: John Brown, WR*

*John Brown has been very productive in Arizona. Unfortunately, Baltimore does not have an explosive offense in place.*

*Hibernators: Chris Moore, WR*

*He's also hurt by the offense's production, but Chris Moore saw his targets increase from 16 in his rookie season to 38 in 2017. A 70 target, 40 reception year is not out of the question.*

# Cincinnati Bengals

## 2017 Fantasy Opportunity Summary (Offensive Positions):

| Position | Player | PPR Rank vs Position | PPR Overall Rank |
|----------|--------|----------------------|------------------|
| Quarterback | Andy Dalton | 29 | 29 |
| Running Back | Joe Mixon | 17 | 23 |
| Running Back 2 | Giovani Bernard | 14 | 13 |
| Wide Receiver 1 | A.J. Green | 10 | 6 |
| Wide Receiver 2 | Brandon LaFell | 21 | 23 |
| Wide Receiver 3 | Tyler Boyd | 29 | 30 |
| Tight End | Tyler Kroft | 21 | 16 |

**Fantasy Opportunity Analysis by Position (Offense Only):**
**Quarterback:**

This was somewhat of a lost year for the Red Rifle. Tyler Eifert and Tyler Boyd played in a combined 5 games last season. Their offensive coordinator was fired/replaced during the season. They could never build much momentum and Dalton's scores were the lowest in his career. However, I should give the Bengals bonus points for leading the league in pass catchers named Tyler.

**Running Back:**

As if the passing game wasn't enough, the running back situation never rose above "toilet water" status. That is to say, it was good enough to sustain … but nothing you'd want to rely on.

**Wide Receiver:**

For the umpteenth year, A.J. Green found himself among league leaders in targets. Unfortunately, of the 143 throws that came in his direction, he only hauled in 75 of them. He was over 1,000 yards, but only just. The entire offense needed increased efficiency. That's something they hope to find this year with John Ross, Tyler Boyd and Tyler Eifert back in the mix.

**Tight End:**

Tyler Kroft was a nice pickup for people in need of a spot start at the position. He was also undervalued in Daily Fantasy for much of the season.

**2018 Offseason Analysis**

**Transactions**

| Position | Player | PPR Rank vs Position | PPR Overall rank | Standard Rank vs Position | Standard Overall Rank |
|---|---|---|---|---|---|
| Quarterback | Andy Dalton | 8 | 82 | 8 | 86 |
| Running Back 1 | Joe Mixon | 29 | 115 | 28 | 68 |
| Running Back 2 | Giovani Bernard | 7 | 113 | 7 | 105 |
| Wide Receiver 1 | A.J. Green | 7 | 10 | 5 | 13 |
| Wide Receiver 2 | Brandon LaFell | 13 | 121 | 14 | 117 |
| Wide Receiver 3 | Tyler Boyd | 26 | 235 | 26 | 237 |
| Tight End 1 | Tyler Eiffert | 10 | 51 | 8 | 71 |
| Kicker | Randy Bullock | 31st Against Kickers | | | |
| Defense/ST | Bengals | 17th Against Defense/ST | | | |

**Draft Summary**

| Round | Overall | Position | Player | College |
|---|---|---|---|---|
| 1 | 21 | C | Billy Price | Ohio St |
| 2 | 54 | S | Jessie Bates | Wake Forest |
| 3 | 77 | DE | Sam Hubbard | Ohio St |
| 3 | 78 | OLB | Malik Jefferson | Texas |
| 4 | 112 | RB | Mark Walton | Miami |
| 5 | 151 | CB | Davontae Harris | Illinois St |
| 5 | 158 | DT | Andrew Brown | Virginia |
| 5 | 170 | CB | Darius Phillips | Western Michigan |
| 7 | 249 | QB | Logan Woodside | Toledo |
| 7 | 252 | G | Rod Taylor | Mississippi |
| 7 | 253 | WR | Auden Tate | Florida St |

**Coaching Changes**

Ken Zampese started the 2017 season as offensive coordinator, but was quickly fired. Bill Lazor assumed control of an offense that had been sputtering for over a year. The Bengals were hit by the injury bug, but Lazor's play calling did appear to improve the fantasy scoring output of his roster. With an entire offseason and a healthy unit returning in 2018, I expect an improvement in overall scoring.

Last year's defensive coordinator, Paul Geunther, was replaced with Teryl Austin. His most recent work came with the Detroit Lions in the same capacity. In Austin's four seasons with the Lions, his defenses finished 3rd, 23rd, 13th and 21st in points against. He will be working closely with head coach, Marvin Lewis, however. I don't anticipate much of a change from a play calling or tactical point of view.

**2018 Fantasy Outlook**

**Projected Position Rankings**

| Position | Player | PPR Rank vs Position | PPR Overall rank | Standard Rank vs Position | Standard Overall Rank |
|---|---|---|---|---|---|
| Quarterback | Andy Dalton | 8 | 81 | 8 | 86 |
| Running Back 1 | Joe Mixon | 29 | 114 | 28 | 69 |
| Running Back 2 | Giovani Bernard | 7 | 112 | 7 | 104 |
| Wide Receiver 1 | A.J. Green | 7 | 9 | 5 | 13 |
| Wide Receiver 2 | Brandon LaFell | 13 | 120 | 14 | 116 |
| Wide Receiver 3 | Tyler Boyd | 26 | 234 | 26 | 236 |
| Tight End 1 | Tyler Eiffert | 10 | 51 | 8 | 72 |
| Kicker | Randy Bullock | 31st Against Kickers | | | |
| Defense/ST | Bengals | 17th Against Defense/ST | | | |

**Position Commentary:**

**Quarterback:**

People will be divided over Andy Dalton this season. He hasn't put up great numbers since Hue Jackson left town. I see this as an opportunity for fantasy GMs. One could make the argument that his decline had correlation with the coaching changes, but I see more correlation with the injuries to Tyler Eifert and the departure of Mohamed Sanu in free agency. When this team has a viable middle-of-the-field option in the passing game and a viable WR2 opposite A.J. Green, they score.

There were flashes last year. With improvements projected on the roster, I see Dalton's Opportunity Rank inside the top-10. He will likely be falling to QB2 status across fantasy drafts, so he'll be an excellent late-round option if you miss the earlier run on QBs.

**Running Back:**

RB Jeremy Hill was the odd man out in Cincinnati and has moved on to New England. This leaves Joe Mixon in charge of the early downs and Gio Bernard the top option on passing downs. This backfield looks a lot like the situation in Baltimore. Mixon, like Collins, is talented, but his Opportunity Score suffers with the influence of Bernard.

Bernard, like Allen of the Ravens, has a firm role on the team as a pass catching running back. He ranks 7th in RB2 opportunity and will be a viable play in the flex spot in deeper leagues.

**Wide Receiver:**

I've always been a bit cool on A.J. Green. I recognize that at the end of the season, he will have WR1 numbers, but he tends to be streaky. He will throw up a 10 catch, 200-yard, 3 TD game a couple of times a year and follow them up with a bunch of 45-yard outings. I find him to be more of a matchup play, but like roulette, when that number hits, it's a beautiful thing.

Brandon LaFell might have to fight off Tyler Boyd and John Ross for WR2 status, but for now, I think his status is safe. I like his potential as a WR2 this year.

**Tight End:**

A healthy Tyler Eifert is the fantasy football equivalent of a snow leopard. It's extremely rare, but when you see it, it's a wonderous experience. If he comes into 2018 healthy, he has the potential to be a tier-1 TE. From a strategic perspective, I'll be ranking Eifert at the bottom of tier-2. Buyer beware.

If Eifert is out, Tyler Kroft is probably a lower-tier starter in this offense.

**Kicker:**

If the Bengals offense returns to form, the kicker position will be worth a start, but there's no competitive advantage that would make them draft-worthy.

**Defense/Special Teams:**

With the additions of Preston Brown and Chris Baker in free agency and S Jessie Bates in the draft, the Bengals have an infusion of talent at all three levels on defense. All told, I don't think there's going to be a major impact on turnovers and sacks, two staples of a high-scoring defense.

I have the Bengals ranked as a mid-tier defense. They will likely be drafted a little too high by your competitors, but they should be available on waivers for spot-play later in the season.

**Sleeper Watch**

*Popular Sleepers: N/A*

*Deep Sleeper: N/A*

*Hibernators: John Ross, WR*

*He had less targets (2) than games played (3) in his rookie year. However, he has a lot of talent and plays on an offense that should improve this season. He's a candidate to get meaningful snaps in the middle of 2018.*

## Cleveland Browns

**2017 Fantasy Opportunity Summary (Offensive Positions):**

| Position | Player | PPR Rank vs Position | PPR Overall Rank |
|----------|--------|----------------------|------------------|
| Quarterback | DeShone Kizer | 18 | 18 |
| Running Back | Isaiah Crowell | 27 | 31 |
| Running Back 2 | Duke Johnson | 4 | 6 |
| Wide Receiver 1 | Corey Coleman/Josh Gordon | 30 | 29 |
| Wide Receiver 2 | Kenny Britt | 30 | 32 |
| Wide Receiver 3 | Ricardo Louis/Rashard Higgins | 28 | 29 |
| Tight End | David Njoku | 24 | 21 |

**Fantasy Opportunity Analysis by Position (Offense Only):**
**Quarterback:**

Cleveland loved DeShone Kizer so much that they shipped him to Green Bay after the season. While he might not have been the answer to Cleveland's QB woe, he did score reasonably well from a fantasy perspective. In many cases, there were better plays on the waiver wire, but he was able to find the end zone through the air and on his feet. Running TDs by a QB are a very underrated stat in the roto world.

**Running Back:**

As someone who had Isiah Crowell on his fantasy team last year, I can attest to the horror of the situation. The rankings showed a 27/31 Opportunity Ranking (PPR/Non-PPR) vs. 4$^{th}$/6$^{th}$ Opportunity Rankings for RB2, Duke Johnson. This displayed a true committee approach. Interestingly, both averaged over 4 yards per carry. Unfortunately, Cleveland was behind so often, they were underutilized.

I mentioned how the Patriots used James White as a receiver. Duke Johnson had more opportunity in the passing game. Those numbers are consistent with a mid-tier WR2.

**Wide Receiver:**

In a PPR league, Browns WRs would be ranked 30$^{th}$, 30$^{th}$ and 28$^{th}$ against their peers. Ouch. The intrigue in this position group comes from Josh Gordon's return. With him serving as a WR1 and bumping the talented Corey Coleman to WR2, the Browns passing game found a bit of life towards the end of the season. 2018 is looking up (but there was really nowhere else to look, frankly).

**Tight End:**

David Njoku was the starter by the end of the year. He ranked in the bottom-third of the league against other tight ends, but I anticipate a surge upward next season thanks to the upward momentum of the Browns offense.

## 2018 Offseason Analysis

**Transactions**

| Key Losses | | | Key Additions | | |
|---|---|---|---|---|---|
| Pos | Player | New Team | Pos | Player | Old Team |
| OT | Zach Banner | Carolina | CB | T.J. Carrie | Oakland |
| WR | Sammie Coates | Houston | TE | Darren Fells | Detroit |
| RB | Isiah Crowell | NY Jets | CB | E.J. Gaines | Buffalo |
| QB | Kevin Hogan | Washington | OT | Chris Hubbard | Pittsburgh |
| QB | Cody Kessler | Jaguars | RB | Carlos Hyde | Cleveland |
| LB | Josh Keyes | Houston | WR | Jeff Janis | Green Bay |
| QB | DeShone Kizer | Green Bay | WR | Jarvis Landry | Miami |
| CB | Jason McCourty | New England | CB | Terrance Mitchell | Kansas City |
| NT | Danny Shelton | New England | LB | Dadi Nicolas | Kansas City |
| CB | C.J. Smith | Seattle | CB | Damarious Randall | Green Bay |
| CB | Jamar Taylor | Arizona | DE | Chris Smith | Cincinnati |
| TE | Randall Telfer | Kansas City | QB | Drew Stanton | Arizona |
| DB | B.W. Webb | NY Giants | OT | Donald Stephenson | Denver |
| *OT* | *Joe Thomas* | *Retired* | QB | Tyrod Taylor | Buffalo |

**Draft Summary**

| Round | Overall | Position | Player | College |
|---|---|---|---|---|
| 1 | 1 | QB | Baker Mayfield | Oklahoma |
| 1 | 4 | CB | Denzel Ward | Ohio St |
| 2 | 33 | G | Austin Corbett | Nevada |
| 2 | 35 | RB | Nick Chubb | Georgia |
| 3 | 67 | DE | Chad Thomas | Miami |
| 4 | 105 | WR | Antonio Callaway | Florida |
| 5 | 150 | ILB | Genard Avery | Memphis |
| 6 | 175 | WR | Damion Ratley | Texas A&M |
| 6 | 188 | DB | Simeon Thomas | Louisiana-Lafayett |

## Coaching Changes

The Browns aggressively pursued, and landed, offensive coordinator Todd Haley when he hit the open market. Though his offenses in Kansas City left something to be desired (when he had no quarterback talent to speak of), the rest of his offenses have produced. He's piloted two offensive schemes that have made deep playoff runs (Pittsburgh and Arizona).

Haley runs an offense predicated on getting the ball out of his quarterback's hands quickly. He will use backs and tight ends, but he commonly prefers distributing to wide receivers. Cleveland has a lot of talent at this position.

Haley hovers around a 60/40 Pass/Run ratio. The scheme and talent in Cleveland have improved. It will be interesting to see if Taylor or Mayfield will win the position battle.

## 2018 Fantasy Outlook

### Projected Position Rankings

| Position | Player | PPR Rank vs Position | PPR Overall rank | Standard Rank vs Position | Standard Overall Rank |
|---|---|---|---|---|---|
| Quarterback | Tyrod Taylor | 25 | 181 | 25 | 184 |
| Running Back 1 | Nick Chubb / Carlos Hyde | 28 | 105 | 29 | 106 |
| Running Back 2 | Duke Johnson Jr. | 5 | 74 | 5 | 104 |
| Wide Receiver 1 | Josh Gordon | 19 | 64 | 19 | 56 |
| Wide Receiver 2 | Jarvis Landry | 1 | 72 | 1 | 75 |
| Wide Receiver 3 | Corey Coleman | 2 | 114 | 2 | 96 |
| Tight End 1 | David Njoku | 23 | 216 | 22 | 217 |
| Kicker | Zane Gonzaelez | 32nd Against Kickers | | | |
| Defense/ST | Browns | 24th Against Defense/ST | | | |

**Position Commentary:**

**Quarterback:**

In Tyrod Taylor, Cleveland obtained a proven NFL talent who can both move and take care of the ball. He is a significant upgrade over last year's starter, Deshone Kizer and could produce nice numbers with his arsenal of wide receivers. Though the Cleveland Browns QB Opportunity Rank is only 25th, Taylor could be a solid fantasy backup if he remains the starter.

Baker Mayfield, the #1 pick in last year's draft, will have a shot to win the starting job. The situation is similar to Buffalo's in that there's a veteran who will likely open the starter, but the rookie will be given every opportunity to take over during the season. Mayfield can move the ball and has solid accuracy. If he can take care of the ball vs. NFL defenses, he might be able to put up points.

For now, I suggest steering clear of the QB situation.

**Running Back:**

The 2017 Browns running game never got off the ground, but the addition of Carlos Hyde in free agency and Nick Chubb in the draft will change things. I expect Chubb to be the number one option this season, but this has the makings of a three-man committee with Duke Johnson ranked as the 5th-best RB2 thanks to his involvement in the passing game.

Similar to the Patriots RB situation, don't pick any of these RBs before the middle rounds. Your most consistent play could be Duke Johnson in a PPR league.

**Wide Receiver:**

The Browns certainly aren't lacking for talent at the WR position. In addition to welcoming Josh Gordon back with open arms late in 2017 and Corey Coleman's continued rise, the Browns acquired heavily targeted Jarvis Landry from the Miami Dolphins.

Cleveland's WR1 Opportunity Rank seems pedestrian at 19th, but WR2 and WR3 both rank within the top 2 against their peers. This shows depth. I think Landry and Gordon will be interchangeable as fantasy options this year. See our overall rankings to make a proper investment on draft day.

**Tight End:**

The Browns TE position has lacked the last couple of years, but Hue Jackson's deployment of Tyler Eifert while coordinating the Bengals offense proves his willingness to use the position. I suspect Jackson will utilize Duke Johnson and slot receivers over the middle of the field, but don't overlook David Njoku. He was targeted 60 times last season and brought in 4 touchdowns in a noteworthy rookie campaign. He will be on everyone's sleeper list and has TE1 potential.

**Kicker:**

The Browns boast the league's worst Opportunity Rank for kicker. Pass.

**D/ST:**

As a fantasy GM, it would have been intriguing to see the Browns draft Bradley Chubb to pair with Myles Garrett. That could have generated more pressures, sacks and turnovers. As an NFL team, yes, they are improving. As a fantasy football D/ST group, I'll pass in the draft.

**Sleeper Watch**

*Popular Sleeper: N/A*

*Deep Sleepers: David Njoku, TE*

*He battled for the starting spot all year ,but still managed 60 targets, 32 receptions, 386 yards and 4 TDs. I don't love the scheme, but he's a candidate to stash.*

*Hibernators: N/A*

# Pittsburgh Steelers

## 2017 Fantasy Opportunity Summary (Offensive Positions):

| Position | Player | PPR Rank vs Position | PPR Overall Rank |
|----------|--------|----------------------|------------------|
| Quarterback | Ben Roethlisberger | 9 | 9 |
| Running Back | Le'Veon Bell | 2 | 2 |
| Running Back 2 | James Conner | 32 | 32 |
| Wide Receiver 1 | Antonio Brown | 1 | 2 |
| Wide Receiver 2 | JuJu Smith-Schuster | 4 | 4 |
| Wide Receiver 3 | Martavis Bryant | 9 | 6 |
| Tight End | Jesse James | 22 | 24 |

**Fantasy Opportunity Analysis by Position (Offense Only):**
**Quarterback:**

Big Ben was a stable QB. Todd Haley's system allowed Roethlisberger to get rid of the ball quickly and his receiving corps was one of the deepest in the league in 2017. There's not much to say about him, honestly. He's consistent and a viable play every week of the season.

**Running Back:**

Le'Veon Bell is in rare company. He's the 2nd-highest ranked RB at his position. He's so dominant within Pittsburgh that Pittsburgh's RB2 last year *barely* averaged more than 2 carries per game. Bell rarely left the field.

**Wide Receiver:**

Fun stat: through the first 8 years of Antonio Brown's career, he's hauled in 723 passes. Jerry Rice caught 610 in his first 8 years. He's a full season and a half ahead of Rice's output. Brown isn't just elite, he's in all-time elite territory.

Juju Smith-Schuster emerged last year, which allowed Pittsburgh to bump Martavis Bryant to their third-targeted WR. This was the top WR group last year with all three positions ranked in the top 10 among their peers.

**Tight End:**

Unfortunately, with so much output by Bell and the WR group, there wasn't a lot of food left on the plate for poor Jesse James. While he played well and was efficient when he had his chances, there weren't enough balls to go around.

**Kicker:**

The Browns boast the league's worst Opportunity Rank for a kicker. Pass.

**D/ST:**

As a fantasy GM, it would have been intriguing to see the Browns draft Bradley Chubb to pair with Myles Garrett. That could have generated more pressures, sacks and turnovers. As an NFL team, yes, they are improving. As a fantasy football D/ST group, I'll pass in the draft.

## 2018 Offseason Analysis

### Transactions

| Key Losses | | | Key Additions | | |
| --- | --- | --- | --- | --- | --- |
| Pos | Player | New Team | Pos | Player | Old Team |
| WR | Martavis Bryant | Oakland | ILB | Jon Bostic | Indianapolis |
| FS | William Gay | Pittsburgh | SS | Morgan Burnett | Green Bay |
| OT | Chris Hubbard | Cleveland | | | |

### Draft Summary

| Round | Overall | Position | Player | College |
| --- | --- | --- | --- | --- |
| 1 | 28 | S | Terrell Edmunds | Virginia Tech |
| 2 | 60 | WR | James Washington | Oklahoma St |
| 3 | 76 | QB | Mason Rudolph | Oklahoma St |
| 3 | 92 | OT | Chuks Okorafor | Western Michigan |
| 5 | 148 | S | Marcus Allen | Penn St |
| 5 | 165 | ILB | Jaylen Samuels | N.C. State |
| 7 | 246 | DT | Joshua Frazier | Alabama |

### Coaching Changes

2017's offensive coordinator, Todd Haley, was not welcomed back in 2018. The Steelers have promoted from within, hiring previous quarterbacks coach Randy Fichtner. Fichtner has been with the organization since 2007, and I don't expect many changes to the playbook. Roethlisberger will likely be given a bit more freedom at the line of scrimmage which could affect Bell's rushing attempt totals. These, however, will likely be mitigated by a corresponding increase in receiving opportunities.

## 2018 Fantasy Outlook

### Projected Position Rankings

| Position | Player | PPR Rank vs Position | PPR Overall rank | Standard Rank vs Position | Standard Overall Rank |
|---|---|---|---|---|---|
| Quarterback | Ben Roethlisberger | 12 | 85 | 12 | 89 |
| Running Back 1 | Le'Veon Bell | 2 | 2 | 2 | 4 |
| Running Back 2 | Stevan Ridley | 32 | 243 | 32 | 245 |
| Wide Receiver 1 | Antonio Brown | 1 | 5 | 1 | 6 |
| Wide Receiver 2 | JuJu Smith-Schuster | 10 | 77 | 9 | 65 |
| Wide Receiver 3 | James Washington | 7 | 211 | 6 | 216 |
| Tight End 1 | Jesse James | 22 | 208 | 23 | 221 |
| Kicker | Chris Boswell | 7th (tied) Against Kickers | | | |
| Defense/ST | Steelers | 4th Against Defense/ST | | | |

### Position Commentary:

### Quarterback:

The loss of Todd Haley as offensive coordinator might improve Roethlisberger's temperament, but I'm not sure it'll improve his play on the field. Big Ben has been an elite quarterback for years and played exceptionally well in Todd Haley's quick release offense. While Pittsburgh's offensive scheme will remain intact, giving Roethlisberger more freedom could leave his aging body vulnerable to more hits. He's still a worthy fantasy QB, but his Opportunity Ranking suffers a setback and I foresee a downgrade in his efficiency.

### Running Back:

Le'Veon Bell ranks #2 overall in fantasy opportunity. He's a highly productive 3-down back. He has a strangle hold on playing time ... so much so that Pittsburgh's RB2 position is ranked 32nd in opportunity for 2018. Draft Bell early and rejoice.

### Wide Receiver:

Pittsburgh has an impressive group of skill positions and WR is no exception. Antonio Brown ranks #1 in fantasy opportunity among WR1s and is at the top of tier-1 picks in the draft. JuJu Smith-Schuster came on strong as a WR2 last year and ranks within the top 10 against his peers at that position.

Trading Martavis Bryant to Oakland leaves a whole at the WR3 position, which also falls in the top 10 in fantasy opportunity against their peers. WR James Washington, Pittsburgh's 2nd round pick, is likely to receive these targets and is a nice deep sleeper in fantasy leagues.

### Tight End:

Between Bell, Brown, Smith-Schuster and James Washington, there aren't many targets left for the tight ends. Jesse James will remain the first-string tight end. He's a solid player, but I don't see any way he significantly improves the 43 receptions and 372 yards he had in 2017. He'll be a match up start at best.

### Kicker:

Pittsburgh puts up a lot of points. I wouldn't spend much more than a last-round pick on this position, but Chris Boswell will be worth a draft selection for you.

### Defense/Special Teams:

You can generally count on Pittsburgh's ability to generate pressure. This leads to sacks and turnovers, which are a fantasy D/ST's best friend. I have their defense ranked 4th in fantasy opportunity in 2018.

### Sleeper Watch

*Popular Sleepers: N/A*

*Deep Sleeper: James Washington, WR*

*Everything is pointing to him assuming Martavis Bryant's role.*

*Hibernators: N/A*

# AFC SOUTH

# AFC South

## Houston Texans

**2017 Fantasy Opportunity Summary (Offensive Positions):**

| Position | Player | PPR Rank vs Position | PPR Overall Rank |
|---|---|---|---|
| Quarterback | Deshaun Watson | 7 | 7 |
| Running Back | Lamar Miller | 14 | 14 |
| Running Back 2 | D'Onta Foreman | 24 | 20 |
| Wide Receiver 1 | DeAndre Hopkins | 2 | 1 |
| Wide Receiver 2 | Will Fuller | 12 | 9 |
| Wide Receiver 3 | Bruce Ellington | 22 | 22 |
| Tight End | C.J. Fiedorowicz/Ryan Griffin | 26 | 26 |

**Fantasy Opportunity Analysis by Position (Offense Only):**
**Quarterback:**

In the games Houston started, Watson was unstoppable. Houston had the top-ranked offense during that stretch. He moved the ball at will against everyone. He was so dominant in that stretch that Houston's position grouping finished 7th overall in spite of Tom Savage and T.J. Yates starting a combined 10 games.

**Running Back:**

Foreman was more prominent in the back half of the year, but Miller was still the starter. Neither inspired much hope if you were leaning on them in key fantasy games last season. Miller averaged 3.7 yards per carry compared to Foreman's 4.2 YPC. This will be an interesting position to watch throughout training camp.

**Wide Receiver:**

Deandre Hopkins finished with 174 targets last season. That's a career for some people. Though he performed the best under Watson (that was the case across the board), his play didn't deteriorate with the backups. That makes a strong case for tier-1 WR status by itself.

Will Fuller was an interesting case. He was unable to produce outside of Watson. His propensity to run deep routes could be the issue. Watson hit him on a few bombs. The others weren't able to.

**Tight End:**

Ryan Griffen and C.J. Fiedorowicz shared primary tight end privileges last season. The offense didn't focus much on the position, so they are only viable as a desperation start in fantasy or Daily Fantasy when the matchup is favorable.

## 2018 Offseason Analysis

### Transactions

| Key Losses | | | Key Additions | | |
|---|---|---|---|---|---|
| Pos | Player | New Team | Pos | Player | Old Team |
| OT | Breno Giacomini | Oakland | CB | Johnson Bademosi | New England |
| SS | Marcus Gilchrist | Oakland | WR | Sammmie Coates | Cleveland |
| QB | Josh Johnson | Oakland | CB | Aaron Colvin | Jacksonville |
| QB | Tom Savage | New Orleans | C | Zach Fulton | Kansas City |
| TE | C.J. Fiedorowicz | Retired | OT | Seantrel Henderson | Buffalo |
| | | | OG | Senio Kelemete | New Orleans |
| | | | LB | Josh Keyes | Cleveland |
| | | | FS | Tyrann Mathieu | Arizona |
| | | | QB | Brandon Weeden | Tennessee |

### Draft Summary

| Round | Overall | Position | | Player | College |
|---|---|---|---|---|---|
| 3 | 68 | S | | Justin Reid | Stanford |
| 3 | 80 | C | | Martinas Rankin | Mississippi St |
| 3 | 98 | TE | | Jordan Akins | UCF |
| 4 | 103 | WR | | Keke Coutee | Texas Tech |
| 6 | 177 | DE | | Duke Ejiofor | Wake Forest |
| 6 | 37 | TE | | Jordan Thomas | Mississippi St |
| 6 | 214 | Edge | | Peter Kalambayi | Stanford |
| 7 | 222 | DB | | Jermaine Kelly | San Jose St |

### Coaching Changes

Previous defensive coordinator Mike Vrabel was hired as the head coach of the Tennessee Titans. Houston promoted from within. Romeo Crennel, who worked closely with the defense under the title of assistant head coach, will assume control of the unit. I don't anticipate much change in tactics. A healthy J.J. Watt and improvements in the linebacking group should pay dividends this year.

### 2018 Fantasy Outlook

### Projected Position Rankings

| Position | Player | PPR Rank vs Position | PPR Overall rank | Standard Rank vs Position | Standard Overall Rank |
|---|---|---|---|---|---|
| Quarterback | Deshaun Watson | 1 | 14 | 1 | 19 |
| Running Back 1 | Lamar Miller | 13 | 46 | 14 | 48 |
| Running Back 2 | D'Onta Foreman | 27 | 138 | 26 | 133 |
| Wide Receiver 1 | DeAndre Hopkins | 2 | 3 | 2 | 5 |
| Wide Receiver 2 | Will Fuller V | 5 | 48 | 3 | 28 |
| Wide Receiver 3 | Bruce Ellington | 30 | 238 | 30 | 240 |
| Tight End 1 | Ryan Griffen | 26 | 218 | 26 | 223 |
| Kicker | Ka'imi Fairbairn | 25th Against Kickers | | | |
| Defense/ST | Texans | 28th Against Defense/ST | | | |

**Position Commentary:**

**Quarterback:**

Deshaun Watson was incredible in his brief time as starter in 2017. During those weeks, Houston ranked first in the NFL in total offense. Had he continued to play at that level, he would have been the top fantasy quarterback last year. His injury history concerns me, but he's legit and worthy of tier-1 QB status.

**Running Back:**

This is an ugly RB situation. Lamar Miller had 3 times as many carries as D'Onta Foreman last year, but Foreman was much more efficient when he ran. I think Miller will be trusted more in passing downs (and with Watson at QB, there will be plenty of them). Foreman will eat into Miller's carries, and I suspect will be the primary ball handler on first and second down by the end of 2018.

**Wide Receiver:**

Analysts say liquor stores are "recession proof". DeAndre Hopkins is "quarterback recession proof". In this offense, he will put up numbers regardless of who is throwing the ball. He's in the elite, tier-1 WR category and will be drafted in the first round of your league this season.

Will Fuller's over-the-top speed makes him reliant on a passer that can hit him deep. While Watson is playing, he has elite potential. Thanks to a few injuries last year and his totals tapering off after Watson's injury, he will be undervalued in fantasy drafts and in the first weeks of Daily Fantasy football. Take advantage.

**Tight End:**

The TE group in Houston has never been particularly exciting from a fantasy perspective. Ryan Griffin, C.J. Fiedorowicz and Stephen Anderson all made a Daily Fantasy lineup or two last year, but I never gave them serious consideration in fantasy football.

The drafting of Jordan Akins at TE in the 3rd round is an interesting selection. If he can fulfill his athletic potential and give Watson an intermediate option over the middle, it could really open things up for Fuller and Hopkins.

**Kicker:**

If Watson is healthy, Houston will have a top-ranked offense in the league. That being the case, Houston's kicker will be valuable. Ka'imi Fairbairn will likely be available in the last round and should every bit the value of a Stephen Gostkowski.

**Defense/Special Teams:**

Houston opens the year with a 28th in Opportunity Ranking, but I will overrule this metric slightly. The return of J.J. Watt will have significant implications on the unit. His presence will impact the key metrics of sack totals, turnover creation and yards per play heavily in Houston's favor.

Based on the last year or two, this group could slip on draft day. If they're sitting there in the last two rounds, they are worth a flyer.

**Sleeper Watch**

***Popular Sleepers: D'Onta Foreman, RB; Will Fuller, WR***

*Foreman is battling Lamar Miller for carries, but was starting to assert himself in 2017. He's dealing with an Achilles injury, but could take over the first and second down carries when healthy.*

*Will Fuller is extremely undervalued. In the few games where he and Deshaun Watson were healthy, Fuller scored a ton of points.*

***Deep Sleepers: N/A***

***Hibernators: N/A***

# Indianapolis Colts

## 2017 Fantasy Opportunity Summary (Offensive Positions):

| Position | Player | PPR Rank vs Position | PPR Overall Rank |
|---|---|---|---|
| Quarterback | Jacoby Brissett | 30 | 30 |
| Running Back | Frank gore | 22 | 21 |
| Running Back 2 | Marlon Mack | 16 | 17 |
| Wide Receiver 1 | T.Y. Hilton | 25 | 19 |
| Wide Receiver 2 | Donte Moncrief | 31 | 30 |
| Wide Receiver 3 | Kamar Aiken | 31 | 31 |
| Tight End | Jack Doyle | 5 | 8 |

**Fantasy Opportunity Analysis by Position (Offense Only):**
**Quarterback:**

I won't speak ill of Jacoby Brissett. He inherited a team with very little time in training camp. Without Andrew Luck, the Colts never had a chance. This roster is built for a defensive-minded head coach and the offensive scheme wasn't doing Brissett any favors.

**Running Back:**

Is it just me, or has Frank Gore been around since the 1980s? Maybe it was the constant churn of high profile running backs from the University of Miami, but the guy just puts up year after year of solid numbers. He's rarely been someone that you'd fight to draft early, but Gore very quietly had over 1,200 combined yards last year.

Marlon Mack is starting to come on. He led Colts Running Backs in yards per carry and matched Gore's output in the passing game.

**Wide Receiver:**

It's hard to say much about this group as the offense was hard to watch. T.Y. Hilton led the team in targets at 109, but Brissett relied heavily on TE Jack Doyle. Fellow receivers seemed non-existent. Donte Moncrief all but disappeared.

**Tight End:**

Jack Doyle was the one bright spot of the Colts offense last season. He amassed 108 targets and hauled 80 of them for 690 yards and 4 TDs.

## 2018 Offseason Analysis

### Transactions

| Key Losses | | | Key Additions | | |
|---|---|---|---|---|---|
| Pos | Player | New Team | Pos | Player | Old Team |
| ILB | Jon Bostic | Pittsburgh | DE | Denico Autry | Oakland |
| CB | Vontae Davis | Buffalo | TE | Eric Ebron | Detroit |
| RB | Frank Gore | Miami | WR | Ryan Grant | WAS |
| DT | Henry Anderson | NY Jets | OG | Matt Slauson | LAC |
| CB | Rashaan Melvin | Oakland | | | |
| OLB | Barkevious Mingo | Seattle | | | |
| WR | Donte Moncrief | Jacksonville | | | |
| DT | Jonathan Hankins | NA | | | |
| CB | Antonio Cromartie | Retired | | | |

### Draft Summary

| Round | Overall | Position | Player | College |
|---|---|---|---|---|
| 1 | 6 | G | Quenton Nelson | Notre Dame |
| 2 | 36 | OLB | Darius Leonard | South Carolina St |
| 2 | 37 | G | Braden Smith | Auburn |
| 2 | 52 | Edge | Kemoko Turay | Rutgers |
| 2 | 64 | DE | Tyquan Lewis | Ohio St |
| 4 | 104 | RB | Nyheim Hines | N.C. State |
| 5 | 159 | WR | Daurice Fountain | Northen Iowa |
| 5 | 169 | RB | Jordan Wilkins | Mississippi |
| 6 | 185 | WR | Deon Cain | Clemson |
| 7 | 221 | LB | Matthew Adams | Houston |
| 7 | 235 | LB | Zaire Franklin | Syracuse |

### Coaching Changes

Indianapolis changed their entire coaching structure. After famously missing out on Josh McDaniels, Indianapolis rebounded and hired Frank Reich, who had previous offensive coordinator stints with the Eagles and Chargers. Reich is experienced and well-respected in NFL circles. Andrew Luck, for the first time in his career, will have an offensive-minded head coach, and I anticipate a return to his fantasy glory.

The Colts have talent on both sides of the ball. I am using the 2015 Chargers offensive play calling structure to feed our analysis as the personnel groupings match well.

The defensive unit in Indianapolis has had success. The hiring of Matt Eberfuls (previously with Dallas as linebackers coach) displays a commitment to aggressive play calling on that side of the ball. The Colts will be an interesting team to watch in 2018.

**2018 Fantasy Outlook**

**Projected Position Rankings**

| Position | Player | PPR Rank vs Position | PPR Overall rank | Standard Rank vs Position | Standard Overall Rank |
|---|---|---|---|---|---|
| Quarterback | Andrew Luck | 11 | 58 | 11 | 60 |
| Running Back 1 | Marlon Mack | 31 | 134 | 31 | 134 |
| Running Back 2 | Nyheim Hines | 14 | 132 | 15 | 127 |
| Wide Receiver 1 | T.Y. Hilton | 27 | 39 | 26 | 30 |
| Wide Receiver 2 | Ryan Grant | 16 | 156 | 21 | 128 |
| Wide Receiver 3 | Chester Rogers | 13 | 207 | 13 | 212 |
| Tight End 1 | Jack Doyle | 12 | 104 | 12 | 83 |
| Kicker | Adam Vinatieri | 20th (tied) Against Kickers | | | |
| Defense/ST | Colts | 31st Against Defense/ST | | | |

**Position Commentary:**

**Quarterback:**

Andrew Luck is on track to start in week 1, and he will be doing so with the best offensive coach he's had since Bruce Arians his rookie season. I anticipate Luck to have one of his best seasons to date. His average draft position will be all over the map, but you can consider him a solid tier-2 QB.

**Running Back:**

Frank Gore is gone, which opens up the backfield for Marlon Mack. Frank Reich likes to use multiple backs in multiple roles, so I have a bit of trepidation on drafting Mack early. Christine Michael and Rookie Nyheim Hines could push for early-down carries.

**Wide Receiver:**

T.Y. Hilton will love having Andrew Luck back in the fold. His draft position might slip due to his production while backups were behind center, but you can feel confident pouncing if he's available in the 25-35 range.

The departure of Donte Moncrief opens the door for Ryan Grant (previously of Washington) to receive his targets. He could represent nice sleeper potential.

**Tight End:**

Jack Doyle was a security blanket for Jacoby Brissett last season and proved he can be a viable threat, catching a ludicrous 74% of his 108 targets.  Reich loves featuring tight ends and although Doyle will be drafted as a TE2, he has legitimate potential to reach tier-1 status by the end of the season.

**Kicker:**

Adam Vinatieri's accuracy was over 85% on FG attempts last season.  With the increased offensive potential of the Colts next year, he'll be worthy of a last-round pick.

**Defense/Special Teams:**

The defense was decent last year, but they'll need more sacks and turnovers to ascend this season. Playing from ahead will naturally put teams in passing situations a little more, but I suggest you take them off your draft boards and monitor their situation throughout the season.

**Sleeper Watch**

*Popular Sleepers: N/A*

*Deep Sleeper: Ryan Grant, WR*

*Ryan Grant had a lot of hype in Washington, but didn't put up many points with increased playing time in 2017.  He will be filling the void Moncrief left behind in free agency and will have ample opportunity to score.*

*Hibernators: Nyheim Hines, RB*

*I suspect Hines will win the RB job by the end of 2018.*

## Jacksonville Jaguars
### 2017 Fantasy Opportunity Summary (Offensive Positions):

| Position | Player | PPR Rank vs Position | PPR Overall Rank |
|---|---|---|---|
| Quarterback | Blake Bortles | 15 | 15 |
| Running Back | Leonard Fournette | 7 | 6 |
| Running Back 2 | Chirs Ivory | 2 | 1 |
| Wide Receiver 1 | Marqise Lee | 20 | 18 |
| Wide Receiver 2 | Keelan Cole | 10 | 11 |
| Wide Receiver 3 | Allen Hurns | 6 | 7 |
| Tight End | Mercedes Lewis | 30 | 27 |

**Fantasy Opportunity Analysis by Position (Offense Only):**
**Quarterback:**

Blake Bortles is an interesting case. Media and fans across the country rail on him quite a bit, but his numbers indicate ascension. After drafting Fournette last year, the team's reliance on him decreased and he's responded with more efficiency. His 60.2% completion percentage and 13 interceptions were the best of his career. He is a solid QB backup and based on his lack of popularity, he represents a competitive opportunity.

**Running Back:**

Fournette and Ivory were a formidable combo last year. While Fournette was a definitely top-10 Running Back (ranked 7th/6th in PPR/Non-PPR, respectively), Ivory also represented tremendous value against his RB2 peers. Jacksonville's commitment to the run is worth noting as you create your draft boards.

**Wide Receiver:**

When Allen Robinson went down with injury, many fantasy owners wrote this position group off. Those who paid attention cashed in. Though Allen Hurns didn't ascend to WR1 status as I hoped last season, Marquise Lee and Keelan Cole teamed up and rounded out the group. Lee has a bit of growing to do as a featured receiver, but there is talent on the roster.

**Tight End:**

Mercedes Lewis is a nice player and a great blocker, but wasn't someone you'd want to play on your fantasy team under any scenario.

**2018 Offseason Analysis**

**Transactions**

| Key Losses | | | Key Additions | | |
|---|---|---|---|---|---|
| Pos | Player | New Team | Pos | Player | Old Team |
| CB | Aaron Colvin | Houston | SS | Don Carey | Detroit |
| QB | Chad Henne | Kansas City | FS | Cody Davis | LA Rams |
| WR | Allen Hurns | Dallas | DB | D.J. Hayden | Detroit |
| RB | Chris Ivory | Buffalo | QB | Cody Kessler | Cleveland |
| OG | Patrick Omameh | NY Giants | WR | Donte Moncrief | Indianapolis |
| WR | Allen Robinson | Chicago | OG | Andrew Norwell | Carolina |
| ILB | *Paul Posluszny* | *NA* | TE | Niles Paul | Washington |
| | | | TE | Austin Seferian-Jenkins | NY Jets |

**Draft Summary**

| Round | Overall | Position | Player | College |
|---|---|---|---|---|
| 1 | 29 | DT | Taven Bryan | Florida |
| 2 | 61 | WR | D.J. Chark | LSU |
| 3 | 93 | S | Ronnie Harrison | Alabama |
| 4 | 129 | DT | Will Richardson | N.C. State |
| 6 | 203 | QB | Tanner Lee | Nebraska |
| 7 | 230 | Edge | Leon Jacobs | Wisconsin |
| 7 | 247 | P | Logan Cooke | Mississippi St |

**Coaching Changes**

There have been no coaching changes at the head coach or coordinator levels. Last year, the team had a run-to-pass ratio of about 50/50. Because our analysis shows that Bortles is growing in terms of dependability and because Chris Ivory has departed in free agency, I expect an increase in passing attempts.

# 2018 Fantasy Outlook

## Projected Position Rankings

| Position | Player | PPR Rank vs Position | PPR Overall rank | Standard Rank vs Position | Standard Overall Rank |
|---|---|---|---|---|---|
| Quarterback | Blake Bortles | 16 | 107 | 16 | 121 |
| Running Back 1 | Leonard Fournette | 11 | 9 | 9 | 8 |
| Running Back 2 | T.J. Yeldon | 4 | 208 | 3 | 197 |
| Wide Receiver 1 | Marqise Lee | 23 | 61 | 22 | 51 |
| Wide Receiver 2 | Keelan Cole | 17 | 80 | 16 | 95 |
| Wide Receiver 3 | Donte Moncrief | 8 | 135 | 10 | 208 |
| Tight End 1 | Austin Sefarian-Jenkins | 28 | 229 | 28 | 222 |
| Kicker | Josh Lambo | 14th Against Kickers | | | |
| Defense/ST | Jaguars | 1st Against Defense/ST | | | |

## Position Commentary:

### Quarterback:

There was a lot made of the Bortles extension this offseason, but what options did the Jaguars have? They could have either extended the Bortles experiment or paid similar money to another quarterback who would have to learn a new offense. I'm not particularly high on Bortles' fantasy potential this year, but I do think he'll be worth a start here or there in backup duty. Also, he'll be so cheap in Daily Fantasy that they will be daring you to start him.

### Running Back:

In 2017, Fournette carried the ball 268 times in 13 games. If he can stay healthy in 2018, I expect that number to eclipse 300. On the passing side of the game, Fournette showed ability out of the backfield, catching 36 of 48 targets. He's worth a first round pick.

Chris Ivory has moved onto Buffalo, which leaves 116 carries to be distributed in the backfield. I believe Fournette will acquire the lion's share. Jacksonville's subdued passing game might limit his opportunities in PPR leagues, but he should be a round-one pick regardless.

### Wide Receiver:

The departures of Allen Hurns and Allen Robinson sound like they'll hurt a lot, but the reality is that Robinson didn't play in 2017 and Hurns was overshadowed by Marquise Lee. Keelan Cole isn't a name a lot of people know about, but he quietly put up 42 receptions and 748 yards in his rookie campaign. 2nd round pick D.J. Clark could take over WR3 duties, which offer top-10 fantasy opportunity against the league.

This group isn't particularly sexy, but they do provide consistent results. Lee and Cole will be worthy of roster spots and should be drafted.

**Tight End:**

I like the additions of Austin Seferian-Jenkins and Niles Paul. They both have put up nice numbers when called into action, but this isn't a position the Jags emphasize in their offense. While I like the talent of this group, I suggest staying away on draft day.

**Kicker:**

The accuracy of the group downgraded Jacksonville kicker's Opportunity Rank. Josh Lambo's output, however, was exceptional in 10 games. He is worthy of a draft pick in the last round.

**Defense/Special Teams:**

Along with Minnesota, the Jaguars are ranked 1st in yards per play. Along with Pittsburgh, they are ranked 1st in sacks generated. Behind Baltimore, they are ranked 2nd in turnovers generated. This is a monster defense. They are so good, that I wouldn't mind you drafting them a couple of rounds earlier thanks to their consistency and competitive advantage relative to their competition.

**Sleeper Watch**

*Popular Sleepers: N/A*

*Deep Sleeper: Keelan Cole, WR*

*In his rookie season, Cole saw 83 targets, 42 receptions, 748 yards and 3 touchdowns. Hurns departed in free agency, so his numbers could improve substantially.*

*Hibernator: D.J. Clark, WR*

I think Jacksonville will pass a bit more. With Allen Robinson and Austin Hurns departing, there is opportunity for Clark to post 40 catches.

# Tennessee Titans
## 2017 Fantasy Opportunity Summary (Offensive Positions):

| Position | Player | PPR Rank vs Position | PPR Overall Rank |
|----------|--------|----------------------|------------------|
| Quarterback | Marcus Mariota | 28 | 28 |
| Running Back | DeMarco Murray | 16 | 20 |
| Running Back 2 | Derrick Henry | 15 | 11 |
| Wide Receiver 1 | Rishard Matthews | 28 | 26 |
| Wide Receiver 2 | Eric Decker | 24 | 27 |
| Wide Receiver 3 | Corey Davis | 12 | 15 |
| Tight End | Delanie Walker | 4 | 5 |

**Fantasy Opportunity Analysis by Position (Offense Only):**
**Quarterback:**

Mariota never grew under head coach Mike Mularkey, and that cost the latter his job. He was one of the few quarterbacks to not have a single WR over 100 targets in 2017. Though Mariota's completion percentage was north of 60%, he had fewer touchdowns (13) than Interceptions (15). The only saving grace was his 5 rushing touchdowns. And if you were a fantasy owner in the playoffs, his TD pass to himself against the Chiefs was a nice touch as well.

**Running Back:**

The tandem of Murray (184 carries) and Henry (176 carries) were about as evenly split as any pair in the league. Henry had the better yards per attempt, but Murry was the better receiver, hauling in 39 of his 47 targets.

The group wasn't featured much in the receiving game, which is why their PPR and overall numbers are low in spite of Tennessee's commitment to their "exotic smashmouth" running attack in 2017.

**Wide Receiver:**

Rishard Matthews led all receivers with 87 targets and 53 receptions. Eric Decker may as well have been selling real estate last year because I certainly didn't notice him on the field. Rookie Corey Davis did well in limited opportunity. 65 targets is a solid number for someone entering the league.

Only Matthews was worth a play here and there in 2017. Had they retained Mularkey in 2018, I'd advise you to avoid them altogether ... but that's not the case. More on this later.

**Tight End:**

Delaine Walker's consistent output was the bright spot of Tennessee's offense. He hauled in 74 of his 111 targets for over 800 yards. His three touchdowns marked his lowest total in 5 years.

## 2018 Offseason Analysis

### Transactions

| Key Losses | | | Key Additions | | |
|---|---|---|---|---|---|
| **Pos** | **Player** | **New Team** | **Pos** | **Player** | **Old Team** |
| QB | Matt Cassel | Detroit | CB | Malcolm Butler | New England |
| QB | Brandon Weeden | Houston | QB | Blaine Gabbert | Arizona |
| ILB | Avery Williamson | NY Jets | RB | Dion Lewis | NE |
| WR | Eric Decker | NA | NT | Bennie Logan | KC |
| RB | DeMarco Murray | NA | OG | Kevin Pamphile | TB |

### Draft Summary

| Round | Overall | Position | Player | College |
|---|---|---|---|---|
| 1 | 22 | OLB | Rashaan Evans | Alabama |
| 2 | 9 | Edge | Harold Landry | Boston College |
| 5 | 15 | S | Dane Crulkshank | Arizona |
| 6 | 25 | QB | Luke Falk | Washington St |

### Coaching Changes

Whether you graded Tennessee's 2017 offense by statistical analysis or the eye test, they received low grades across the board. Mike Mularkey was given an ultimatum: fire coordinators or face the consequences. He chose the guillotine.

Tennessee followed the recent trend of hiring youth. Mike Vrabel obviously comes from the Bill Belichick coaching tree. On one hand, there hasn't been a lot of success at the HC level. On the other hand, Vrabel brings youth, energy and fresh ideas. Tennessee's defense in 2017 was stout and is filled with talent. I expect the defense to transition from a predominantly 4-3 alignment to 3-4. There will be a bit of transition, but the talent on this unit shouldn't make the adjustment problematic.

From an NFL organizational point of view, I have a preference to hire offensive-minded head coaches in today's NFL. The thought is that aggressive offenses tend to win more games. Defensive coaches tend to play conservatively with a lead on both sides of the ball and have confidence in their ability to win low-scoring games. There are exceptions to this rule, however.

Aggressive-minded defensive head coaches who empower creative offensive coordinators to attack can offer a potent combination of offensive and defensive attacking. Atlanta offers an example. Dan Quinn was hired after a successful stint as Seattle's defensive coordinator. He hired aggressive coordinator, Kyle

Shanahan, to run the offense. The Falcons were two missed chip blocks away from being Super Bowl Champions.

Mike Vrabel seems to be following the Falcons' lead. The hiring of ex-Rams coach Matt LeFleur is very encouraging. LeFleur comes from the Shanahan line and has also spent time in the Gruden system in Washington. The Shanahan and Gruden systems are widely considered two of the top three offensive designs in the game (along with the McDaniels system in New England). The Functional Sportsaholic is very high on this staff's potential.

## 2018 Fantasy Outlook

### Projected Position Rankings

| Position | Player | PPR Rank vs Position | PPR Overall rank | Standard Rank vs Position | Standard Overall Rank |
|----------|--------|---------------------|------------------|---------------------------|----------------------|
| Quarterback | Marcus Mariota | 17 | 151 | 17 | 160 |
| Running Back 1 | Dion Lewis | 9 | 42 | 10 | 63 |
| Running Back 2 | Derrick Henry | 22 | 137 | 20 | 135 |
| Wide Receiver 1 | Rishard Matthews | 12 | 45 | 10 | 33 |
| Wide Receiver 2 | Corey Davis | 11 | 118 | 8 | 109 |
| Wide Receiver 3 | Tajae' Sharpe | 17 | 164 | 19 | 139 |
| Tight End 1 | Delanie Walker | 5 | 52 | 5 | 57 |
| Kicker | Ryan Succop | 13th Against Kickers | | | |
| Defense/ST | Titans | 10th Against Defense/ST | | | |

### Position Commentary:

### Quarterback:

Do I like Mariota? Yeah, but 13 TDs vs. 15 INTs for a veteran quarterback is not good enough. I'm removing him from my draft board, and I advise you to do the same. He will likely be available via waivers.

### Running Back:

RBs Derrick Henry and Dion Lewis both have a ton of talent. This will be an offense that continues to run the ball, but it's hard to predict how this offense will divvy out carries. I'm anticipating Henry to handle 1st and 2nd down and Lewis to work in as a 3rd down back. They will try to emulate the success of the 2017 Saints.

### Wide Receiver:

The Titans had 496 passing attempts compared to 443 rushing attempts in 2017. Expect those numbers to swing toward a heavier pass rate. I expect Rishard Matthews' stock to increase substantially in the new offensive system. Higher completion percentages + higher target rates = higher fantasy potential.

Matthews ranks 12<sup>th</sup> and 10<sup>th</sup> against his fellow WR1s in PPP/Non-PPR opportunity. He will be a great mid-round pick in your league.

Don't forget about Tajae Sharpe. In his 2016 rookie campaign, he saw 83 targets, 41 receptions, 522 yards and 2 TDs. If he can return to form, he could accumulate 100 targets and 60-70 catches in this system. He should be available late in your fantasy drafts and represents a hibernation sleeper.

**Tight End:**

Delaine Walker has been a standout for a few years now and I think he's going to reach his potential in this offensive system. Last year's "exotic smashmouth" afforded Walker 74 receptions and 807 yards, but only 3 TDs. I expect 6 TDs or more and have ranked him 5<sup>th</sup> in the opportunity rankings vs. tight ends.

**Kicker:**

I think the offense will improve, but not enough for me to suggest you spend a draft pick on their kicker. You can pull a name out of a hat and get similar production.

**Defense/Special Teams:**

This defense was strong, but they are transitioning from a 4/3 to a 3/4. Nose tackle, Bennie Logan and CB Malcolm Butler will help the defense initially, but I have concerns on the edge. Moving a 4/3 end to a 3/4 LB is a recipe for disaster in pass coverage. The Opportunity Rank is within the top 10, but a lot could go wrong in the transition. I suggest passing, but flagging as a waiver watch.

**Sleeper Watch**

*Popular Sleepers: Rishard Matthews, WR*

*I have to include him year because we project him much higher than his draft position. You'll be able to get a bargain on draft day with him.*

*Deep Sleepers: N/A*

*Hibernator: Tajae Sharpe, WR*

*40 catches, 522 yards and 2 TDs in his rookie year. He missed 2017 with injury, but is ready for 2018.*

AFC WEST

# AFC West

## Denver Broncos

### 2017 Fantasy Opportunity Summary (Offensive Positions):

| Position | Player | PPR Rank vs Position | PPR Overall Rank |
|----------|--------|----------------------|------------------|
| Quarterback | Trevor Siemian | 26 | 26 |
| Running Back | C.J. Anderson | 18 | 18 |
| Running Back 2 | Devontae Booker | 17 | 18 |
| Wide Receiver 1 | Demaryius Thomas | 17 | 22 |
| Wide Receiver 2 | Emmanuel Sanders | 17 | 17 |
| Wide Receiver 3 | Bennie Fowler/Cody Latimer | 10 | 4 |
| Tight End | Virgil Green | 32 | 32 |

**Fantasy Opportunity Analysis by Position (Offense Only):**
**Quarterback:**

In a standard 10 or 12 team league, there are generally 7 or 8 quarterbacks on the waiver wire that would have been a better play than Trevor Siemian and his ragtag band of mediocre QBs. DeShone Kizer was obviously superior as a fantasy start last year. That says enough about Denver's 2017 QB situation, I think.

**Running Back:**

Like Miami, Denver is a team that seems to stick to a committee approach out of pure stubbornness. CJ Anderson was over 1,000 yards and 4 YPC in the running game and caught 28 of 40 passes. Unfortunately, he gave away carries to Devontae Booker (3.8 YPC) as the season went on.

**Wide Receiver:**

Demaryius Thomas had a similar year to A.J. Green. He hauled in 83 of 140 targets for 949 yards and a lackluster 5 TDs. I'd say this is more of an indictment of his offensive system and quarterback. That said, DeAndre Hopkins produced with Tom Savage under center.

Emmanuel Sanders barely caught half of his targets last season (47 receptions on 94 targets). This story carries on throughout the grouping. There weren't a lot of bright spots last season.

**Tight End:**

There are many backup tight ends that averaged more points than Denver's primary TE. Offenses that feature neither running back nor TE in the passing game tend to stall, and Denver's 2017 season is no exception.

## 2018 Offseason Analysis

**Transactions**

| | Key Losses | | | Key Additions | |
|---|---|---|---|---|---|
| Pos | Player | New Team | Pos | Player | Old Team |
| P | Riley Dixon | NY Giants | DB | Tramaine Brock | Minnesota |
| TE | Virgil Green | LA Chargers | S | Su'a Cravens | Washington |
| WR | Cody Latimer | NY Giants | QB | Case Keenum | Minnesota |
| QB | Brock Osweiler | Miami | P | Marquette King | Oakland |
| DT | Donald Stephenson | Cleveland | DT | Clinton McDonald | Tampa Bay |
| CB | Aquib Talib | LA Rams | OT | Jared Veldheer | Cleveland |
| QB | Trevor Siemian | Minnesota | | | |
| P | Riley Dixon | NY Giants | | | |

**Draft Summary**

| Round | Overall | Position | Player | College |
|---|---|---|---|---|
| 1 | 5 | DE | Bradley Chubb | N.C. State |
| 2 | 40 | WR | Courtland Sutton | SMU |
| 3 | 71 | RB | Royce Freeman | Oregon |
| 3 | 99 | CB | Isaac Yiadom | Boston College |
| 4 | 106 | ILB | Josey Jewell | Iowa |
| 4 | 113 | WR | Desean Hamilton | Penn St |
| 5 | 156 | TE | Troy Fumagalli | Wiscon |
| 6 | 183 | CB | Sam Jones | Arizona St |
| 6 | 217 | ILB | Keishawn Bierria | Washington |
| 7 | 226 | RB | David Williams | Arkansas |

## Coaching Changes

There are no coaching changes at the head coach or coordinator levels to report. Bill Musgrave is in a similar position to Cincinnati's Bill Lazor. Like Lazor, Musgrave was promoted to OC during the 2018 season. I expect Denver's offense to improve this season, but it will have more to do with changes at quarterback than play calling.

## 2018 Fantasy Outlook

## Projected Position Rankings

| Position | Player | PPR Rank vs Position | PPR Overall rank | Standard Rank vs Position | Standard Overall Rank |
|---|---|---|---|---|---|
| Quarterback | Case Keenum | 21 | 183 | 21 | 182 |
| Running Back 1 | Royce Freeman | 20 | 73 | 21 | 49 |
| Running Back 2 | Devontae Booker | 17 | 180 | 17 | 180 |
| Wide Receiver 1 | Demaryius Thomas | 9 | 65 | 11 | 77 |
| Wide Receiver 2 | Emmanuel Sanders | 8 | 152 | 10 | 154 |
| Wide Receiver 3 | Courtland Sutton | 10 | 205 | 8 | 206 |
| Tight End 1 | Jeff Heuerman | 31 | 241 | 31 | 241 |
| Kicker | Brandon McManus | 20th (tied) Against Kickers | | | |
| Defense/ST | Broncos | 18th (tied) Against Defense/ST | | | |

## Position Commentary:

### Quarterback:

Denver's quarterback situation will be much-improved in 2018 with the addition of Case Keenum. The rotation of quarterbacks in 2017 proved to be ineffective with one of the lowest team completion rates in the league. Keenum's completion percentage was 9 points higher last season. Although there will be an acclimation period as he adjusts to a new offensive system, Keenum has proven he's worthy of a starting role.

### Running Back:

The release of C.J. Anderson was interesting considering he was one of the bright spots in a bad Denver offense last season. Many point to Devontae Booker as the starting RB, but his 3.8 yards per carry isn't going to cut it. The smarter money to receive the bulk of carries is rookie Royce Freeman out of Oregon.

This has the makings of committee, but watch this situation closely throughout training camp. If Freeman can win the job clean by week 3 of the preseason, He'll be in line for over 250 carries and 1,000 yards. For now, I am giving Denver's starting RB an Opportunity Ranking of 21/20 in PPR/non-PPR leagues, but that could increase as I watch Freeman's growth.

### Wide Receiver:

These receivers accumulate targets, but as I mentioned above, they weren't working with top-notch passers. Demaryius Thomas led Broncos with 140 targets in 2018, but caught only 83 of them and found himself under 1,000 yards and with only 5 TDs. For anyone who drafted him in the earlier rounds last year, that did not meet expectations. I anticipate a resurgence of sorts in 2018 and his Opportunity Ranking has him as a mid-tier WR2.

Emmanuel Sanders saw 92 targets in limited action last season. His catch percentage was a disappointing 51.8%. Expect these numbers to increase sharply with a full slate of games. He ranks well against his WR2 competition in opportunity, and he'll be a valuable mid or late round WR pick, if available.

Last year's 3rd and 4th receivers (Bennie Fowler and Cody Latimer) have moved on. Denver has theoretically replaced their output with the drafting of Courtland Sutton from Texas A&M. Thanks to Denver's increased efficiency at quarterback and because they have to replace 87 targets from last year, it's not unreasonable to think Sutton could put up a 70 target, 40 reception, 4 TD type season. I have him labeled as a hibernation-level sleeper.

**Tight End:**

Virgil Green left Denver to sign with the Chargers in the offseason and the team hasn't made a significant investment in the offseason to fill the position. Green's targets from last year (22) will likely fall to Jeff Heuerman. Denver's TE opportunity score is 31st in the league for both PPR/non-PPR leagues. However, this is a situation you'll want to keep an eye on. As I mentioned, Fowler and Latimer have moved on. If you add Virgil Green's departure into the fold, that equates to over 100 targets in line for redistribution.

Heuerman should go undrafted, but watch the preseason snap counts and targets closely. Keenum loved passing to Rudolph in Minnesota. I like Heuerman as a hibernation sleeper and a possible early-season Daily Fantasy play.

**Kicker:**

Even with the addition of Keenum and increased scoring potential, I don't see anything with Denver that would lead me to draft their kicker.

**Defense/Special Teams:**

Last year's tough season leaves Denver's defense a bit undervalued. At 18, their Opportunity Score projects them as a bye week or matchup play. I don't love that Talib was sent to the Rams, but there is still talent in the secondary. The addition of Bradley Chubb to rush passers opposite Von Miller will be the key to this team's potential. Denver had a decent sack total of 2.1 per game. If they can boost that into the high 2s or low 3s, this will be a viable starting defense.

**Sleeper Watch:**

*Popular Sleepers: N/A*

*Deep Sleepers: N/A*

**Hibernators: Courtland Sutton, WR; Jeff Heuerman, TE**

*I like Sutton a lot, but he has to fight Thomas and Sanders for targets. If Case Keenum can bring the magic to Denver, Sutton might be a Daily Fantasy or spot start.*

*With Virgil Green gone, Jeff Heuerman is line to see more targets.*

## Kansas City Chiefs
### 2017 Fantasy Opportunity Summary (Offensive Positions):

| Position | Player | PPR Rank vs Position | PPR Overall Rank |
|---|---|---|---|
| Quarterback | Alex Smith | 3 | 3 |
| Running Back | Kareem Hunt | 3 | 3 |
| Running Back 2 | Charcandrick West | 27 | 27 |
| Wide Receiver 1 | Tyreek Hill | 5 | 3 |
| Wide Receiver 2 | Albert Wilson | 27 | 24 |
| Wide Receiver 3 | Demarcus Robinson | 26 | 26 |
| Tight End | Travis Kelce | 1 | 2 |

### Fantasy Opportunity Analysis by Position (Offense Only):
### Quarterback:

Alex Smith responded to the drafting of Patrick Mahomes by putting together arguably his best season to date. Prior to his interior offensive line having injury issues, the offense was unstoppable. Smith's thank you for his 67.5% completion rate, 4,000 yards and 5:1 TD to INT rate was a trade to Washington.

### Running Back:

Hunt was dynamic last year. As you can see by the disparity between his ranking (3) vs. the Chiefs RB2 peer ranking (27), he has attained bell-cow status. Injuries on the O-line hurt his productivity in the middle of the season, but he regained form toward the end of the year.

### Wide Receiver:

The Chiefs WR group is basically Tyreek Hill and a bunch of guys. Kansas City tries to get the ball into his hands as much as possible. His presence in the running game and on the punt return team is a bonus to solid WR1 production. Outside of Hill, the group struggled.

### Tight End:

Travis Kelce led all TEs in PPR "Opportunity Rank, which demonstrates Kansas City's desire to get him involved in the game plan. He has matched Gronkowski's level of productivity and is healthier year-to-year.

### 2018 Offseason Analysis

### Transactions

| | Key Losses | | | Key Additions | |
|-----|-----------------|------------|-----|------------------|-------------|
| Pos | Player | New Team | Pos | Player | Old Team |
| C | Zach Fulton | Houston | CB | David Amerson | Oakland |
| CB | Phillip Gaines | Buffalo | CB | Kendall Fuller | Washington |
| ILB | Derrick Johnson | Oakland | QB | Chad Henne | Jacksonville |
| NT | Bennie Logan | Tennessee | MLB | Anthony Hitchens | Dallas |
| CB | Terrance Mitchell | Cleveland | WR | Sammy Watkins | LA Rams |
| LB | Dadi Nicolas | Cleveland | TE | Randall Telfer | Kansas City |
| CB | Marcus Peters | LA Rams | RB | Damien Williams | Miami |
| QB | Alex Smith | Washington | | | |
| WR | Albert Wilson | Miami | | | |
| ILB | Ramik Wilson | LA Rams | | | |

**Draft Summary**

| Round | Overall | Position | Player | College |
|-------|---------|----------|--------|---------|
| 2 | 46 | DT | Breeland Speaks | Mississippi |
| 3 | 75 | DT | Derrick Nnadi | Florida St |
| 3 | 100 | OLB | Dorian O'Daniel | Clemson |
| 4 | 124 | S | Armani Watts | Texas A&M |
| 6 | 196 | CB | Tremon Smith | Central Arkansas |
| 6 | 198 | DT | Kahlil McKenzie | Tennessee |

**Coaching Changes**

2017 offensive coordinator Matt Nagy was hired to be Chicago's head coach. The Chiefs promoted running backs coach Eric Bieniemy in his place. Because this offense is engineered by head coach Andy Reid, I don't anticipate much change from a tactics point of view. The move from Alex Smith to Patrick Mahomes, however, will have an impact.

**2018 Fantasy Outlook**

## Projected Position Rankings

| Position | Player | PPR Rank vs Position | PPR Overall rank | Standard Rank vs Position | Standard Overall Rank |
|---|---|---|---|---|---|
| Quarterback | Patrick Mahomes | 24 | 108 | 24 | 122 |
| Running Back 1 | Kareem Hunt | 3 | 4 | 3 | 2 |
| Running Back 2 | Damien Williams | 16 | 198 | 13 | 191 |
| Wide Receiver 1 | Tyreek Hill | 4 | 25 | 4 | 35 |
| Wide Receiver 2 | Sammy Watkins | 3 | 117 | 4 | 115 |
| Wide Receiver 3 | Demarcus Robinson | 22 | 198 | 21 | 228 |
| Tight End 1 | Travis Kelce | 4 | 34 | 4 | 39 |
| Kicker | Harrison Butker | 2nd Against Kickers | | | |
| Defense/ST | Chiefs | 22nd (tied) Against Defense/ST | | | |

### Position Commentary:

### Quarterback:

Patrick Mahomes is a media darling. The Chiefs brass are saying a lot of positive things about him, and he put up a nice stat line in his lone start in 2017. I watched his week 17 performance and while I don't argue his talent on the field, I was reminded of RG3 in Washington. He has a lot of positive traits, but did throw the ball up for grabs a little too often to make me feel comfortable. He threw 2-3 passes that should have been intercepted, but weren't. You won't hear that kind of feedback in the 2018 hype machine.

Andy Reid did great things coaching Donovan McNabb. From what I saw in week 17 last year, Mahomes could have a McNabb-like season. Based on personnel, I'm projecting this Chiefs team to be similar to the 2007 Eagles in terms of QB output (over 60% passing, solid number of yards), WR targets and RB attempt distribution. The only change we'll make is to give Kelce a boost in targets due to his playmaking ability.

### Running Back:

The Chiefs seemingly hit a home run with Kareem Hunt in 2017. He has proven himself an explosive runner and dependable in the passing game. He handled most of the RB work in all downs and packages. I have his Opportunity Rank at #3 against RB1s. With a young quarterback, he could see more targets and receptions. You can draft him early and feel great about the pick.

### Wide Receiver:

The Chiefs give Tyreek Hill plenty of opportunities to touch the ball. He's ranked 4th against his fellow WR1s. In addition to his 75 receptions and 1183 yards, the Chiefs also give him 1-2 rushing attempts per game and allow him to return kicks. Even with a new quarterback, I think his production can be replicated. With only 7 TDs in 2017, there is room for improvement.

The Chiefs have had trouble finding an adequate WR2, but Sammy Watkins hopes he's found a place to finally reach his full potential. People may not recall, but Buffalo traded a future first round pick to move up and draft him. He was taken before Odell Beckham. Ouch.

Andy Reid will find a way to get Watkins the ball. I have his Opportunity Rank at WR2 ranked at 3rd/4th in PPR/non-PPR leagues relative to his peers at the position. As a fantasy GM, you should consider him a depth player or fringe flex start in the early part of the year, with the potential to be a solid WR2 play by season's end.

## Tight End:

Kelce is a monster. Along with Ertz in Philadelphia and Gronk in New England, he should be valued as a tier-1 TE. The insertion of a new, young QB gives me a bit of trepidation, but he could also be a trusted outlet to a growing QB.

## Kicker:

Kansas City puts up points. Harrison Butker's Opportunity Rank is 2nd in the league. Not only is he worthy of a draft pick, you could argue his competitive advantage makes him draftable a round or two early.

## Defense/Special Teams:

The departures of Marcus Peters and nose tackle Bennie Logan are going to have an impact on this unit's scoring. I have them ranked 22nd in fantasy opportunity. Also, don't forget they have to play 6 games against Derek Carr (with Gruden now calling plays), Philip Rivers and an improving Broncos team. I don't have them on my draft-worthy list.

**Sleeper Watch**

*Popular Sleepers: N/A*

*Deep Sleepers: N/A*

*Hibernators: N/A*

## Los Angeles Chargers
### 2017 Fantasy Opportunity Summary (Offensive Positions):

| Position | Player | PPR Rank vs Position | PPR Overall Rank |
|---|---|---|---|
| Quarterback | Philip Rivers | 14 | 14 |
| Running Back | Melvin Gordon | 5 | 5 |
| Running Back 2 | Austin Ekeler / Branden Oliver | 19 | 16 |
| Wide Receiver 1 | Keenan Allen | 3 | 4 |
| Wide Receiver 2 | Tyrell Williams | 22 | 18 |
| Wide Receiver 3 | Travis Benjamin | 4 | 9 |
| Tight End | Hunter Henry | 10 | 9 |

**Fantasy Opportunity Analysis by Position (Offense Only):**
**Quarterback:**

Philip Rivers displays the disparity between *fantasy* sports and *real* sports. Rivers was one of the top-graded quarterbacks last season, but his overall fantasy Opportunity Rank was pedestrian. The problem from his fantasy perspective isn't his yards or TD passes, it's his lack of presence in the running game. He was the only QB to average negative yards per attempt. Even Tom Brady averaged 1.2 YPC!

All of this said, Rivers is a solid start on any given week thanks to his TD potential and solid group of pass catchers.

**Running Back:**

Depending on your opinion, Melvin Gordon could either be at the bottom of tier-1 or top of tier-2 RB rankings. I'd place him at the top of tier-2 because Bell, Gurley, Elliott and Hunt have separated themselves a bit in terms of opportunity. The culprit here isn't Gordon's ability level, but the Chargers do give him rest from time to time. Austin Ekeler was particularly effective in spot duty averaging 5.5 yards per carry and 10.3 yards per reception.

**Wide Receiver:**

Daily Fantasy sites slept on Keenan Allen for most of the year, but I don't see that happening again. It's hard to ignore 159 targets and 102 receptions. 1,393 yards and 6 touchdowns are nothing to sneeze at either. Allen has been a favorite of mine for years because he produces like a top WR1, but tends to slip in drafts year after year.

Tyrell Williams was on everyone's radar last season after catching 69 passes in 2016. With Allen healthy, his productivity slipped. In 2017, he received 69 *targets*.

Travis Benjamin keeps defenses honest with his downfield speed. From a fantasy perspective, he's a matchup play against teams with below-average safeties. Daily Fantasy players love his potential given his consistently low price.

**Tight End:**

It feels a little weird to write this section with Hunter Henry as the primary target instead of Antonio Gates, but that's the world we live in. As a group, the Chargers are blessed with two standout TEs. Gates has become a TD specialist, which will eat into Henry's scoring potential.

## 2018 Offseason Analysis

**Transactions**

| Key Losses | | | Key Additions | | |
|---|---|---|---|---|---|
| Pos | Player | New Team | Pos | Player | Old Team |
| DE | Jeremiah Attaochu | San Francisco | TE | Virgil Green | Denver |
| OG | Matt Slauson | Indianapolis | C | Mike Pouncey | Miami |
| DB | Tre Boston | NA | QB | Geno Smith | NY Giants |
| | | | K | Caleb Sturgis | Philadelphia |
| | | | CB | Jayden Watkins | Philadelphia |

**Draft Summary**

| Round | Overall | Position | Player | College |
|---|---|---|---|---|
| 1 | 17 | S | Derwin James | Florida St |
| 2 | 48 | Edge | Uchenna Nwosu | USC |
| 3 | 84 | DT | Justin Jones | N.C. State |
| 4 | 19 | S | Kyzir White | West Virginia |
| 5 | 155 | C | Scott Quessenberry | UCLA |
| 6 | 191 | WR | Dylan Cantrell | Texas Tech |
| 7 | 251 | RB | Justin Jackson | Northwestern |

**Coaching Changes**

There are no changes at the head coach or coordinator levels to report.

## 2018 Fantasy Outlook

**Projected Position Rankings**

| Position | Player | PPR Rank vs Position | PPR Overall rank | Standard Rank vs Position | Standard Overall Rank |
|---|---|---|---|---|---|
| Quarterback | Philip Rivers | 15 | 86 | 15 | 90 |
| Running Back 1 | Melvin Gordon | 6 | 8 | 6 | 7 |
| Running Back 2 | Austin Ekeler | 21 | 204 | 22 | 193 |
| Wide Receiver 1 | Keenan Allen | 3 | 20 | 3 | 17 |
| Wide Receiver 2 | Tyrell Williams | 30 | 194 | 29 | 195 |
| Wide Receiver 3 | Travis Benjamin | 12 | 201 | 15 | 219 |
| Tight End 1 | Virgil Green | 13 | 126 | 14 | 119 |
| Kicker | Caleb Sturgis | 17th Against Kickers | | | |
| Defense/ST | Chargers | 5th Against Defense/ST | | | |

**Position Commentary:**

**Quarterback:**

Philip Rivers is playing well, and he has a number of weapons behind him. His Opportunity Ranking is an underwhelming 15th against his QB1 peers, but his ranking improves once I factor in his efficiency and ability to take care of the ball. Like Dalton, he'll probably slip in the draft, but will be a nice mid-to-late-round pick up as a starter.

**Running Back:**

Melvin Gordon ranks 6th against his peers in both PPR/non-PPR fantasy opportunity. He plays all three downs and doesn't give much away to his backup in goal line or passing situations. I don't quite place him in the top tier of RBs, but he's definitely at the top of the tier-2 list. The addition of Mike Pouncey on the interior line could boost his output a bit more. He's a definite RB1 and, if healthy, will produce throughout the year.

Branden Oliver and Austin Ekeler will vie for backup duty and take a few catches away from Gordon in the process. I don't see either as worthy of a roster spot unless Gordon is injured. They do, however, represent excellent matchup plays in Daily Fantasy.

**Wide Receiver:**

I love Keenan Allen. He gets a ton of targets and red zone opportunities. Year after year, he's drafted in the 2nd through 4th rounds of fantasy drafts around the world and he gives WR1 production. He's ranked 3rd overall in our fantasy Opportunity Rankings against WR1s because of his production and chemistry he has with Philip Rivers. If he's sitting there at the end of round 2, you can feel safe grabbing him. If he's there in round 3 or later, take him!

Tyrell Williams has potential, but his targets decreased substantially in 2017 compared to 2016. This was due to Keenan Allen's return to health last season. The moral of the story here is that unless Allen is injured, Williams is more of a matchup play in Daily Fantasy.

**Tight End:**

Hunter Henry has asserted himself as the dominant tight end on this team, but he's out for the season. The Chargers will move on to Free Agent acquisition Virgil Green. This offense utilizes the TE position, so he is worth of a roster spot. Don't be shocked if they bring Gates back for one more year. If that happens, Gates will get the best goal line looks, and diminish Green's potential.

**Kicker:**

The only reason the Chargers missed the playoffs last year is because they couldn't find a kicker to start the year. There is yet another training camp battle in 2018. Stay away.

**Defense/Special Teams:**

Already a defense that could put a lot of pressure on the quarterback, the Chargers tripled down on defense with the first three picks of their draft in standout safety, Derwin James, Edge Rusher Uchenna Nwosu and Defensive Tackle Justin Jones. I have San Diego ranked at #5 in terms of fantasy opportunity, but they are ascending as their yards per play will likely decrease from the 5.3 they averaged in 2017. If you have a high pick in the 2nd-to-last round, take them. You might consider selecting them a bit earlier as a competitive-advantage defense.

**Sleeper Watch**

*Popular Sleepers: N/A*

*Deep Sleepers: N/A*

*Hibernators: N/A*

## Oakland Raiders

### 2017 Fantasy Opportunity Summary (Offensive Positions):

| Position | Player | PPR Rank vs Position | PPR Overall Rank |
|---|---|---|---|
| Quarterback | Derek Carr | 21 | 21 |
| Running Back | Marshawn Lynch | 19 | 15 |
| Running Back 2 | DeAndre Washington | 25 | 26 |
| Wide Receiver 1 | Michael Crabtree | 22 | 21 |
| Wide Receiver 2 | Amari Cooper | 5 | 6 |
| Wide Receiver 3 | Seth Roberts | 15 | 17 |
| Tight End | Jared Cook | 13 | 13 |

**Fantasy Opportunity Analysis by Position (Offense Only):**
**Quarterback:**

After putting the NFL on notice in 2016, Derek Carr fell back to earth in 2017. He ranked in the bottom-third of quarterbacks. Part of this could be attributed to an abridged offseason program due to injury. Statistically speaking, this might have been his worst season to date. Only his rookie season compares.

Carr's completion percentage dipped slightly, but was still respectable (62.7%). The noticeable difference was his interception rate. Perhaps defensive coordinators across the league had a solid game plan, but that would be odd for a 4th-year starter. My instincts say that after a successful 2016 campaign, he pressed a bit too much in 2017.

**Running Back:**

Marshawn Lynch looked to be the perfect addition to a young team on the verge of contender status. He averaged 4.3 yards per carry, but received only 207 attempts. And while he has displayed solid pass catching ability in his career, the Raiders only threw to him 31 times all year. The combination of DeAndre Washington and Jalen Richard received 81 Targets. I suppose the takeaway is that Lynch owners were more the disappointed victims of play calling and personnel packages than of Lynch's poor play.

**Wide Receiver:**

When you look at the rankings and see Amari Cooper sitting at 5th and 6th relative to his WR2 peers, it might come across as a positive stat. I, however, do not view Cooper as a WR2. I doubt he does either.

Cooper was targeted a rather paltry 96 times for a player of his caliber. He caught half (48) of these targets. His saving grace is that he found pay dirt 7 times.

After playing the Robin to Cooper's Batman the past few seasons, Crabtree rose to the top of Oakland's passing game, having caught 58 passes on 101 targets. He's produced in both spots.

Seth Roberts is a standard WR3, but there are too many mouths to feed in this offense.

**Tight End:**

Jared Cook has perpetually searched for a home in his career. The awful Titans and Rams teams of the late 00s and early 10s wasted the best years of his life. He finally hooked onto a team with a stable QB in Green Bay in 2016 and Oakland in 2017. He was a borderline weekly starter and definitely someone worth stashing if you had enough bench for a 2nd TE.

## 2018 Offseason Analysis

### Transactions

| Key Losses | | | Key Additions | | |
|---|---|---|---|---|---|
| Pos | Player | New Team | Pos | Player | Old Team |
| CB | David Amerson | Kansas City | WR | Martavis Bryant | Pittsburgh |
| DE | Denico Autry | Indianapolis | DE | Tank Carradine | San Francisco |
| CB | T.J. Carrie | Cleveland | TE | Derek Carrier | LA Rams |
| WR | Michael Crabtree | Baltimore | OT | Breno Giacomini | Houston |
| K | Sebastian Janikowski | Seattle | SS | Marcus Gilchrist | Houston |
| P | Marquette King | Denver | QB | Christian Hackenberg | Ny Jets |
| OT | Marshall Newhouse | Buffalo | DB | Leon Hall | San Francisco |
| RB | Jamize Olawale | Dallas | ILB | Derrick Johnson | Kansas City |
| WR | Cordarrelle Patterson | New England | QB | Josh Johnson | Houston |
| DE | Jihad Ward | Dallas | RB | Doug Martin | Tampa Bay |
| LB | Navorro Bowman | NA | CB | Rashaan Melvin | Indianapolis |
| | | | WR | Jordy Nelson | Green Bay |
| | | | FB | Keith Smith | Dallas |
| | | | WR | Ryan Switzer | Dallas |
| | | | WR | Griff Whalen | Baltimore |
| | | | OLB | Tahir Whitehead | Detroit |
| | | | OLB | Kyle Wilber | Dallas |
| | | | CB | Daryl Worley | Phi/Car |
| | | | CB | Shareece Wright | Buffalo |

### Draft Summary

| Round | Overall | Position | Player | College |
|---|---|---|---|---|
| 1 | 15 | OT | Kolton Miller | UCLA |
| 2 | 57 | NT | P.J. Hall | Sam Houston St |
| 3 | 65 | OT | Brandon Parker | North Carolina A&T |
| 3 | 87 | Edge | Arden Key | LSU |
| 4 | 110 | CB | Nick Nelson | Wisconsin |
| 5 | 140 | DT | Maurice Hurst | Michigan |
| 5 | 173 | P | Johnny Townsend | Florida |
| 6 | 216 | ILB | Azeem Victor | Washington |
| 7 | 228 | WR | Marcell Ateman | Oklahoma St |

## Coaching Changes

Everyone, including The Functional Sportsaholic, thought the 2017 Oakland Raiders were entering a championship contention window. Unfortunately, Derek Carr's play regressed, and the team eroded. Jack Del Rio was fired as a result.

Enter Chucky.

Jon Gruden was wooed out of retirement after close to a decade in the TV booth of ESPN. Critics of the move liken his return to the return of Joe Gibbs to the Redskins after a longer absence. I don't see that parallel. Unlike Gibbs, who spent his sabbatical building a NASCAR team, Gruden stayed close the game and continued to study film. Moreover, Gruden's offensive philosophy (a descendent of the Walsh coaching tree) is relevant today. His key protégé (brother, Jay Gruden) and mentor (Andy Reid) continue to have success in the NFL today.

Gruden was noted for running simple concepts in a seemingly endless combination of personnel packages. This type of strategy will help Carr adapt to the system quickly. The hiring of ex-Rams QB coach, Greg Olsen brings familiarity as the two worked together in Gruden's last year in Tampa. Olsen has had steady work and experience at the coordinator level (including a previous stint in Oakland). He will help Gruden adapt to the 2018 NFL ... if such help is needed.

On the defensive side of the ball, Paul Geunther (ex Bengals defensive coordinator) is taking over a talented group. Geunther is experienced, and I expect them to properly unleash Khalil Mack. Gruden has shown trust in previous defensive coordinators to run that side of the ball, and I expect that trend to hold this season.

## 2018 Fantasy Outlook

**Projected Position Rankings**

| Position | Player | PPR Rank vs Position | PPR Overall rank | Standard Rank vs Position | Standard Overall Rank |
|---|---|---|---|---|---|
| Quarterback | Derek Carr | 26 | 187 | 26 | 186 |
| Running Back 1 | Doug Martin / Marshawn Lynch | 5 | 17 | 5 | 27 |
| Running Back 2 | DeAndre Washington | 23 | 234 | 24 | 231 |
| Wide Receiver 1 | Amari Cooper | 25 | 41 | 24 | 32 |
| Wide Receiver 2 | Jordy Nelson | 19 | 79 | 17 | 80 |
| Wide Receiver 3 | Martavis Bryant | 15 | 136 | 14 | 138 |
| Tight End 1 | Jared Cook | 16 | 129 | 16 | 131 |
| Kicker | Giorgio Tavercchio | 27th Against Kickers | | | |
| Defense/ST | Raiders | 29th (tied) Against Defense/ST | | | |

**Position Commentary:**

**Quarterback:**

Jon Gruden has been able to call his shots as a head-coaching candidate and decided to come out of retirement to reunite with the Raiders and to coach Derek Carr. Carr seemed to be pushing last season and had his worst fantasy output in years. I expect Gruden to simplify the play calling and put Carr in positions to hit open receivers. For now, his Opportunity Ranking has been lowered because we are likening this year's Raiders to the 2007 Tampa Bay Buccaneers, but I will be pushing his rank up based on efficiency expectations.

**Running Back:**

Marshawn Lynch never got it going last year, but the addition of Doug Martin in 2018 is intriguing. Jon Gruden stayed close to Tampa Bay and is familiar with Martin. To Martin's credit, he's been able to produce if put in the right system. Gruden will feed him the ball. I have the Raiders RB1 position ranked at #5 in terms of opportunity. Proceed with caution, however. Lynch could win carries and turn this backfield into a 2, 3 or even 4 RB committee.

This offense will produce a top RB in one person separates themselves from the rest. For now, I'm linking Martin and Lynch together, but downgrading their ranking until the picture comes into focus. If one of these backs is dominating carries throughout preseason, he will be in the second tier of my rankings. If the running backs are splitting carries, downgrade them to tier-5.

**Wide Receiver:**

General Manager Raleigh McKenzie certainly went to work building a receiving unit for Jon Gruden this offseason. Last year's WR1, Michael Crabtree, left for Baltimore, but Amari Cooper will reassume those responsibilities and be targeted often. He has a lowered player Opportunity Ranking, but Carr's increase in efficiency will improve his ranking. I have him as a solid WR2 or lower-tier WR1.

Jordy Nelson was signed quickly after Green Bay let him go. I love his potential at the WR2 position — particularly if Derek Carr and he can replicate the back-shoulder game on the sideline that Nelson/Rodgers so effectively utilized in Green Bay. He's ranked #3 against his WR2 peers.

Martavis Bryant was brought over from Pittsburgh in a draft day trade. If he outduels Nelson for the WR2 spot in training camp, you should snap him up in the middle rounds. If he plays as a WR3, I view him as a bye week starter in the fantasy world and a great Daily Fantasy valued player.

### Tight End:

I like Jared Cook, but don't view him as an elite fantasy tight end. The offense has a lot of weapons, and I don't see him getting significant targets ahead of Oakland's trio of talented receivers. He'll be a mid-tier TE2 this season.

### Kicker:

The kicking opportunity is low enough that you should not use a draft selection on Giorgio Tavecchio.

### Defense/Special Teams:

The fantasy Opportunity Ranking for this unit is low in spite of having talent on the roster. Thanks to the changes at the head coach and coordinator levels, there is going to be a lot of turnover and a significant learning curve. Don't use a draft spot on this unit.

### Sleeper Watch

*Popular Sleeper: Doug Martin, RB*

*If he wins the job, he'll be significantly undervalued in your fantasy draft.*

*Deep Sleepers: N/A*

*Hibernators: N/A*

# NFC EAST

# NFC East

## Dallas Cowboys

### 2017 Fantasy Opportunity Summary (Offensive Positions):

| Position | Player | PPR Rank vs Position | PPR Overall Rank |
|---|---|---|---|
| Quarterback | Dak Prescott | 13 | 13 |
| Running Back | Ezekiel Elliott | 8 | 4 |
| Running Back 2 | Alfred Morris | 23 | 19 |
| Wide Receiver 1 | Dez Bryant | 21 | 20 |
| Wide Receiver 2 | Terrance Williams | 26 | 29 |
| Wide Receiver 3 | Cole Beasley | 20 | 21 |
| Tight End | Jason Witten | 9 | 10 |

**Fantasy Opportunity Analysis by Position (Offense Only):**
**Quarterback:**

Moving on from Romo to Dak Prescott was the right decision, but that does not mean it has been a seamless transition. Prescott is finding success at quarterback, but it's clear he's not as effective without Ezekiel Elliott in the lineup.

Prescott ranked 13th in opportunity. This score would have been higher if he found more success throwing to his wide receivers. Elliott and TE Jason Witten were his key outlets in 2017.

**Running Back:**

When Elliott is on the field, this team is tough to beat. Having only played in 10 weeks, the running back 1 positioned showed an Opportunity Ranking of 8th and 4th respectively. Elliot's ability to stay on the field in obvious pass catching situations combined with his dominance in running ability makes him a clear tier-1 running back.

**Wide Receiver:**

Whether it was the effect of Dez Bryant demanding targets, Dak's continued acclimation to the professional game or a reliance on Ezekiel Elliott, this WR group disappointed in 2017. For the past 2 seasons, I advised owners to stay away from Dez Bryant (correctly, I might add). He had 139 targets in 2017, but only 69 receptions. Whether you assign the blame to Dez or Dak, the WR1 position needs more productivity.

This unit has a lot of improvement to be made before I'd advise anyone to be drafted inside the top 7 rounds.

**Tight End:**

Jason Witten had a great 2017 campaign with top-10 Opportunity Ranking. He will be missed in 2018.

## 2018 Offseason Analysis

### Transactions

| Key Losses | | | Key Additions | | |
|---|---|---|---|---|---|
| Pos | Player | New Team | Pos | Player | Old Team |
| DB | Bene' Benwikere | Arizona | WR | Tavon Austin | LA Rams |
| OG | Jonathan Cooper | San Francisco | DE | Kony Ealy | Ny Jets |
| MLB | Anthony Hitchens | Kansas City | OT | Cameron Fleming | New England |
| P | Sam Irwin-Hill | Washington | WR | Allen Hurns | Jacksonville |
| CB | Orlando Scandrick | Washington | RB | Jamize Olawale | Oakland |
| FB | Keith Smith | Oakland | WR | Deonte Thompson | Buffalo |
| WR | Ryan Switzer | Oakland | DE | Jihad Ward | Dallas |
| OLB | Kyle Wilber | Oakland | | | |
| WR | *Dez Bryant* | *NA* | | | |
| TE | *Jason Witten* | *Retired* | | | |

### Draft Summary

| Round | Overall | Position | Player | College |
|---|---|---|---|---|
| 1 | 19 | ILB | Leighton Vander Esch | Boise St |
| 2 | 50 | G | Connor Williams | Texas |
| 3 | 81 | WR | Michael Gallup | Colorado St |
| 4 | 116 | Edge | Dorance Armstrong | Kansas |
| 4 | 137 | TE | Dalton Schultz | Stanford |
| 5 | 171 | QB | Mike White | Western Kentucky |
| 6 | 193 | OLB | Chris Covington | Indiana |
| 6 | 208 | WR | Cedrick Wilson | Boise St |
| 7 | 236 | RB | Bo Scarbrough | Alabama |

### Coaching Changes

There are no changes at the head coach or coordinator levels to report. With Ezekiel Elliot slated to play a full 16-game season, I expect last year's run to pass ratio (roughly 47% - 53%) to hold.

## 2018 Fantasy Outlook

### Projected Position Rankings

| Position | Player | PPR Rank vs Position | PPR Overall rank | Standard Rank vs Position | Standard Overall Rank |
|----------|--------|----------------------|------------------|---------------------------|------------------------|
| Quarterback | Dak Prescott | 6 | 57 | 6 | 59 |
| Running Back 1 | Ezekiel Elliott | 4 | 6 | 4 | 3 |
| Running Back 2 | Rod Smith | 30 | 244 | 30 | 230 |
| Wide Receiver 1 | Austin Hurns | 18 | 93 | 16 | 79 |
| Wide Receiver 2 | Terrance Williams | 29 | 192 | 30 | 199 |
| Wide Receiver 3 | Tavon Austin | 16 | 221 | 18 | 227 |
| Tight End 1 | Geoff Swaim | 8 | 100 | 10 | 192 |
| Kicker | Dan Bailey | 19th Against Kickers | | | |
| Defense/ST | Cowboys | 15th (tied) Against Defense/ST | | | |

### Position Commentary:

### Quarterback:

Dak Prescott receives the hype of a Cowboys quarterback, but he's not a world-beater as a passer. What you do get with him, however, is an ability to move the pocket and accumulate fantasy points as a rusher. For this reason, he has a fantasy Opportunity Rank of #6 against his fellow QBs. The departures of Jason Witten and Dez Bryant, however, cast a large shadow. This will hurt his final ranking.

### Running Back:

Ezekiel Elliott makes this offense go. The team was completely different when he was in the game vs. when he missed time with suspension. If I adjust the 2017 Cowboys output to include only Elliot's performance, you can see Elliott firmly plants himself in the tier-1 RB category. He's a 3-down back and does not give many rushing attempts to his backup. He's worth a first round pick to be sure.

### Wide Receiver:

Personnel changes make this group a very interesting watch in 2018. Dallas did their best to feed Dez Bryant last year. Between Bryant and Witten, there are 219 targets that will be redistributed in 2018. Some will go to RB Ezekiel Elliott and some will go to their new TE. But what about the rest?

Terrance Williams accumulated 78 targets last season. The Cowboys have added WR Tavon Austin via trade and spent a 3rd round pick on WR Michael Gallup. One or two of these players will be draft-worthy, but it's hard to figure out where the targets are going to go. One thing is for sure, whoever ranks at the top of the list will be a fantastic bargain for fantasy GMs and a great early-season Daily Fantasy play.

### Tight End:

Witten's sudden retirement was jarring. There wasn't a lot of depth behind him in terms of fantasy output, and the Cowboys were left scrambling in the draft. 4th round pick Dalton Schultz or 4th-year player

Geoff Swaim could see TE1 responsibilities. Don't be shocked to see the Cowboys bring in another player during camp.

**Kicker:**

K Dan Bailey is extremely accurate and has deep range. I don't love the fantasy opportunity of the Cowboys offense, but he is worthy of a last-round draft pick.

**Defense/Special Teams:**

Dallas was a middle-of-the-road defense in 2017. I'd argue this was less about the talent level of their team and more about the division they play in. Philadelphia and Washington have top-tier offenses and the Giants will likely score quite a bit with Pat Shurmur on the team. Playing 6 games against those teams is going to hurt the overall ranking. Making matter worse, they have Deshaun Watson, Andrew Luck, and a high-scoring NFC South on their schedule. I suspect they'll be a backup defense for much of the season.

### Sleeper Watch

***Popular Sleeper: Tavon Austin, WR***

*Look for him to be used as a hybrid RB and slot WR.*

***Deep Sleeper: Michael Gallup, WR***

*The Cowboys will have heavy competition at WR this year. Gallup could easily win targets.*

***Hibernator: Geoff Swaim, TE***

*Dak uses his Tight Ends and Swaim is in line to start.*

# New York Giants

## 2017 Fantasy Opportunity Summary (Offensive Positions):

| Position | Player | PPR Rank vs Position | PPR Overall Rank |
|---|---|---|---|
| Quarterback | Eli Manning | 27 | 27 |
| Running Back | Orleans Darkwa | 26 | 30 |
| Running Back 2 | Wayne Gallman | 18 | 22 |
| Wide Receiver 1 | Sterling Shepard / Odell Beckham | 15 | 24 |
| Wide Receiver 2 | Roger Lewis | 19 | 22 |
| Wide Receiver 3 | Brandon Marshall / tavarres King | 13 | 13 |
| Tight End | Evan Engram | 7 | 7 |

**Fantasy Opportunity Analysis by Position (Offense Only):**
**Quarterback:**

This was a lost year in Manning's career. He finished 27th against his peers in our quarterback index. Injuries to his top three WRs last year didn't help, but that does nothing to comfort fantasy owners who were burned last year.

**Running Back:**

The running back situation was one of the worst in the league. The team seemed to be searching for answers for the entirety of 2017, but only found more questions. Orleans Darkwa and Wayne Gallman rotated between primary ball handlers, but neither found much success.

**Wide Receiver:**

When and Sterling Shepard were both healthy, this group was as potent as ever. Unfortunately, they weren't on the field much in 2017. While all position groupings were in the middle of the pack against their peers, outside of Sterling Shepard, there weren't many reasons to start a Giants receiver in 2017. Look for this to change in a big way in 2018.

**Tight End:**

Evan Engram was a bright spot in 2017. As a rookie, he made immediate impact for the Giants and for tight end needy fantasy teams around the globe. His Opportunity Ranking fell within the top 7 against his peers in 2017. How will a healthy Beckham and Shepard impact him in 2018?

## 2018 Offseason Analysis

**Transactions**

| | Key Losses | | | Key Additions | |
|---|---|---|---|---|---|
| Pos | Player | New Team | Pos | Player | Old Team |
| DB | Ross Cockrell | | P | Riley Dixon | NY Giants |
| OG | D.J. Fluker | | FS | William Gay | Pittsburgh |
| OLB | Devon Kennard | | WR | Cody Latimer | Denver |
| DE | Jason Pierre-Paul | Tampa Bay | ILB | Kareem Martin | Arizona |
| OT | Justin Pugh | | DE | Josh Mauro | Arizona |
| C | Weston Richburg | | LB | Alec Ogletree | NY Giants |
| QB | Geno Smith | | OG | Patrick Omameh | Jacksonville |
| DB | *Dominique Rodgers-Cromartie* | | OT | Nate Solder | New England |
| | | | RB | Jonathan Stewart | Carolina |
| | | | SS | Michael Thomas | Miami |
| | | | DB | B.W. Webb | Cleveland |
| | | | DB | Teddy Williams | Carolina |

**Draft Summary**

| Round | Overall | Position | Player | College |
|---|---|---|---|---|
| 1 | 2 | RB | Saquon Barkley | Penn St. |
| 2 | 34 | G | Will Hernandez | Texas-El Paso |
| 3 | 66 | Edge | Lorenzo Carter | Georgia |
| 3 | 69 | DT | B.J. Hill | N.C. State |
| 4 | 108 | QB | Kyle Lauletta | Richmond |
| 5 | 139 | DT | R.J. McIntosh | Miami |

**Coaching Changes**

I was extremely critical when the Giants promoted Ben McAdoo to head coach in 2016. He always struck me as someone more likely to sell me a used jet ski than lead a winning NFL team. Credit the Giants brass for realizing this mistake and "failing fast".

The New York Giants made what I consider to be the best hiring of the offseason in Pat Shurmur. Certainly, his work in the past two seasons with Sam Bradford and Case Keenum at quarterback can't be underestimated. More impressive, I think, was his work with Cleveland as head coach in 2011 and 2012. Critics will say he only won 9 games in those seasons. While I admit that leaves something to be desired, you must also consider that in those 32 games, his starting quarterbacks were: Colt McCoy, Seneca Wallace, Thaddeus Lewis and then-rookie Brandon Weeden. Nine wins wasn't a travesty; it was a miracle.

Previous Panthers offensive coordinator, Mike Shula, will assume the same role with the Giants. While his experience will help coach up the younger players, make no mistake – this will be Shurmur's offense. From a personnel standpoint, the skill positions translate very well to Minnesota's 2017 team. Diggs and Thielen map to Beckham and Shepard at WR. Rudolph and Engram have similarities at tight end. Newly drafted Saquon Barkley has similar skills to last year's rookie Viking standout, Dalvin Cook. Given the output of Case Keenum in Shumur's system last year, it's not out of the question that Eli has a bounce back season in a major way.

There's a lot to be excited about on the defensive side of the ball too. James Bettcher was hired as defensive coordinator, having spent the last three seasons behind the Arizona Cardinals defense. They were a tough, aggressive unit, and I expect him to bring the same energy to New York.

Things are looking up for Giants fans.

## 2018 Fantasy Outlook

### Projected Position Rankings

| Position | Player | PPR Rank vs Position | PPR Overall rank | Standard Rank vs Position | Standard Overall Rank |
|---|---|---|---|---|---|
| Quarterback | Eli Manning | 30 | 90 | 30 | 94 |
| Running Back 1 | Saquon Barkley | 8 | 19 | 8 | 10 |
| Running Back 2 | Jonathan Stewart | 15 | 206 | 19 | 211 |
| Wide Receiver 1 | Odell Beckham | 20 | 11 | 25 | 11 |
| Wide Receiver 2 | Sterling Shepard | 25 | 60 | 24 | 62 |
| Wide Receiver 3 | Cody Latimer | 14 | 214 | 12 | 218 |
| Tight End 1 | Evan Engram | 6 | 103 | 6 | 130 |
| Kicker | TBD | 26th Against Kickers | | | |
| Defense/ST | Giants | 29th (tied) Against Defense/ST | | | |

### Position Commentary:

### Quarterback:

Eli Manning had a tough year in 2017, but those days are in his rear-view mirror. The Giants have a new system in place, and Manning will see the return of Odell Beckham and infusion of talented rookie RB, Saquon Barkley.

Pat Shurmur will look to improve Manning's efficiency while cutting down on costly interceptions. Manning ranks 30th in fantasy opportunity. I'm a believer in the Shurmur offense and consider Manning an undervalued talent. He could put up starter numbers while being drafted late.

### Running Back:

The Giants haven't found a significant contributor in the running game, but Saquon Barkley will change that. In Barkley, Shurmur will have a player he can deploy much like he utilized Dalvin Cook in Minnesota last season. My only concern with his output is that he didn't get many touches in his days at Penn St. Still, his RB1 value is ranked 8th in both PPR and Non-PPR leagues. You can feel safe picking him in the second round.

### Wide Receiver:

While Sterling Shepard played exceptionally well as a WR1 for much of 2017, this is Odell Beckham's group. He and Manning have a level of trust that is rare in today's NFL. Much like Big Ben and Antonio Brown and Philip Rivers and Keenan Allen, the Manning/Beckham combo is special. The overall Opportunity Rank for Beckham is an underwhelming 20th, but he will maximize those opportunities.

Shepard, along with Juju Smith-Schuster, will be a high-impact WR2. Again, his WR2 ranking doesn't stack well against his competition, but I am boosting his ranking based on Shurmur's impact.

Cody Latimer gives the Giants an intriguing #3 option next year. I won't recommend spending a draft pick on him, but add him to your waiver watch list and track his targets in weeks 1-3. If he is averaging 6 or 7 a game, you can give him a roster spot if you have the space.

### Tight End:

Evan Engram scored well last season and I expect him to have a Kyle Rudolph-like impact in 2018. I do think his total targets will decrease with Beckham back in the fold. He's worth a starting TE spot, but don't assume he will build on his numbers from last year. It's far more likely that he matches or slightly degrades.

### Kicker:

Due to the Giants poor play in 2017, the kicker position will be undervalued. Thus, you'll probably be able to grab their kicker on waivers after your draft. Don't waste a pick here.

### Defense/Special Teams:

The Giants were pedestrian-to-poor in the major Defensive/ST rankings of yards per play, sacks and turnovers generated. While the new coaching staff will have an impact, the strength of this team will be offense. Steer clear on draft day.

### Sleeper Watch

*Popular Sleepers: N/A*

*Deep Sleepers: N/A*

*Hibernators: N/A*

## Philadelphia Eagles

### 2017 Fantasy Opportunity Summary (Offensive Positions):

| Position | Player | PPR Rank vs Position | PPR Overall Rank |
|---|---|---|---|
| Quarterback | Carson Wentz | 2 | 2 |
| Running Back | LeGarrette Blount / Jay Ajayi | 25 | 22 |
| Running Back 2 | Wendell Smallwood / Corey Clement | 20 | 15 |
| Wide Receiver 1 | Alshon Jeffery | 18 | 11 |
| Wide Receiver 2 | Nelson Agholor | 3 | 3 |
| Wide Receiver 3 | Torrey Smith | 11 | 10 |
| Tight End | Zach Ertz | 2 | 3 |

**Fantasy Opportunity Analysis by Position (Offense Only):**
**Quarterback:**

Fantasy players welcomed Carson Wentz into the elite club in 2017. He takes care of the ball; his coach gives him plenty of opportunities to distribute, and his receivers are talented.

**Running Back:**

LeGarrette Blount and Jay Ajayi found success in 2017. Philadelphia boasts a deep and talented backfield. Ajayi and Blount hammered teams in early downs and Corey Clement, and Wendell Smallwood found success shredding defenses in passing situations.

**Wide Receiver:**

If you're an Eagles fan, you have to be very pleased with this group. Fantasy owners, however, do need to proceed with caution. The Eagles distribute the ball across all pass catchers including running backs and tight ends. WR1 Alshon Jeffery had a surprisingly low PPR Opportunity Ranking with respect to his peers. In spite of 120 targets, Jeffery only hauled in 57 passes. Yes, he caught less than half of his targets. Ouch.

**Tight End:**

Zach Ertz has blossomed in Doug Pederson's offense. He was an elite TE in 2017, and that is likely to continue into 2018 and beyond.

### 2018 Offseason Analysis

**Transactions**

| Key Losses | | | Key Additions | | |
|---|---|---|---|---|---|
| Pos | Player | New Team | Pos | Player | Old Team |
| DT | Beau Allen | Tampa Bay | DE | Michael Bennett | Philadelphia |
| RB | LeGarrette Blount | Detroit | DT | Haloti Ngata | Detroit |
| TE | Trey Burton | Chicago | WR | Mike Wallace | Baltimore |
| DE | Vinny Curry | Tampa Bay | | | |
| WR | Marcus Johnson | Seattle | | | |
| CB | Patrick Robinson | New Orleans | | | |
| WR | Torrey Smith | Carolina | | | |
| K | Caleb Sturgis | LA Chargers | | | |
| CB | Jaylen Watkins | LA Chargers | | | |

**Draft Summary**

| Round | Overall | Position | Player | College |
|---|---|---|---|---|
| 2 | 49 | TE | Dallas Goedert | South Dakota St |
| 4 | 125 | CB | Avonte Maddox | Pittsburgh |
| 4 | 130 | Edge | Josh Sweat | Florida St |
| 6 | 206 | OT | Matt Pryor | TCU |
| 7 | 233 | OT | Jordan Mailata | (Australian Football) |

**Coaching Changes**

Having lost Frank Reich to the Colts, the Eagles have promoted Mike Groh (previous WR coach) into the offensive coordinator vacancy. I don't expect much change as this unit will still be led by head coach Doug Pederson.

# 2018 Fantasy Outlook

## Projected Position Rankings

| Position | Player | PPR Rank vs Position | PPR Overall rank | Standard Rank vs Position | Standard Overall Rank |
|---|---|---|---|---|---|
| Quarterback | Carson Wentz | 31 | 35 | 31 | 40 |
| Running Back 1 | Jay Ajayi | 19 | 145 | 19 | 103 |
| Running Back 2 | Corey Clement | 9 | 297 | 9 | 190 |
| Wide Receiver 1 | Alshon Jeffery | 32 | 26 | 32 | 16 |
| Wide Receiver 2 | Nelson Agholor | 32 | 71 | 32 | 50 |
| Wide Receiver 3 | Mike Wallace | 23 | 199 | 20 | 200 |
| Tight End 1 | Zach Ertz | 9 | 15 | 9 | 23 |
| Kicker | Jake Elliott | 4th Against Kickers | | | |
| Defense/ST | Eagles | 8th Against Defense/ST | | | |

**Position Commentary:**

**Quarterback:**

Carson Wentz is a stud. I have him ranked at #2 in terms of fantasy opportunity and he is highly valued in our final rankings. This is an efficient quarterback in a system that features passing. If that weren't enough, he has weapons at every position. Draft him early.

**Running Back:**

Jay Ajayi produces, yes. Unfortunately for fantasy GMs, the Eagles rotate running backs based on matchups. He will get the most rushing attempts and put up a nice average. He'll even catch passes out of the backfield, but he will give too many fantasy opportunities away to his teammates, which include Corey Clement, Wendell Smallwood and newly acquired Matt Jones.

**Wide Receiver:**

The Eagles will feature different WRs based on position matchups, which is why they are so successful on the field. Fantasy GMs need to proceed with a bit of caution here. Alshon Jeffery and Nelson Agholor will have similar numbers at the end of the year. Strategically speaking, targeting Agholor will be the wiser move because you'll receive similar output, but you will be able to grab him a couple of rounds later.

I like the Mike Wallace signing quite a bit. Last year's deep thread (Torrey Smith) caught 36 passes for 436 yards and 2 TDs. I think Wallace will give the Eagles a bit more than that, but not much. He can offer depth on your roster and will be a great daily fantasy value player.

**Tight End:**

Ertz is at the top of the TE tiers. With injury concerns for Gronk and Kelce adapting to a new QB, you can make the argument he's the top TE available.

**Kicker:**

The Eagles score quite a bit. I have Jake Elliott ranked at #4 in terms of fantasy opportunity. He's at the bottom part of our tier-1 kicker rankings.

**Defense/Special Teams:**

This defensive line plays as fast as any unit I've ever watched. At the snap, they look like a nest of angry hornets. They get to the quarterback and are a nightmare for opposing offenses. They've also added Haloti Ngata in the offseason. This is a deep, talented group.

Losing Patrick Robinson at CB hurts a bit, but they added Avonte Maddux in the draft. The strength of the unit will come with the pass rush. I have their defense ranked 8th in opportunity in spite of playing in a tough offensive position. They're worthy of a roster spot and season-long starter position.

**Sleeper Watch**

*Popular Sleepers: N/A*

*Deep Sleepers: N/A*

*Hibernators: N/A*

# Washington Redskins

## 2017 Fantasy Opportunity Summary (Offensive Positions):

| Position | Player | PPR Rank vs Position | PPR Overall Rank |
|---|---|---|---|
| Quarterback | Kirk Cousins | 4 | 4 |
| Running Back | Robert Kelley / Samaje Perine | 30 | 29 |
| Running Back 2 | Chris Thomas | 5 | 4 |
| Wide Receiver 1 | Jamison Crowder | 27 | 27 |
| Wide Receiver 2 | Josh Doctson | 20 | 15 |
| Wide Receiver 3 | Ryan Grant | 8 | 8 |
| Tight End | Jordan Reed | 11 | 14 |

**Fantasy Opportunity Analysis by Position (Offense Only):**
**Quarterback:**

After seeing DeSean Jackson and Pierre Garcon depart in free agency, Kirk Cousins had trouble finding chemistry with newly minted starters, Josh Doctson and WR Terrelle Pryor. The Redskins offense likes to spread the ball around. In spite of the degradation of offensive talent around him, Cousins found himself at #4 in terms of fantasy opportunity last season.

**Running Back:**

The early down backs, Samaje Perine and Robert Kelly, found trouble getting anything going. Granted, the entire offensive line was hurt for long stretches in 2017, but there are no excuses in the NFL (or in fantasy land). There are only results. Perine and Kelly were only worth emergency-start status.

Pass catching/third-down back Chris Thompson, however, was a bright spot in 2017. He was also cut by injury, but his pass catching prowess and ability to find the end zone lifted his fantasy Opportunity Rankings to 4th and 5th in PPR/Non-PPR leagues against his peers.

**Wide Receiver:**

Slot receiver Jamison Crowder ended up the primary pass catcher in Washington last year thanks to the inability of Josh Doctson, Terrelle Pryor and Ryan Grant to reach their potential. While you could make the argument that, similar to the Eagles, the offensive distribution works against Washington receivers, the reality is that this unit was bad across the board. Crowder was the only reasonable play here week-to-week and was the only player to crack 100 targets.

**Tight End:**

When Jordan Reed was on the field, he was effective. Unfortunately, injury concerns continue to chase Reed wherever he goes. Though not quite as elite, I categorize Reed with Gronkowski in the "buyer beware" category.

## 2018 Offseason Analysis

### Transactions

| Key Losses | | | Key Additions | | |
|---|---|---|---|---|---|
| Pos | Player | New Team | Pos | Player | Old Team |
| QB | Kirk Cousins | Minnesota | P | Sam Irwin-Hill | Dallas |
| S | Su'a Cravens | Denver | QB | Kevin Hogan | Cleveland |
| CB | Kendall Fuller | Kansas City | OLB | Pernell McPhee | Chicago |
| WR | Ryan Grant | Indianapolis | WR | Paul Richardson | Seattle |
| C | Spencer Long | NY Jets | CB | Orlando Scandrick | Dallas |
| LB | Trent Murphy | Buffalo | QB | Alex Smith | Chiefs |
| TE | Niles Paul | Jacksonville | | | |
| WR | Terrelle Pryor | NY Jets | | | |
| CB | *Breshad Breeland* | *NA* | | | |
| DB | *DeAngelo Hall* | *Retired* | | | |

### Draft Summary

| Round | Overall | Position | Player | College |
|---|---|---|---|---|
| 1 | 13 | DT | Da'ron Payne | Alabama |
| 2 | 59 | RB | Derrius Guice | LSU |
| 3 | 74 | DT | Geron Christian | Louisville |
| 4 | 109 | S | Troy Apke | Penn St |
| 5 | 163 | DT | Tim Settle | Virginia Tech |
| 6 | 197 | ILB | Shaun dion Hamilton | Alabama |
| 7 | 241 | CB | Greg Stroman | Virginia Tech |
| 7 | 256 | WR | Trey Quinn | SMU |

### Coaching Changes

There have been no coaching changes at the head coach or coordinator levels. Washington was particularly devastated by injuries last year, so I expect an improvement in offensive output. The 41%-61% run to pass ratio should slide a little more in favor of running with a healthy offensive line and personnel improvements.

### 2018 Fantasy Outlook

## Projected Position Rankings

| Position | Player | PPR Rank vs Position | PPR Overall rank | Standard Rank vs Position | Standard Overall Rank |
|----------|--------|----------------------|------------------|---------------------------|-----------------------|
| Quarterback | Alex Smith | 7 | 56 | 7 | 58 |
| Running Back 1 | Derrius Guice | 32 | 146 | 32 | 136 |
| Running Back 2 | Chris Thompson | 2 | 16 | 2 | 24 |
| Wide Receiver 1 | Jamison Crowder | 31 | 157 | 31 | 156 |
| Wide Receiver 2 | Paul Richardson Jr. | 31 | 160 | 31 | 159 |
| Wide Receiver 3 | Josh Doctson | 20 | 224 | 23 | 233 |
| Tight End 1 | Jordan Reed | 14 | 54 | 17 | 70 |
| Kicker | Dustin Hopkins | 22th Against Kickers | | | |
| Defense/ST | Redskins | 11th (tied) Against Defense/ST | | | |

## Position Commentary:

### Quarterback:

The Gruden offenses always move the ball. The franchise famously bungled the Kirk Cousins situation, but they also feel they've upgraded at the position having acquired Alex Smith in the offseason. Scouts and analysts agree.

The Redskins offer the 7th-best quarterback opportunity. Alex Smith possesses superior ability escaping the pocket. If he can have a firm grasp of the offense, he'll be a potent player and worthy of a start.

### Running Back:

Gruden and the coaching staff have yet to be enamored with a first and second down running back. They've tried and moved on from Alfred Morris and Matt Jones in recent years. Last year's starters, Robert Kelley and Samaje Perine were unable to clear 3.4 yards per carry. That's not going to cut it.

The Redskins saw standout RB Derrius Guice fall to them in the second round and they pounced. Draft analysis from various publications mentioned Guice had a few warts from a personality standpoint, but Washington did not share those concerns. If Guice is properly motivated, he has the talent to make a difference on a team that ranks 32nd in fantasy opportunity at the RB1 position. Because of the question marks, I've categorized Guice as a sleeper.

Pass catching running back Chris Thompson was by far the best fantasy RB on this list. It's rare for a back who only accumulated about 6.4 attempts per game to be the top fantasy scorer, but averaging 4 catches and 54 yards make him intriguing in PPR leagues. He's worth a roster spot, but don't pounce on him too quickly. He will not be getting first and second down carries unless Guice is injured.

### Wide Receiver:

Washington is a great NFL offense, but fantasy GMs don't get a ton of production at this spot. The only Redskins receiver to consistently contribute is WR Jamison Crowder. Thanks to the injury to Jordan Reed last year, Crowder was the only pass catcher to exceed 100 targets in 2017. He's worthy of a roster spot and thanks to his low TD totals in 2017, he should be attainable in the later rounds of your draft, or perhaps even waivers.

Two of their key contributors last year (Ryan Grant and Terrelle Pryor) are gone, but these two totaled only 102 targets combined in 2017. The acquisition of Paul Richardson will provide an infusion of talent. Place Paul Richardson on your waiver watch list and consider both Crowder and Richardson as Daily Fantasy sleepers.

Josh Doctson hasn't reached his first-round draft pick potential. Though he'll see plenty of snaps, I want to see more regular season production before placing him on my fantasy team or Daily Fantasy lineup.

### Tight End:

When Jordan Reed is healthy, he's elite. Unfortunately, that's not often. Like Tyler Eifert in Cincinnati, he has boom-or-bust potential thanks to his injury history. I rank him in the 2nd tier of tight ends, but proceed with caution.

### Kicker:

Washington does consistently move the ball and score. An improved running game could increase the kicking output. Dustin Hopkins hasn't scored well in fantasy opportunity, however. I suggest holding off until waivers, but he has low-tier starting potential.

### Defense/Special Teams:

The Redskins do get to the passer, which is important in a fantasy defense. Unfortunately, they often blitz and have a history of giving up chunks of yardage to slot receivers and tight ends. Making matters worse, they traded their top-rated CB (Kendall Fuller) and are letting Breshaud Breeland depart. They brought in Orlando Scandrick in free agency, but this group will degrade. They are a backup group at best.

### Sleeper Watch

***Popular Sleepers: Paul Richardson, WR***

*Based on what he showed in Seattle last year, he could fill the hole left by Garcon and Jackson in 2017.*

***Deep Sleepers: N/A***

***Hibernators: N/A***

NFC NORTH

# NFC North

## Chicago Bears

### 2017 Fantasy Opportunity Summary (Offensive Positions):

| Position | Player | PPR Rank vs Position | PPR Overall Rank |
|----------|--------|----------------------|------------------|
| Quarterback | Mitch Trubisky | 31 | 31 |
| Running Back | Jordan Howard | 13 | 12 |
| Running Back 2 | Tarik Cohen | 11 | 12 |
| Wide Receiver 1 | Kendall Wright | 31 | 31 |
| Wide Receiver 2 | Dontrelle Inman | 32 | 31 |
| Wide Receiver 3 | Deonte Thompson | 16 | 11 |
| Tight End | Zach Miller | 25 | 25 |

### Fantasy Opportunity Analysis by Position (Offense Only):
### Quarterback:

Mitch Trubisky took over the quarterback position early in 2017, but he never had the training wheels removed. Last year's coaching staff acted a bit like helicopter parents. They clearly never put much on his shoulders and his growth was stunted. Expect different things with a new coaching staff in 2018.

### Running Back:

Jordan Howard continues to have success. Unfortunately, thanks to Tarik Cohen's productivity, Howard's fantasy Opportunity Rankings dipped into RB2 territory. He was certainly someone you wanted to have on your starting roster in 2017, but he wasn't *the* guy you wanted.

Cohen was great for PPR leagues and Daily Fantasy players last year.

### Wide Receiver:

The Bears were unable to get much going with their top two receivers last year. The WR3 position found a bit of success, finishing 16th and 11th in fantasy opportunity against their peers. Based on my analysis, this was due as much to play calling as it was to offensive talent.

### Tight End:

Zach Miller had established himself as Trubiski's go-to receiver prior to his devastating injury against the Saints. After that, the position grouping never rebounded.

## 2018 Offseason Analysis

### Transactions

| Key Losses | | | Key Additions | | |
|---|---|---|---|---|---|
| Pos | Player | New Team | Pos | Player | Old Team |
| OG | Tom Compton | Minnesota | TE | Trey Burton | Philadelphia |
| QB | Mike Glennon | Arizona | QB | Chase Daniel | New Orleans |
| ILB | Christian Jones | Detroit | WR | Taylor Gabriel | Atlanta |
| OLB | Pernell McPhee | Washington | DE | Aaron Lynch | San Francisco |
| K | Cairo Santos | NY Jets | K | Cody Parkey | Miami |
| OG | Josh Sitton | Miami | WR | Allen Robinson | Jacksonville |
| DE | Mitch Unrein | Tampa Bay | | | |
| WR | Kendall Wright | Minnesota | | | |
| ILB | Jerrell Freman | Retired | | | |

### Draft Summary

| Round | Overall | Position | Player | College |
|---|---|---|---|---|
| 1 | 8 | Georgia | Roquan Smith | Georgia |
| 2 | 39 | Iowa | james Daniels | Iowa |
| 2 | 51 | Memphis | Anthony Miller | Memphis |
| 4 | 115 | Westeron Kentucky | Joel Iyiebuniwe | Westeron Kentucky |
| 5 | 145 | Delaware | Bilal Nichols | Delaware |
| 6 | 181 | Utah | Kyle Fitts | Utah |
| 7 | 224 | Georgia | Javon Wims | Georgia |

### Coaching Changes

I have a bit of mixed feelings with Chicago releasing head coach Jon Fox. Certainly, he was criticized by fans and media alike. The team, however, overachieved in the win/loss column. If you are a fan of defense, there was a lot to like about the Bears in 2017 and their potential moving forward.

The success of Sean McVay with Jared Goff and the Rams last year stood out. While Jon Fox was finding success in running a defense, it was clear the team had no plan for Mitch Trubisky. There were three games where Trubisky had fewer than 20 passing attempts. Against the Panthers, he only attempted 7 passes … and they won!

If Chicago hopes to compete in a division with Minnesota, Green Bay and Detroit, they need to go all-in with Trubisky and this is where new head coach Matt Nagy comes in. Having spent his career in the Andy

Reid coaching tree, Nagy brings an NFL-ready system. He spent 2017 helping groom fellow top-10, Patrick Mahomes. Scouts loved what they saw with Mahomes in week 17 last season.

Nagy put together an interesting staff. Ex-Oregon head coach Mark Helfrich will be running the offense. On the defensive side of the ball, he's retained the highly respected Vic Fangio.

Overall, this offensive unit should be much improved. If the defense can remain stable, the NFC North will challenge the NFC West and AFC South as the toughest top-to-bottom divisions in football.

### 2018 Fantasy Outlook

### Projected Position Rankings

| Position | Player | PPR Rank vs Position | PPR Overall rank | Standard Rank vs Position | Standard Overall Rank |
|---|---|---|---|---|---|
| Quarterback | Mitch Trubisky | 31 | 188 | 31 | 187 |
| Running Back 1 | Jordan Howard | 19 | 31 | 19 | 12 |
| Running Back 2 | Tarik Cohen | 9 | 127 | 9 | 129 |
| Wide Receiver 1 | Allen Robinson | 32 | 159 | 32 | 158 |
| Wide Receiver 2 | Dontrelle Inman | 32 | 220 | 32 | 224 |
| Wide Receiver 3 | Kevin White | 23 | 216 | 20 | 209 |
| Tight End 1 | Trey Burton | 9 | 76 | 9 | 85 |
| Kicker | Cody Parkey | 28th Against Kickers | | | |
| Defense/ST | Bears | 7th Against Defense/ST | | | |

### Position Commentary:

### Quarterback:

The hope for the Bears brass and their fans is that Mitch Trubisky's 2018 will be similar to Jared Goff's 2017 in LA. For fantasy GMs out there, pump the breaks. The Bears didn't put a ton of weight on his shoulders last season, and he will take a bit of time to adjust. Do not draft him, but put him on your watch list to begin the year.

### Running Back:

Matt Nagy's system calls for a bell cow running back, and he's stated as much in interviews. Jordan Howard has been a consistent contributor on what can only be described as a bad offense. I don't think he'll match the Kansas City output of Kareem Hunt or Jamaal Charles in recent years, but he is a solid RB2 and could creep into RB1 status. The only thing that will get in the way of fantasy greatness is teammate Tarik Cohen, who is dynamic in the passing game.

You should be able to grab Howard in rounds 3-5. Tarik Cohen's primary value will be for Daily Fantasy players and PPR leagues.

### Wide Receiver:

Chicago's top receiver, Kendall Wright, has left for Minnesota. To the Bears' credit, they made an investment in pass catchers this offseason. Allen Robinson was signed in free agency, and he has WR1 potential in this scheme. The new Bears offense offers their WR1 the 9th-best Opportunity Ranking among their peers. This puts Robinson in the sleeper category for me because he figures to be undervalued on draft day.

WR2 duties will likely fall to Kevin White. After spending an early first-round pick on him, he's battled injuries and has only played in 5 games over those two seasons. In his 4 starts in 2016, he averaged 9 targets per game. For this reason, I'm including him in our hibernation sleeper category.

**Tight End:**

Nagy's offense will need a top TE. The Bears have two options. First is last year's Adam Shaheen. Having only received 14 targets in 2017, I doubt he is ready to make much of an impact.

Newly-signed TE Trey Burton brings talent and a familiarity with the offense thanks to his time in Philadelphia (under Doug Pederson, another coach in the Andy Reid tree). Burton will be a popular sleeper pick this offseason, but that hype will drive up his draft stock. If you're a believer in his fantasy potential (I have him ranked 9th in opportunity against TE1s), you might need to splurge in the first run on tight ends.

**Kicker:**

Cairo Santos was effective in his time in Kansas City, but I don't think the Bears offense scores enough to warrant a draft pick at this stage.

**Defense/Special Teams:**

Chicago's D/ST unit is underrated. They have a talented squad, and Nagy retained DC Vic Fangio. Because they don't carry much of a reputation, they should be available in the last two rounds. If your higher targeted defenses are gone, you can feel good about this group.

**Sleeper Watch**

**_Popular Sleeper: Trey Burton, TE_**

_He couldn't crack the lineup in Philadelphia because Zach Ertz had a firm grasp on the TE targets. Nagy will want to use Burton in that Ertz/Kelce-like TE role the Andry Reid tree loves so much._

**_Deep Sleepers: N/A_**

**_Hibernator: Kevin White, WR_**

_When he plays, he produces. If he's healthy, he's worth a roster spot._

# Detroit Lions

## 2017 Fantasy Opportunity Summary (Offensive Positions):

| Position | Player | PPR Rank vs Position | PPR Overall Rank |
|---|---|---|---|
| Quarterback | Matthew Stafford | 11 | 11 |
| Running Back | Ameer Abdullah | 23 | 24 |
| Running Back 2 | Theo Riddick | 12 | 14 |
| Wide Receiver 1 | Golden Tate | 14 | 23 |
| Wide Receiver 2 | Marvin Jones | 1 | 1 |
| Wide Receiver 3 | T.J. Jones | 14 | 14 |
| Tight End | Eric Ebron | 12 | 11 |

### Fantasy Opportunity Analysis by Position (Offense Only):
### Quarterback:

For as many throws as Matt Stafford makes, you'd think he'd be a more elite fantasy quarterback, but it never turns out that way. For fantasy players, Stafford is a lower-tier QB1 play. I'd say he's better used when stacking with his WR1 or WR2 (Golden Tate and Marvin Jones).

### Running Back:

The Lions haven't found a consistent run game, but it hasn't appeared to be an emphasis for offensive coordinator Jim Bob Cooter to find one. Ameer Abdullah and Theo Riddick have shown playmaking ability when they have the ball in their hands. It will take a shift in offensive philosophy for them to have much more than spot-play or matchup-based Daily Fantasy value.

### Wide Receiver:

The Lions boast a group of three or four receivers that could all be draftable. Golden Tate received a massive number of targets, and Marvin Jones leads all WR2s in fantasy potential. Jones was a bit of a boom-or-bust player last year. The Lions WRs are among my favorite week-to-week Daily Fantasy plays.

### Tight End:

Eric Ebron has long confused fantasy owners. After writing him off in recent years, Ebron found himself as a TE1 in fantasy leagues this past season. With an offense that passes as often as the Lions did, Ebron produced 53 catches on 86 targets and found pay dirt 4 times.

# 2018 Offseason Analysis

## Transactions

| Key Losses | | | Key Additions | | |
|---|---|---|---|---|---|
| Pos | Player | New Team | Pos | Player | Old Team |
| SS | Don Carey | Jacksonville | RB | LeGarrette Blount | Philadelphia |
| DE | Brandon Copeland | NY Jets | QB | Matt Cassel | Tennessee |
| TE | Eric Ebron | Indianapolis | LB | Jonathan Freeney | New Orleans |
| TE | Darren Fells | Celveland | C | Wesley Johnson | NY Jets |
| DB | D.J. Hayden | Jacksonville | ILB | Christian Jones | Chicago |
| P | Jeff Locke | San Francisco | OLB | Devon Kennard | NY Giants |
| DT | Haloti Ngata | Philadelphia | CB | DeShawn Snead | Seattle |
| DT | Akeem Spence | Miami | TE | Levine Toilolo | Atlanta |
| C | Travis Swanson | NY Jets | TE | Luke Wilson | Seattle |
| OLB | Tahir Whitehead | Oakland | | | |

## Draft Summary

| Round | Overall | Position | Player | College |
|---|---|---|---|---|
| 1 | 20 | C | Frank Ragnow | Arkansas |
| 2 | 43 | RB | Kerryon Johnson | Auburn |
| 3 | 82 | S | Tracy Walker | Louisiana-Lafayett |
| 4 | 114 | DE | Da'shawn Hand | Alabama |
| 5 | 153 | G | Tyrell Crosby | Oregon |
| 7 | 237 | RB | Nick Bawden | San Diego St |

## Coaching Changes

Matt Patricia brings a Super Bowl pedigree with him from New England to Detroit. I have two concerns. First, there's never been a hire from the Belichick coaching tree that has found success. Second, the defenses in New England have given up a lot of yards.

From an offensive standpoint, Detroit has retained Jim Bob Cooter to run the unit. They had one of the higher pass ratios (over 60%) in 2017. The Lions have invested in running back talent, however, so I expect the rushing totals to increase this season.

Paul Pasqualoni was brought on board to coach the defense. He most recently served as the defensive line coach for Boston College, but does have a ton of NFL experience including a 2-year stint as the Dolphins defensive coordinator in 2007 and 2008. Pasqualoni brings a wealth of experience to a young staff. Because the Lions are so talented offensively, a bit of toughness and intrigue on the defensive side of the ball could make them playoff contenders in 2018.

**2018 Fantasy Outlook**

**Projected Position Rankings**

| Position | Player | PPR Rank vs Position | PPR Overall rank | Standard Rank vs Position | Standard Overall Rank |
|----------|--------|---------------------|------------------|--------------------------|----------------------|
| Quarterback | Matthew Stafford | 14 | 84 | 14 | 88 |
| Running Back 1 | LeGarrette Blount / Kerryon Johnson | 25 | 119 | 26 | 102 |
| Running Back 2 | Theo Riddick | 13 | 179 | 14 | 178 |
| Wide Receiver 1 | Golden Tate | 22 | 49 | 27 | 72 |
| Wide Receiver 2 | Mike Jones Jr | 2 | 69 | 2 | 34 |
| Wide Receiver 3 | TJ Jones | 19 | 215 | 17 | 213 |
| Tight End 1 | Levine Toilolo | 15 | 193 | 15 | 198 |
| Kicker | Matt Prater | 7th Against Kickers | | | |
| Defense/ST | Lions | 11th (tied) Against Defense/ST | | | |

**Position Commentary:**

**Quarterback:**

Offensive coordinator Jim Bob Cooter was retained, so I anticipate similar Lions passing output for Matt Stafford. On my list? That makes him a top-tier QB2 on your team rather than a weekly starter. I do, however, love him in Daily Fantasy play. Stacking him with undervalued WR2 Mike Jones will be a potent bargain play.

**Running Back:**

The Lions haven't found much spark in their running game. Ameer Abdullah and Theo Riddick have both flashed, but no fantasy GM feels good about starting them as an RB2. Both have historically held value only if the other was injured or in Daily Fantasy matchup plays.

LeGarrette Blount produced well when called upon in Philly last year. He will likely get the bulk of first and second down carries. I don't love his fantasy potential (ranked 25th and 26th in PPR/non-PPR) fantasy opportunity. Making matters worse, rookie Kerryon Johnson figures to be in the mix.

This looks like a 3-4 member running back committee. Similar to Philadelphia's situation, the smart move is to avoid all of them unless you see Blount or Johnson winning the bulk of the carries in preseason. You are likely to see Johnson on sleeper lists around the different publications, but that is likely to overvalue his position. If you have an irresistible urge to fill your roster with a Lion running back, make it a late pick.

**Wide Receiver:**

I like the output from Golden Tate, but this is a deep group of receivers. His fantasy opportunity suffers as a result of this, but you can feel great about drafting him in rounds 3 or 4 if he's available.

Marvin Jones is one of the most underrated receivers in the league. He ranks 2nd against his fellow WR2s and is worthy of a roster spot. He tends to get his TDs in chunks, so pay close attention to our weekly matchup rankings.

WR3 will score. Keep an eye out for T.J. Jones and Kenny Golladay. Whoever wins most of the snaps could be a valued spot-starter or Daily Fantasy bargain.

### Tight End:

Eric Ebron produced last year, but he left in free agency. New additions Levine Toilolo (Atlanta) and Luke Wilson (Seattle) don't inspire much confidence. My gut says Luke Wilson will win the job, but don't spend a draft spot on him.

### Kicker:

Detroit moves the ball and scores. Matt Prater ranks 7th in our Opportunity Rankings. He's worth a last-round draft pick.

### Defense/Special Teams:

Matt Patricia will be installing a new defense. The team has talent, but it doesn't make sense to draft them on speculation. They should be available in waivers if you want to wait and see.

### Sleeper Watch

*Popular Sleepers: N/A*

*Deep Sleepers: Kenny Golladay, WR; T.J. Jones, WR*

*Whoever wins the WR3 duties in Detroit will score well.*

*Hibernators: N/A*

## Green Bay Packers

**2017 Fantasy Opportunity Summary (Offensive Positions):**

| Position | Player | PPR Rank vs Position | PPR Overall Rank |
|---|---|---|---|
| Quarterback | Aaron Rodgers | 12 | 12 |
| Running Back | Jamaal Williams / Aaron Jones | 10 | 10 |
| Running Back 2 | Ty Montgomery | 30 | 28 |
| Wide Receiver 1 | Davante Adams | 11 | 7 |
| Wide Receiver 2 | Randall Cobb | 8 | 13 |
| Wide Receiver 3 | Jordy Nelson | 1 | 1 |
| Tight End | Martellus Bennett | 27 | 31 |

**Fantasy Opportunity Analysis by Position (Offense Only):**
**Quarterback:**

*It was the best of times. It was the worst of times.* When Aaron Rodgers is on the field, the Packers offense is dynamic. He was elite and worthy of an early draft pick. Unfortunately for anyone who used an early draft pick on Rodgers last year, he only played in 6 games (7 if you count his early exit vs. Minnesota, but I don't).

Brett Hundley seems nice. Maybe he'll be a good starting QB someday. He wasn't last year. Let's move on...

**Running Back:**

For years, the Packers have had no running game to speak of. 2016 saw converted WR Ty Montgomery win carries. As a fantasy player, he was a great play. With Rodgers out in 2017, we learned why more teams aren't converting WRs into RBs. With Hundley behind center, Montgomery gave way to Aaron Jones and Jamaal Williams in the backfield after injuries.

If Packers fans could find one positive last year, it's that there is room for optimism at the RB position. Aaron Jones averaged over 5 yards per carry (on 81 attempts) and though Jamaal Williams only averaged 3.6 YPC, he brought stability to the backfield and was able to get tough yards. In Jones and Montgomery, the Packers now have a realistic run option on third-and-2, and that should open opportunities across the board.

**Wide Receiver:**

The 2017 WR group didn't produce well, but this had more to do with Rodgers being out than their viability as fantasy players. Only Davante Adams cleared 100 targets in 2017. You can expect three WRs to top triple digits in 2018.

**Tight End:**

Martellus Bennet played pretty well with Rodgers. He was catching over 60% of his targets, but he fell off the map after his own injury situation and was eventually waived.

## 2018 Offseason Analysis

### Transactions

| Key Losses | | | Key Additions | | |
|---|---|---|---|---|---|
| Pos | Player | New Team | Pos | Player | Old Team |
| SS | Morgan Burnett | Pittsburgh | TE | Jimmy Graham | Seattle |
| WR | Jeff Janis | Cleveland | QB | DeShone Kizer | Cleveland |
| WR | Jordy Nelson | Oakland | DE | Muhammad Wilkerson | NY Jets |
| CB | Damarious Randall | Cleveland | DB | Tramon Williams | Arizona |

### Draft Summary

| Round | Overall | Position | Player | College |
|---|---|---|---|---|
| 1 | 18 | CB | Jaire Alexander | Louisville |
| 2 | 45 | CB | Josh Jackson | Iowa |
| 3 | 88 | LB | Oren Burks | Vanderbilt |
| 4 | 133 | WR | J'mon Moore | Missouri |
| 5 | 138 | DL | Cole Madison | Washington St |
| 5 | 172 | P | JK Scott | Alabama |
| 5 | 174 | WR | Marquez Valdes-Scantling | South Florida |
| 6 | 207 | WR | Equanimeous St. Brown | Notre Dame |
| 7 | 232 | DE | James Looney | California |
| 7 | 239 | LS | Hunter Bradley | Mississipi St |
| 7 | 248 | Edge | Kendall Donnerson | Southeast Missouri |

### Coaching Changes

When a starting quarterback goes down with injury, particularly one as incredible as Aaron Rodgers, you get a truer sense of what your football team is made of. In Green Bay last year, we saw that there were glaring needs in personnel and on the coaching staff.

Joe Philbun, most recently with the Colts, returns to Green Bay where he spent 5 years coaching the offense under Mike McCarthy.

The more interesting hire is defensive coordinator Mike Pettine. Pettine made his mark as defensive coordinator of the New York Jets and Buffalo Bills under Rex Ryan. He's piloted several standout defenses and even won 7 games as the head coach of the Cleveland Browns in 2014.

## 2018 Fantasy Outlook

### Projected Position Rankings

| Position | Player | PPR Rank vs Position | PPR Overall rank | Standard Rank vs Position | Standard Overall Rank |
|---|---|---|---|---|---|
| Quarterback | Aaron Rodgers | 5 | 38 | 5 | 43 |
| Running Back 1 | Ty Montgomery | 12 | 44 | 12 | 46 |
| Running Back 2 | Aaron Jones | 29 | | 29 | 143 |
| Wide Receiver 1 | Davante Adams | 8 | 27 | 8 | 18 |
| Wide Receiver 2 | Randall Cobb | 4 | 96 | 6 | 76 |
| Wide Receiver 3 | Geronimo Allison / J'Mon Moore | 1 | 140 | 1 | 188 |
| Tight End 1 | Jimmy Graham | 18 | 55 | 18 | 84 |
| Kicker | Mason Crosby | 28th (tied) Against Kickers | | | |
| Defense/ST | Packers | 20th Against Defense/ST | | | |

### Position Commentary:

### Quarterback:

When Rodgers is healthy, he's at the top of the tier-1 QB rankings. Draft him early.

### Running Back:

Jamaal Williams asserted himself as an early down running back last season. That said, Aaron Jones was actually the most productive back on the roster with 5.5, yards per rush. My hesitation comes because WR/RB Ty Montgomery produces well for Rodgers. Any of these three could easily win the RB role. Watch preseason position groupings closely because the Packers RB1 will be a viable starter at RB or flex.

### Wide Receiver:

The departure of Rodgers' favorite receiver, Jordy Nelson will have a ripple effect throughout the offense. The likely beneficiary is Devante Adams. I have Adams ranked in the back half of the league in WR1 opportunity, but thanks to Rodgers' accuracy, the efficiency of his WR corps will raise them in the rankings.

Randall Cobb is aging, but still productive, and represents the 8th-best WR2 ranking in both PPR/Non-PPR leagues. He's worth a roster spot, but understand that you're drafting the 2018 Randall Cobb and not the 2014 Randall Cobb.

WR3 will have value. This spot should either go to Geronimo Allison, rookie J'mon Moore or even Ty Montgomery if he is moved back to receiver.

**Tight End:**

TE Jimmy Graham is an intriguing acquisition. The McCarthy offense made Jermichael Finley a standout tight end years ago, and I think Graham will also be a standout. Though the offensive output leaves the TE1 position ranked at a disappointing 18th, Graham's playmaking ability will drive up his overall ranking.

**Kicker:**

With a healthy Rodgers, the Packers score ... but they kick a lot of extra points instead of field goals. You can feel OK drafting Crosby in the last round.

**Defense/Special Teams:**

This is another defense that is going through a transition. Mike Pettine will have this group reaching its potential, but it's hard to know exactly what that means in fantasy output. I suggest passing on this unit in the draft, but they can be a nice matchup play through the season if you can grab them from waivers.

**Sleeper Watch**

*Popular Sleepers: Aaron Jones, RB; Jamaal Williams, RB*

*Deep Sleeper: Geronimo Allison, WR*

*Green Bay's WR3 spot is worth a lot of points. If he can hold off his competition, Allison will score well.*

*Hibernator: Jamaal Williams, RB; J'mon Moore, WR*

*Williams will probably open camp as the third running back, but he has potential to win the carries.*

*Green Bay is back to drafting WR talent early. Moore will push Allison for playing time.*

# Minnesota Vikings
## 2017 Fantasy Opportunity Summary (Offensive Positions):

| Position | Player | PPR Rank vs Position | PPR Overall Rank |
|----------|--------|----------------------|------------------|
| Quarterback | Case Keenum | 16 | 16 |
| Running Back | Dalvin Cook / Latavius Murray | 9 | 8 |
| Running Back 2 | Jerick McKinnon | 8 | 8 |
| Wide Receiver 1 | Adam Thielen | 9 | 10 |
| Wide Receiver 2 | Stefon Diggs | 2 | 2 |
| Wide Receiver 3 | Laquon Treadwell | 32 | 32 |
| Tight End | Kyle Rudolph | 8 | 6 |

**Fantasy Opportunity Analysis by Position (Offense Only):**
**Quarterback:**

Case Keenum was graded well by scouts across the league and was also a nice waiver play or Daily Fantasy play week-to-week. He only scored 16th in our fantasy Opportunity Rankings, but gelled well with his offensive personnel and distributed the ball well.

**Running Back:**

When Dalvin Cook played, he was ascending into T2, or possibly even T1, status. He was explosive in the run game and was a weapon in the pass game. He has potential to be a 3-down back in this league for a long time.

After losing Dalvin Cook for the season early in 2017, Latavius Murray and Jerrick McKinnon played exceptionally well. The committee worked so well that both RB1 and RB2 finished in the top 10 in our fantasy Opportunity Rankings.

**Wide Receiver:**

Adam Thielen was a gem in last year's fantasy draft, having caught 91 balls on 142 targets. He's a solid player, but benefits from something I call the *Houshmandzadeh Effect*. Stefon Diggs is dynamic and commands the attention of opposing defenses. This opens opportunities for Thielen (in the same way Chad OchoCinco opened opportunities for teammate T.J. Houshmandzadeh). Both members in this tandem are viable WR1 plays week-to-week.

**Tight End:**

Kyle Rudolph ranked third on the Vikings in targets (81) and tied Stefon Diggs for the top mark in TDs (8). He was a weekly play at tight end, and 2018 will be no different.

## 2018 Offseason Analysis

### Transactions

| Key Losses | | | Key Additions | | |
|---|---|---|---|---|---|
| Pos | Player | New Team | Pos | Player | Old Team |
| QB | Sam Bradford | Arizona | OG | Tom Compton | Chicago |
| QB | Teddy Bridgewater | Ny Jets | QB | Kirk Cousins | Washington |
| DB | Tramaine Brock | Denver | DT | Sheldon Richardson | Seattle |
| DT | Tom Johnson | Seattle | WR | Kendall Wright | Chicago |
| QB | Case Keenum | Denver | QB | Trevor Siemian | Denver |
| RB | Jerick McKinnon | San Francisco | | | |
| OG | Jeremiah Sirles | Carolina | | | |
| WR | Jarius Wright | Carolina | | | |
| OG | Joe Berger | Retired | | | |

### Draft Summary

| Round | Overall | Position | Player | College |
|---|---|---|---|---|
| 1 | 30 | CB | Mike Hughes | UCF |
| 2 | 62 | OT | Brian O'Neill | Pittsburgh |
| 4 | 102 | DE | Jalyn Holmes | Ohio St |
| 5 | 157 | TE | Tyler Conklin | Central Michigan |
| 5 | 167 | K | Daniel Carlson | Auburn |
| 6 | 213 | G | Colby Gossett | Appalachina St |
| 6 | 218 | Edge | Ade Aruna | Tulane |
| 7 | 225 | LB | Devante Downs | California |

### Coaching Changes

Unfortunately for Vikings fans, Pat Shurmur was hired as the head coach of the New York Giants. Enter new offensive coordinator John DeFilippo.

Filippo is young but has well over a decade of NFL coaching experience. He most recently served as the Eagles quarterbacks coach and has worked very closely with Carson Wentz. Unfortunately for DeFilippo, he was also the offensive coordinator for a 3-13 Browns team. On the other hand, that Browns squad won more games that season than 2016 and 2017 combined for Cleveland.

The Vikings offense is as talented as any unit in football. I expect the unit to perform similarly to its 2017 output. They key for this group will be how fast Kirk Cousins can adapt to the offense.

## 2018 Fantasy Outlook

**Projected Position Rankings**

| Position | Player | PPR Rank vs Position | PPR Overall rank | Standard Rank vs Position | Standard Overall Rank |
|---|---|---|---|---|---|
| Quarterback | Kirk Cousins | 23 | 87 | 23 | 91 |
| Running Back 1 | Dalvin Cook | 16 | 32 | 15 | 20 |
| Running Back 2 | Latavius Murray | 10 | 161 | 11 | 167 |
| Wide Receiver 1 | Stefon Diggs | 11 | 30 | 13 | 38 |
| Wide Receiver 2 | Adam Thielen | 7 | 63 | 7 | 37 |
| Wide Receiver 3 | Laquon Treadwell | 29 | 236 | 29 | 236 |
| Tight End 1 | Kyle Rudolph | 17 | 130 | 13 | 118 |
| Kicker | Kai Forbath | 10th (tied) Against Kickers | | | |
| Defense/ST | Vikings | 15th (tied) Against Defense/ST | | | |

**Position Commentary:**

**Quarterback:**

The addition of Kirk Cousins was an aggressive move designed to stabilize the QB position and extend a Super Bowl window. The departure of Pat Shurmur to New York casts a bit of a shadow on the offense. I have only given Cousins and the Vikings an Opportunity Ranking of 23rd. Given his undoubtedly high draft position, I suggest you let one of your competitors take him.

**Running Back:**

Dalvin Cook was electric last year before his season-ending injury. While the RB1 Opportunity Rank is only 16th/15th between PPR/non-PPR leagues, he has home run potential that can't be accurately measured over a 15-game fantasy season. I will be moving his ranking upward as a result.

**Wide Receiver:**

In Adam Thielen and Stefon Diggs, the Vikings have one of the best one-two punches in the league at WR. Both can be considered a WR1 across your fantasy league, and both are worthy of early selections in your draft. But beware of the WR2 fantasy potential score. New OC John DeFilippo has shown a desire to feature one WR over another. For this reason, I will boost Stefon Diggs' ranking and drop Thielen's ranking a bit.

New addition, Kendall Wright could be a solid spot-start or Daily Fantasy sleeper. The Vikings offense gives their WR3 the 7th-highest Opportunity Ranking against WR3 peers. Defenses will be trying to slow down Diggs/Thielen and Rudolph. Wright will likely have opportunities for chunk yardage.

**Tight End:**

Cousins likes to pass to his TEs, and Kyle Rudolph gives offers a ton of potential. Because he doesn't get a ton of targets relative to his peers, his opportunity ranks a bit lower. The catches he does make count, having tied for a team-high 8 TD receptions in 2017. I have him ranked as a lower-level TE starter, but that could improve based on his chemistry with Cousins throughout the preseason.

**Kicker:**

Minnesota will score points, and Kai Forbath is accurate. He's worth a draft pick in the final round.

**Defense/Special Teams:**

This unit is incredible in the NFL, but that doesn't necessarily translate to fantasy points. While their yards per play is low (which correlates to fewer points over a season), they don't get much bonus via sack or turnover totals. This makes sense because they force a lot of punts, so they have less opportunity to rush the QB or pick off passes. Your competition will draft them based on reputation. Let them do it.

**Sleeper Watch**

*Popular Sleepers: N/A*

*Deep Sleepers: N/A*

*Hibernators: N/A*

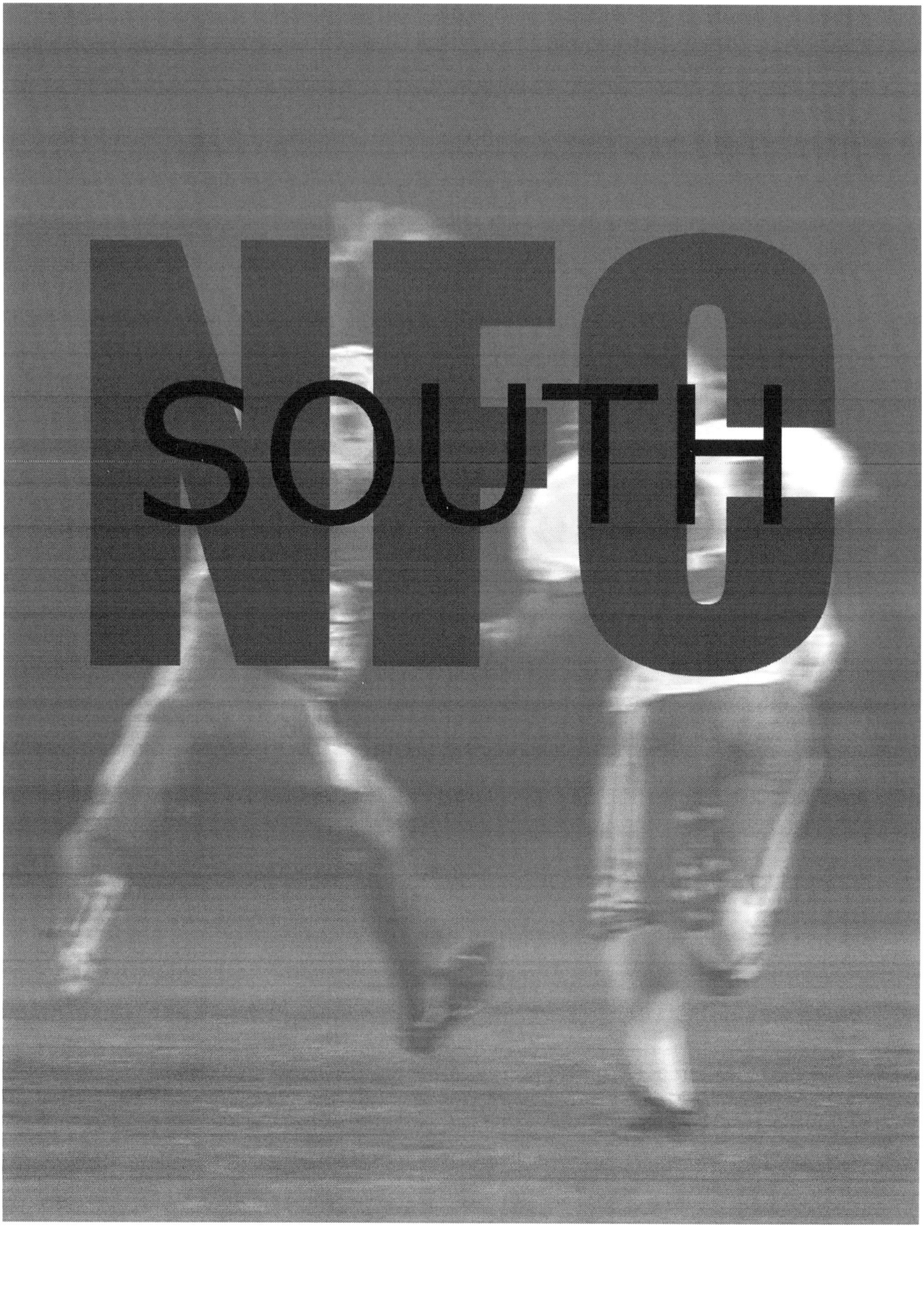
NFC
SOUTH

# NFC South

## Atlanta Falcons

### 2017 Fantasy Opportunity Summary (Offensive Positions):

| Position | Player | PPR Rank vs Position | PPR Overall Rank |
|---|---|---|---|
| Quarterback | Matt Ryan | 19 | 19 |
| Running Back | Devonta Freeman | 12 | 11 |
| Running Back 2 | Tevin Coleman | 7 | 5 |
| Wide Receiver 1 | Julio Jones | 7 | 5 |
| Wide Receiver 2 | Mohamed Sanu | 9 | 12 |
| Wide Receiver 3 | Taylor Gabriel | 19 | 20 |
| Tight End | Austin Hooper | 19 | 19 |

**Fantasy Opportunity Analysis by Position (Offense Only):**
**Quarterback:**

Matt Ryan seemed to have an adjustment period with new offensive coordinator Steve Sarkisian to start the 2017 season. While duplicating his 2016 TD/INT numbers (38 and 7) seemed like a long shot, I also wasn't expecting him to throw 20 TDs and 12 INTs. Still, by the end of the year, the offense seemed to have found its way and this remains one of the most talented offenses in the league.

**Running Back:**

This unit is now a definite committee. Devonta Freeman remains the primary ball carrier (196 carries to 153), but Coleman's production while starting can't be ignored. They both finished with 8 total touchdowns, but Freeman had 4 fumbles compared to Coleman's 1.

Freeman finished 12th/11th in PPR/Non-PPR fantasy opportunity vs. his RB1 peers. Coleman finished 7th/5th. This could be a position battle in 2018 and worth monitoring during training camp.

**Wide Receiver:**

As expected, Atlanta's WR1 and WR2 position groupings were both ranked in the top-10 against their peers. Julio Jones is a no-brainer starter week-to-week. He caught 88 passes on 148 carries. Unfortunately, he was only able to haul in 3 TDs.

Mohamed Sanu caught 67 passes and led the team in receiving touchdowns with 5. If you needed a flex player or a bye week starter, you could have done a lot worse than Sanu in 2017.

**Tight End:**

Austin Hooper finished 2017 with the 19th-ranked fantasy opportunity against his fellow TE1s. He was the beneficiary of 3 of Matt Ryan's 20 touchdown passes. I expect the overall offensive production to increase next year and Hooper's output to improve as well.

## 2018 Offseason Analysis

### Transactions

| Key Losses | | | Key Additions | | |
|---|---|---|---|---|---|
| Pos | Player | New Team | Pos | Player | Old Team |
| DE | Adrian Clayborn | New England | CB | Austin Bethel | Arizona |
| WR | Taylor Gabriel | Chicago | OG | Brandon Fusco | San Francisco |
| DT | Dontari Poe | Carolina | TE | Logan Paulsen | San Francisco |
| TE | Levine Toilolo | Detroit | | | |

### Draft Summary

| Round | Overall | Position | Player | College |
|---|---|---|---|---|
| 1 | 26 | WR | Calvin Ridley | Alabama |
| 2 | 58 | CB | Isiah Oliver | Colorado |
| 3 | 90 | OT | Deadrin Senat | South Florida |
| 4 | 126 | RB | Ito Smith | Southern Miss |
| 6 | 194 | WR | Russell Gage | LSU |
| 6 | 200 | LB | Foye Oluokun | Yale |

### Coaching Changes
There were no changes to the coaching staff at the head coach or coordinator levels.

# 2018 Fantasy Outlook

## Projected Position Rankings

| Position | Player | PPR Rank vs Position | PPR Overall rank | Standard Rank vs Position | Standard Overall Rank |
|----------|--------|---------------------|------------------|--------------------------|----------------------|
| Quarterback | Matt Ryan | 28 | 109 | 28 | 123 |
| Running Back 1 | Devonta Freeman | 14 | 28 | 13 | 26 |
| Running Back 2 | Tevin Coleman | 11 | 128 | 10 | 110 |
| Wide Receiver 1 | Julio Jones | 14 | 23 | 14 | 14 |
| Wide Receiver 2 | Mohamed Sanu | 14 | 111 | 15 | 108 |
| Wide Receiver 3 | Calvin Ridley | 24 | 225 | 24 | 141 |
| Tight End 1 | Austin Hooper | 21 | 202 | 21 | 210 |
| Kicker | Matt Bryant | 10th (tied) Against Kickers | | | |
| Defense/ST | Falcons | 18th (tied) Against Defense/ST | | | |

## Position Commentary:

### Quarterback:

Matt Ryan's output plummeted in 2017 after the offense transitioned from Kyle Shanahan to Steve Sarkisian. TD totals were down significantly, and I don't see much changing for the better. I have given Ryan an Opportunity Rank of 20th which sounded low until I dug further. Your competition will likely view last year as a fluke when in reality, the 2016 season appears to be the fluke. Let your competition draft him early and take a better-valued QB.

### Running Back:

Devonta Freeman is losing his grip on RB1 opportunities. He carried the ball 196 times in 14 games compared to Tevin Coleman's 156 in 15 games. Because of this, Freeman sees an opportunity score of 14/13 in PPR/Non-PPR leagues, and Coleman remains lower against RB2s with Opportunity Rankings of 11th and 10th vs. his peers.

Freeman will be drafted earlier based on reputation, but like Ryan, let your competitors risk using an early-round pick on a situation that could turn into a 50/50 committee in the 2018 season.

### Wide Receiver:

Julio Jones has an Opportunity Ranking of 5th/6th in spite of catching only 3 TDs last year. The Falcons threw his direction 148 times, which shows a commitment to keeping him a focal point on the roster. Expect him to at least double his TD output in 2018.

The Falcons saw WR Calvin Ridley slip to them at the bottom of the first round of the 2018 draft. I still believe Mohamed Sanu will remain the WR2 in 2-receiver formations, but Ridley will eat into Sanu's targets. I'd still take a flyer on Sanu in the late rounds of the draft, as Ridley's inclusion should open things up from a coverage point of view.

Ridley is a sleeper on my board, but his 1st round pedigree could push his draft position up into overvalued territory.

**Tight End:**

Austin Hooper produced reasonably well last season, having received 65 targets and catching 3 touchdown passes. If the offense can improve as a unit, he could be worth a roster spot. For now, flag him and watch him during the preseason.

His target total increased from 27 to 65 in 2017. If you have a deep roster, he'll be worth drafting and stashing as your 2nd tight end.

**Kicker:**

Atlanta had the 10th-best kicker Opportunity Rank, and Matt Bryant is a trusted kicker. I think Atlanta's offense will improve in 2018, so for that reason, he will be a draftable kicker. Do not take him before the last round of the draft, however.

**Defense/Special Teams:**

Atlanta gets to the quarterback, but they don't have a particularly inspiring yards-per-play average or turnover generation ratio. In my opinion, they are a squad that should be available on waivers for most of the year and only picked up based on matchup.

**Sleeper Watch**

**Popular Sleeper: Calvin Ridley, WR**

*I love his potential, but perhaps more for 2019 and beyond. Ridley will be fighting Jones and Sanu for WR targets.*

**Deep Sleeper: Austin Hooper, TE**

*He's very quietly improved his fantasy output. If Atlanta can get more scoring this year, he could easily be a top-10 TE.*

**Hibernators: N/A**

# Carolina Panthers
## 2017 Fantasy Opportunity Summary (Offensive Positions):

| Position | Player | PPR Rank vs Position | PPR Overall Rank |
|---|---|---|---|
| Quarterback | Cam Newton | 5 | 5 |
| Running Back | Jonathan Steward | 32 | 28 |
| Running Back 2 | Chris McCaffrey | 3 | 3 |
| Wide Receiver 1 | Devin Funchess / Kelvin Benjamin | 23 | 17 |
| Wide Receiver 2 | Russell Shepard | 14 | 16 |
| Wide Receiver 3 | Curtis Samuel | 30 | 28 |
| Tight End | Greg Olsen / Ed Dickson | 20 | 17 |

**Fantasy Opportunity Analysis by Position (Offense Only):**
**Quarterback:**

Cam Newton's running ability continues to vault him into the top tier of fantasy quarterbacks. He finished 5th overall in fantasy Opportunity Ranking in spite of losing his preferred WR, Kelvin Benjamin, via trade and TE Greg Olsen to injury last season.

The offense began a transition towards short and intermediate pass concepts. His passing efficiency improved in 2017, but he did throw the second-most interceptions of his career.

**Running Back:**

Jonathan Stewart isn't producing as a number 1 running back anymore. Part of his degradation was due to the change in offensive approach. Christian McCaffrey came on board and received 113 pass targets last year. Although Stewart led the team in rushing attempts, this backfield was McCaffrey's for all intents and purposes.

**Wide Receiver:**

Trading Kelvin Benjamin to Buffalo in the middle of the season was an odd move for a playoff contender to make, but it didn't seem to hurt the team much. Devin Funchess assumed WR1 status and picked up where Benjamin left off, hauling in 63 passes on 111 targets.

The interesting thing to watch moving forward will be the use of RB/WR Curtis Samuel. He was bogged down by injuries in 2017 but did manage to start 4 of 9 games he participated in. He showed promise.

**Tight End:**

Thanks to injury, it seemed like TE Greg Olsen spent more time as an NFL commentator than he did on the field. Playing in only 7 games, Olsen saw the worst yards-per-game average of his Panthers career. By far.

## 2018 Offseason Analysis

### Transactions

| Key Losses | | | Key Additions | | |
|---|---|---|---|---|---|
| Pos | Player | New Team | Pos | Player | Old Team |
| WR | Kaelin Clay | Buffalo | OT | Zach Banner | Cleveland |
| FS | Kurt Coleman | New Orleans | DB | Ross Cockrell | NY Giants |
| TE | Ed Dickson | Seattle | DT | Dontari Poe | Atlanta |
| DT | Star Lotulelei | Buffalo | OG | Jeremiah Sirles | Minnesota |
| OG | Andrew Norwell | Jacksonville | WR | Torrey Smith | Philadelphia |
| RB | Jonathan Stewart | NY Giants | WR | Jarius Wright | Minnesota |
| DB | Teddy Williams | Ny Giants | | | |
| CB | Daryl Worely | Oakland | | | |

### Draft Summary

| Round | Overall | Position | Player | College |
|---|---|---|---|---|
| 1 | 24 | WR | D.J. Moore | Maryland |
| 2 | 55 | CB | donte Jackson | LSU |
| 3 | 21 | S | Rashaan Gaulden | Tennessee |
| 4 | 101 | TE | Ian Thomas | Indiana |
| 4 | 136 | Edge | Marquis Haynes | Mississippi |
| 5 | 161 | ILB | Jermaine Carter | Maryland |
| 7 | 234 | ILB | Andre Smith | North Carolina |
| 7 | 242 | DT | Kendrick Norton | Miami |

### Coaching Changes

Previous offensive coordinator Mike Shula is now on the Giants. The experienced Norv Turner will be taking his place. Turner's resume shows sustained success at the coordinator level, and I anticipate the same holding true in Carolina. Carolina will show a commitment to the run in 2018. Already a playoff team, it won't take much to open a new Super Bowl contention window for this unit. If Turner can improve Cam Newton's efficiency, this could be a scary team in 2018.

With Steve Wilks taking the head coaching job in Arizona, Carolina has promoted Eric Washington into the coordinator position. There have been personnel changes, but I don't foresee a difference in play calling or tactics.

### 2018 Fantasy Outlook

## Projected Position Rankings

| Position | Player | PPR Rank vs Position | PPR Overall rank | Standard Rank vs Position | Standard Overall Rank |
|---|---|---|---|---|---|
| Quarterback | Cam Newton | 4 | 37 | 4 | 42 |
| Running Back 1 | C.J. Anderson | 15 | 92 | 16 | 98 |
| Running Back 2 | Christian McCaffrey | 3 | 22 | 4 | 29 |
| Wide Receiver 1 | Devin Funchess | 28 | 70 | 28 | 53 |
| Wide Receiver 2 | D.J. Moore | 18 | 153 | 20 | 153 |
| Wide Receiver 3 | Torrey Smith | 32 | 239 | 31 | 239 |
| Tight End 1 | Greg Olsen | 3 | 33 | 3 | 69 |
| Kicker | Graham Gano | 15th Against Kickers | | | |
| Defense/ST | Panthers | 8th Against Defense/ST | | | |

## Position Commentary:

### Quarterback:

The combination of Cam's ability to pick up rushing yards and the addition of Norv Turner calling plays improves Cam's Opportunity Ranking. Depending on your opinion, he can rank anywhere from the bottom portion of QB tier-1 starter to the top of QB tier-2 starter. I like his potential, and he'll be at the top of your draft's first run on QBs.

### Running Back:

It's rare for a running back with more carries to be less favorable than his counterpart. Washington was in this situation with Chris Thompson/Rob Kelley, and Carolina experienced this with Christian McCaffrey/Jonathan Stewart. I believe that McCaffrey will lead the team in rushing attempts in Norv Turner's offense this season, making him a true RB1. Regardless, he will have a lot of receptions and targets and be viable in both PPR and Non-PPR leagues.

The addition of C.J. Anderson is intriguing. He was one of the few bright spots for the Denver Broncos offense last year and showed an ability to get tough yards. I believe he will take over Jonathan Stewart's role from the 2017 season. I don't like his season-long draft value, but there will be several high scoring weeks. Keep an eye out for our weekly matchup report to capitalize on a bye-week spot start or in daily fantasy sports.

### Wide Receiver:

Devin Funchess will come into the season as the unquestioned WR1. He produced well last year after the departure of Kelvin Benjamin. His overall Opportunity Rank (28th) doesn't jump off the page, but he does make big catches and will get a lot of red zone targets, making him one of the more efficient WR producers in the league.

There hasn't been a lot to like behind Funchess and Benjamin in recent years, but the Panthers investment of a first round pick in WR D.J. Moore could put an end to that. You can expect Moore to clear 60 targets this season, if healthy.

I'm intrigued at the potential of RB/WR Curtis Samuel. He only played in 9 games (starting 4), and only saw 26 targets, but showed promise as a versatile slot weapon. I want to monitor feedback in training camp and see how Carolina lines him up in preseason weeks 2 and 3, but I'm adding him to hibernation status. You'll likely be able to draft him very late.

**Tight End:**

Greg Olsen never gained momentum after an early-season injury. He had an uncharacteristically lackluster year. He has tier-2 TE potential, but 2018's lack of efficiency concerns me. His Opportunity Rank is 3rd in PPR and Non-PPR leagues, but that could be inflated if he's lost a step. I suggest targeting a round for him and sticking to that. That will be the best way to mitigate risk where Olsen is concerned.

**Kicker:**

Graham Gano is a solid kicker, but you can replicate his production on the waiver wire during the season. There is no need to draft him.

**Defense/Special Teams:**

Carolina has lost their defensive coordinator to a head coaching vacancy for the second year in a row. Ron Rivera remains in charge of the unit, and they've promoted from within to fill the position. I don't like that the team lost Star Lotulelei in free agency, but he didn't play up to standard last season. The addition of Dontari Poe could easily be an upgrade on the line.

Carolina also fortified their CB position by investing in Donte Jackson in the second round. I still have this group ranked in the top-10 in spite of playing in a very talented NFC South. They get sacks, but the turnovers are low and yards-per-play averages declined. You can draft them in the later rounds and plug them in as a season-long starter, but do not draft them prior to the last two rounds unless there's an inexplicable run on backup defenses in your league.

**Sleeper Watch**

**Popular Sleeper: D.J. Moore, WR**

*Somebody has to get targets somewhere on this team, right? The Panthers invested early draft capital on Moore and I expect him to be a starter in week 1.*

**Deep Sleepers: N/A**

**Hibernator: Curtis Samuel, RB/WR**

*He didn't play a ton in 2018, but he is a weapon. It wouldn't shock me if he can produce numbers like Percy Harvin in his prime.*

# New Orleans Saints

## 2017 Fantasy Opportunity Summary (Offensive Positions):

| Position | Player | PPR Rank vs Position | PPR Overall Rank |
|----------|--------|----------------------|------------------|
| Quarterback | Drew Brees | 17 | 17 |
| Running Back | Mark Ingram | 4 | 7 |
| Running Back 2 | Alvin Kamara | 1 | 2 |
| Wide Receiver 1 | Michael Thomas | 6 | 9 |
| Wide Receiver 2 | Ted Ginn | 18 | 20 |
| Wide Receiver 3 | Brandon Coleman | 21 | 16 |
| Tight End | Josh Hill | 31 | 30 |

**Fantasy Opportunity Analysis by Position (Offense Only):**
**Quarterback:**

I know you'll bristle at Brees' fantasy Opportunity Ranking with respect to his peers, but the truth is Brees only threw 23 TDs last year. In terms of fantasy output, this team was built on the run. In real-world output? Brees completed 72% of his passes last year. He's still elite, but many fantasy owners were burned in the early rounds. Proceed with caution.

**Running Back:**

I'm going to name this backfield Marvin Kingram because it's a true and rare committee. Mark Ingram and Alvin Kamara both rank in the top 5 against their peers in PPR leagues. You could start either at the RB1 slot week-to-week. There was a lot to like in 2017.

**Wide Receiver:**

Michael Thomas is a bona fide WR1, having hauled in 104 of his 149 targets. With so many receptions, I would expect more than 5 total touchdowns, but pay dirt will come.

Teddy Ginn can still blow the top off the defense and hauled in 4 TDs of his own. As a fantasy player, I'd prefer to use him off the bench in bye weeks or from time to time in Daily Fantasy, but he's worthy of a roster spot.

**Tight End:**

The TE situation in New Orleans left a lot to be desired. The Saints rotated between Coby Fleener and Josh Hill last year but never found the consistency they desired. Look for that to change in 2018.

## 2018 Offseason Analysis

**Transactions**

| Key Losses | | | Key Additions | | |
|---|---|---|---|---|---|
| Pos | Player | New Team | Pos | Player | Old Team |
| DB | Rafael Bush | Buffalo | OG | Jermon Bushrod | Miami |
| QB | Chase Daniel | Chicaog | FS | Kurt Coleman | Carolina |
| LB | Jonathan Freeny | Detroit | ILB | Demario Davis | NY Jets |
| OG | Senio Kelemete | Houston | CB | Patrick Robinson | Philadelphia |
| DB | *Kenny Vaccaro* | *NA* | QB | Tom Savage | Houston |
| OT | *Zach Strief* | *Retired* | | | |

**Draft Summary**

| Round | Overall | Position | Player | College |
|---|---|---|---|---|
| 1 | 14 | DE | Marcus Davenport | Texas-San Antonio |
| 3 | 91 | WR | Tre'quan Smith | UCF |
| 4 | 127 | DT | Rick Leonard | Florida St |
| 5 | 164 | S | Natrell Jamerson | Wisconsin |
| 6 | 189 | CB | Kamrin Moore | Boston College |
| 6 | 201 | RB | Boston Scott | Louisiana Tech |
| 7 | 245 | CB | Will Clapp | LSU |

**Coaching Changes**

There were no changes at the head coach or coordinator levels.  This is one of the most talented teams in the league and will be one to watch in 2018.

# 2018 Fantasy Outlook

## Projected Position Rankings

| Position | Player | PPR Rank vs Position | PPR Overall rank | Standard Rank vs Position | Standard Overall Rank |
|---|---|---|---|---|---|
| Quarterback | Drew Brees | 20 | 88 | 20 | 92 |
| Running Back 1 | Mark Ingram | 7 | 18 | 7 | 25 |
| Running Back 2 | Alvin Kamara | 1 | 7 | 1 | 9 |
| Wide Receiver 1 | Michael Thomas | 5 | 12 | 6 | 15 |
| Wide Receiver 2 | Tedd Ginn Jr | 26 | 131 | 26 | 132 |
| Wide Receiver 3 | Brandon Coleman | 25 | 227 | 25 | 220 |
| Tight End 1 | Benjamin Watson | 29 | 230 | 29 | 232 |
| Kicker | Wil Lutz | 5th Against Kickers | | | |
| Defense/ST | Saints | 13th Against Defense/ST | | | |

## Position Commentary:

### Quarterback:

The name Drew Brees carries more value than the player Drew Brees – at least as far as fantasy scoring is concerned. Yes, Brees is a great NFL quarterback, but remember you're looking for passing touchdowns and rushing yards at the position. Brees has never been mobile and with the one-two punch of Kamara and Ingram at running back, his total touchdown output has decreased as well.

Though his fantasy Opportunity Ranking is only at 20, remember that Brees remains remarkably efficient. He will move up our draft rankings as a result.

### Running Back:

New Orleans is stacked at running back. Mark Ingram averaged 4.9 yards per carry and caught 58 passes. He eclipsed 1,500 all-purpose yards and added 12 touchdowns. He is 7th in fantasy RB opportunity. The fact that he can score so well in spite of last year's standout rookie, Alvin Kamara, as such a large part of the offense is incredible.

Speaking of Kamara, he is by far the best RB2 in the league and is worthy of a starting spot week-to-week. Ingram's 4.9 yards per carry is impressive. Kamara averaged 6.1 yards per carry! He added 81 receptions for 826 yards, 13 total touchdowns and over 1,550 yards. Whether Ingram or Kamara, you can draft them. Draft both if you feel so inclined and have the opportunity.

The suspension of Ingram will lead to an early increase in Kamara's workload. While I think both are elite, I will boost Kamara's overall ranking. I will also downgrade Ingram's ranking slightly.

### Wide Receiver:

Michael Thomas has asserted himself as a true WR1. He saw 149 targets and caught over 100 of them. This 70% catch rate is phenomenal and is a testament to both his ability and the accuracy of Drew Brees.

Another 1,200-yard, 12 touchdown season is likely. You might find three Saints players drafted in the first round of your draft this season.

Behind Michael Thomas, Ted Ginn will flash from time to time. He only had 70 targets, but caught over 75% of balls thrown his way. He finished with 787 yards and 4 TDs. He'll also get a rushing attempt more often than not. Ginn has big play potential and should be stashed on a roster somewhere in your league. He's best utilized as a matchup start, so be sure to check our weekly forecasts if he's on your roster.

I've been looking for a third receiver on this team for a few years. Snead popped a couple of years ago. Brandon Coleman showed promise but never made the leap. The most likely WR to grab the next crop of targets will be rookie Tre-quan Smith out of UCF. He has the physical tools to contribute on this team, but there aren't a lot of NFL-ready secondaries in the American Athletic Conference. There will be a period of adjustment for the young WR.

### Tight End:

The Saints missed Ben Watson's production so much that they re-signed him in free agency. Drew Brees trusted and targeted him quite a bit in Watson's first tenure. If he hasn't lost a step, he could be in line for meaningful targets.

### Kicker:

The Saints score a ton of TDs and will even kick a field goal from time to time. Wil Lutz is worth a draft selection and a season-long start.

### Defense/Special Teams:

Philosophically, I'm against trading a future year's draft pick for anything other than a quarterback. That said, New Orleans did this last year for Alvin Kamara and it worked out. They've done it again this season for standout, small school DE Marcus Davenport. New Orleans' defensive potential ranking was 13th. Before the arrival of Davenport, they were already getting nice sack output. The next step on this team's journey will be to decrease their yards per play and increase their turnover totals. If they can improve their sack average from 2.7 per game to the 3.0 range (which is feasible), they will be a starting defense.

I could go either way. If you're one of the last teams to pick a defense, they'll be worth a pick. There are, however, better teams out there to select and start. I view them more as a matchup play or bye-week starter.

### Sleeper Watch

### *Popular Sleeper: Ben Watson, TE*

*Brees called his number quite a bit the last time he was in New Orleans.*

### *Deep Sleepers: N/A*

### *Hibernator: Tre-quan Smith, WR*

*He has the tools to win the WR2 or WR3 job.*

# Tampa Bay Buccaneers

## 2017 Fantasy Opportunity Summary (Offensive Positions):

| Position | Player | PPR Rank vs Position | PPR Overall Rank |
|---|---|---|---|
| Quarterback | Jameis Winston | 8 | 8 |
| Running Back | Doug Martin | 29 | 27 |
| Running Back 2 | Peyton Barber / Jacquizz Rodgers | 28 | 30 |
| Wide Receiver 1 | Mike Evans | 12 | 15 |
| Wide Receiver 2 | DeSean Jackson | 16 | 14 |
| Wide Receiver 3 | Adam Humphries | 7 | 19 |
| Tight End | Cameron Brate | 14 | 12 |

**Fantasy Opportunity Analysis by Position (Offense Only):**
**Quarterback:**

Dirk Koetter followed his trend of heavy-passing. Tampa Bay split 605 targets between Jameis Winston and Ryan Fitzpatrick last season. Fantasy owners saw a receiving corps that included Mike Evans and DeSean Jackson and loved Winston's potential. Unfortunately, in 13 games, he only put up 19 touchdowns compared to 11 touchdowns. He has yet to reach the potential of a top quarterback in the NFL or in the fantasy world.

**Running Back:**

With a heavy emphasis on passing, I suppose a weaker running output was to be expected. That said, Tampa was particularly ineffective at the position. The Buccaneers rotated between Doug Martin, Peyton Barber and Jacquizz Rodgers. They seemed to take a "ride the hot hand" approach. Unfortunately, nobody got hot. Charles Sims was the only RB on the roster to average more than 4 yards per carry (4.5). He only had 21 attempts.

**Wide Receiver:**

Mike Evans caught 71 of 136 targets for 1001 yards and 5 touchdowns. We'd like to see his total TDs increase. He hovers around 12th in the WR1 fantasy Opportunity Ranking. Given his average draft position last year, many fantasy players were disappointed in 2017.

DeSean Jackson was hyped coming into 2017, but was a non-factor. He caught 50 of 90 targets for a lackluster 668 yards and 3 touchdowns.

Adam Humphries continued to produce as a WR3. He caught 61 passes for 631 yards, but only found the end zone once. Though I don't consider Humphries a draft-worthy player, I do like him as a value Daily Fantasy player.

**Tight End:**

Although Tampa Bay used an early draft pick on O.J. Howard, Cameron Brate continued to be the heaviest producing TE in 2017. Brate caught 48 passes last season and scored a team-high 6 TDs.

## 2018 Offseason Analysis

### Transactions

| Key Losses | | | Key Additions | | |
|---|---|---|---|---|---|
| Pos | Player | New Team | Pos | Player | Old Team |
| DT | Chris Baker | Tampa Bay | DT | Beau Allen | Philadelphia |
| RB | Doug Martin | Oakland | K | Chandler Catanzaro | NY Jets |
| DT | Clinton McDonald | Denver | DE | Vinny Curry | Philadelphia |
| OG | Kevin Pamphile | Tennessee | C | Ryan Jensen | Baltimore |
| | | | DE | Jason Pierre-Paul | NY Giants |
| | | | DE | Mitch Unrein | Chicago |

### Draft Summary

| Round | Overall | Position | Player | College |
|---|---|---|---|---|
| 1 | 12 | DT | Vita Vea | Washington |
| 2 | 38 | RB | Ronald Jones | USC |
| 2 | 53 | CB | M.J. Stewart | North Carolina |
| 2 | 163 | CB | Carlton Davis | Auburn |
| 3 | 94 | G | Alex Cappa | Humboldt St |
| 4 | 117 | S | Jordan Whitehead | Pittsburgh |
| 5 | 144 | WR | Justin Watson | Pennsylvania |
| 6 | 202 | ILB | Jack Cichy | Wisconsin |

### Coaching Changes

There were no changes at the head coach or coordinator levels to report. Dirk Koetter has historically been a heavy pass team. Expect a lot of targets to Mike Evans.

## 2018 Fantasy Outlook

## Projected Position Rankings

| Position | Player | PPR Rank vs Position | PPR Overall rank | Standard Rank vs Position | Standard Overall Rank |
|---|---|---|---|---|---|
| Quarterback | Jameis Winston | 9 | 106 | 9 | 120 |
| Running Back 1 | Ronald Jones | 27 | 124 | 27 | 101 |
| Running Back 2 | Peyton Barber | 26 | 162 | 27 | 168 |
| Wide Receiver 1 | Mike Evans | 15 | 62 | 15 | 36 |
| Wide Receiver 2 | DeSean Jackson | 20 | 155 | 19 | 116 |
| Wide Receiver 3 | Adam Humphries | 5 | 200 | 11 | 225 |
| Tight End 1 | Cameron Brate | 11 | 102 | 11 | 125 |
| Kicker | Chandler Catanzaro | 16th Against Kickers | | | |
| Defense/ST | Tampa Bay | 32nd Against Defense/ST | | | |

## Position Commentary:

### Quarterback:

This is an offense that loves to throw the ball. Unfortunately, calling a sharp percentage of passes gives opponents a better feel for game planning. This also leaves an inefficient quarterback in a tough position. As the football community knows, Jameis Winston had accuracy issues in college. He has yet to post a 2:1 TD to INT ratio in his career. The media mentions him as a breakout candidate, but I haven't seen it and I would not hitch my fantasy wagon to him. Let someone else invest a draft pick on him. For me, he caps out as a stash and trade or bye-week play.

### Running Back:

Based on film and situational football, the lack of commitment to running the ball in Tampa and during his time in Atlanta is interesting. The only logical conclusion I can reach is that calling running plays gives Dirk Koetter an allergic reaction. You're going to see rookie Ronald Jones on a lot of "Rookie Impact" or "Fantasy Sleeper" lists, but don't be fooled. Under Koetter's guidance, his top RB has put up the following numbers: 2017 – 138 carries, 406 yards; 2016 – 144 attempts, 421 yards; 2014 (Atlanta) – 190 attempts, 707 yards; 2013 (Atlanta) – 157 attempts, 543 yards...

The best season for an RB I could find in Koetter's play calling history was the Falcons 2012 season where Michael Turner had 202 carries, 800 yards and 10 TDs. Doug Martin also had 288 carries in 2015 in Koetter's first year in Tampa, but he was overseen by head coach Lovie Smith.

...so yeah, stay away from Ronald Jones unless he's still on the board late in your draft.

### Wide Receiver:

Mike Evans' fantasy Opportunity Rank is a mediocre 15th against WR1s thanks to Tampa's inability to get consistent movement on offense. His total targets, receptions, yards and TDs were down in 2017 as Tampa began targeting WR2 (Desean Jackson). Evans has big play potential, but he'll be overvalued by fantasy players more focused on a name than output. Remember, he has an inaccurate quarterback throwing to him and is giving deep targets away to Jackson. He's a 2nd or 3rd round player to me.

Desean Jackson saw 90 targets, but only pulled in 50 of them. He had a lot of hype heading into 2017, but those expectations are properly calibrated for the 2018 campaign. Is he worth a roster spot? Sure. Would I play him? Only on a bye week. His value comes on the Daily Fantasy side of things where you can stack him with another low-cost, high-potential player and fill out the rest of your team with consistently scoring monsters.

**Tight End:**

Cameron Brate continues to produce, and he has great chemistry with Jameis Winston, but Tampa seems intent on replacing him. They drafted O.J. Howard early last year. The two will be fighting for targets all season. Don't prospect here. Let the dust settle and claim the starter off waivers.

**Kicker:**

Unfortunately, the offense isn't consistent enough to warrant drafting their kicker.

**Defense/Special Teams:**

Tampa's defense ranks dead-last in fantasy opportunity. They've added talent to their line in Vinny Curry and rookie Vita Vea but this unit has a long way to go. They gave up 6 yards per play last season and couldn't make up ground with sack totals or turnovers. Do not draft. Do not play on a bye week. Do not pass go, and do not collect $200.

**Sleeper Watch**

*Popular Sleepers: N/A*

*Deep Sleepers: N/A*

*Hibernators: N/A*

# NFC WEST

# NFC West

## Arizona Cardinals

### 2017 Fantasy Opportunity Summary (Offensive Positions):

| Position | Player | PPR Rank vs Position | PPR Overall Rank |
|---|---|---|---|
| Quarterback | Carson Palmer / Glaine Gabbert / Drew Stanton | 24 | 24 |
| Running Back | Adrian Peterson | 24 | 25 |
| Running Back 2 | Kerwynn Williams / Chris Johnson | 22 | 23 |
| Wide Receiver 1 | Larry Fitzgerald | 4 | 8 |
| Wide Receiver 2 | Jaron Brown | 23 | 21 |
| Wide Receiver 3 | JJ Nelson | 18 | 12 |
| Tight End | Jermaine Gresham | 28 | 29 |

**2017 Fantasy Opportunity Analysis by Position (Offense Only):**
**Quarterback:**

Once Palmer went down with injury, the potential for the Cardinals went out the window. The quarterback position was 24th in fantasy Opportunity Ranking last season. This unit will be changing scheme in 2018, as well as adding two new players to the QB position.

**Running Back:**

The injury to Palmer might not have even been the most devastating loss to the Cardinals. Dynamic RB David Johnson was out for the year in the first quarter of the first game. Adrian Peterson, Chris Johnson and Kerwynn Williams did their best to replace Johnson's output, but there was very little upside to this group outside of one or two big days for Adrian Peterson.

**Wide Receiver:**

With two of their biggest three stars out for the year, Arizona relied heavily on Larry Fitzgerald. Hauling in 109 of his 161 targets, Fitzgerald enjoyed a typical, highly productive season. His fantasy Opportunity Ranking (4th and 8th in PPR/Non-PPR leagues) marked the only position in the top half of the league.

Jaron Brown, John Brown and J.J. Nelson split the bulk of the other targets. Only J.J. Nelson cleared 500 receiving yards. Their primary value came via Daily Fantasy bargain starts and desperation matchup plays.

**Tight End:**

Jermaine Gresham's output was lackluster as well. He caught only 33 passes on 46 targets for 2 touchdowns. He was not worth a roster spot on fantasy teams last year.

## 2018 Offseason Analysis

### Transactions

| Key Losses | | | Key Additions | | |
|---|---|---|---|---|---|
| Pos | Player | New Team | Pos | Player | Old Team |
| QB | Matt Barkley | Cincinnati | DB | Bene' Benwikere | Dallas |
| CB | Justin Bethel | Atlanta | QB | Sam Bradford | Minnesota |
| WR | Jaron Brown | Seattle | QB | Mike Glennon | Chicago |
| WR | John Brown | Baltimore | OT | Justin Pugh | NY Giants |
| QB | Blaine Gabbert | Tennessee | OT | Andre Smith | Cincinnati |
| ILB | Kareem Martin | NY Giants | CB | Jamar Taylor | Arizona |
| FS | Tyrann Mathieu | Houston | | | |
| DE | Josh Mauro | NY Giants | | | |
| QB | Drew Stanton | Cleveland | | | |
| OT | Jared Veldheer | Denver | | | |
| DB | Tramon Williams | Green Bay | | | |
| DB | Tyvon Branch | NA | | | |
| RB | Adrian Peterson | NA | | | |
| QB | Carson Palmer | Retired | | | |

### Draft Summary

| Round | Overall | Position | Player | College |
|---|---|---|---|---|
| 1 | 10 | QB | Josh Rosen | UCLA |
| 2 | 47 | WR | Christian Kirk | Texas A&M |
| 3 | 97 | C | Mason Cole | Michigan |
| 4 | 134 | RB | Chase Edmonds | Fordham |
| 6 | 182 | CB | Chris Campbell | Penn St. |
| 7 | 254 | OT | Korey Cunningham | Cincinnati |

### Coaching Changes

Head Coach Steve Wilks was hired after several years of success as Carolina's defensive coordinator. The Cardinals defensive unit has talent and has performed well in the previous seasons. Wilks has tabbed previous Carolina linebackers coach Al Holcomb to run the defense. I expect Wilks and Holcomb to harness this talent and play tough, aggressive football.

The offensive coordinator duties will fall to Mike McCoy. McCoy's most successful run leading an offense came in Denver with Peyton Manning. Then again, every coordinator who's coached Manning would say the same thing.

McCoy's offensive play calling won't be as important as his ability to bring Sam Bradford and rookie QB Josh Rosen along.

## 2018 Fantasy Outlook

### Projected Position Rankings

| Position | Player | PPR Rank vs Position | PPR Overall rank | Standard Rank vs Position | Standard Overall Rank |
|----------|--------|----------------------|------------------|---------------------------|-----------------------|
| Quarterback | Sam Bradford | 21 | 185 | 21 | 183 |
| Running Back 1 | David Johnson | 20 | 29 | 21 | 44 |
| Running Back 2 | Elijah Penny | 17 | 191 | 17 | 207 |
| Wide Receiver 1 | Larry Fitzgerald | 9 | 40 | 11 | 31 |
| Wide Receiver 2 | J.J. Nelson | 8 | 112 | 10 | 194 |
| Wide Receiver 3 | Christian Kirk | 10 | 226 | 8 | 201 |
| Tight End 1 | Jermaine Gresham | 31 | 203 | 31 | 242 |
| Kicker | Phil Dawson | 12th Against Kickers | | | |
| Defense/ST | Cardinals | 14th Against Defense/ST | | | |

**Position Commentary:**

**Quarterback:**

This is going to be a position battle throughout the season. Expect Sam Bradford to hold rookie Josh Rosen off until after their bye week. I suspect Rosen will be starting by week 9. For this reason, I'd avoid drafting any of their QBs.

**Running Back:**

David Johnson will be back. He'll contribute well, but I'm not sure how Mike McCoy intends to utilize him. In theory, Johnson's talent should make him a 3-down back, but I've seen McCoy deploy annoying committees in the past. I have Arizona's RB1 ranked at 20th and 21st in PPR/non-PPR leagues. I'll bump Johnson up in the rankings due to his playmaking ability, but proceed with caution and avoid using a 1st round pick on him.

**Wide Receiver:**

Larry Fitzgerald produces no matter who is behind center. I have him ranked 9th and 11th in fantasy opportunity for PPR/non-PPR leagues. McCoy will figure out a way to get him the ball. You can feel safe drafting Fitzgerald this season. He'll be consistent for you.

Behind Fitzgerald, Arizona has evenly spread targets out during the Bruce Arians era. This year could go the same way. Rookie Christian Kirk and veteran J.J. Nelson figure to be a key part of the offense. If the QB situation was stable, I'd like their potential. Because there looks to be transition this year, I suggest avoiding both in the draft. Nelson and Christian Kirk are labeled deep sleepers in my rankings.

**Tight End:**

Jermaine Gresham is in line to receive the most targets. I aren't big believers in the potential of Cardinals tight ends this season, ranking them 31st in both PPR and non-PPR fantasy opportunity.

**Kicker:**

Phil Dawson made the most of his opportunities last year, but I'm not high on this offense. He should be available on waivers, but if you are one of the last teams to take a kicker and he's on the board, you could do worse. How's that for a ringing endorsement?

**Defense/Special Teams:**

Head coach Stephen Wilks will bring a new, aggressive system. Arizona has talent on the defense. This unit is ranked 14th in fantasy opportunity. My concern is that the 49ers and Rams will have standout offenses next year. Russell Wilson is dynamic enough to put up points even if they can't get a running game going. I see them as a matchup play this season thanks to the transition. This is a unit, however, that could start to gel in the middle of the year. If you have an underwhelming defense going on bye week in the middle of the season, you can pick up the Cardinals in week 9 and ride them through the playoffs.

**Sleeper Watch**

*Popular Sleepers: N/A*

*Deep Sleepers J.J. Nelson, WR; Christian Kirk, WR*

*Jaron Brown and John Brown are gone. Nelson has proven his ability in Arizona and Kirk was a high pick. If Sam Bradford can stay healthy and provide stability at the position, there's a lot of upside. If Arizona loses a few games early and switch to Rosen at QB, it could be rocky for everyone except Fitzgerald.*

*Hibernators: N/A*

# Los Angeles Rams

## 2017 Fantasy Opportunity Summary (Offensive Positions):

| Position | Player | PPR Rank vs Position | PPR Overall Rank |
|---|---|---|---|
| Quarterback | Jared Goff | 10 | 10 |
| Running Back | Todd Gurley | 1 | 1 |
| Running Back 2 | Malcolm Brown | 31 | 31 |
| Wide Receiver 1 | Cooper Kupp | 13 | 16 |
| Wide Receiver 2 | Robert Woods | 10 | 5 |
| Wide Receiver 3 | Sammy Watkins | 17 | 18 |
| Tight End | Tyler Higbee / Gerald Everett | 29 | 28 |

**Fantasy Opportunity Analysis by Position (Offense Only):**
**Quarterback:**

Jared Goff shook the "bust" label off last year in his first year with Sean McVay. In 15 games, he completed over 62% of his passes and had a 4:1 TD to INT ratio. Available on the waiver wire in most leagues after draft day, Goff was a rags-to-riches story for fantasy owners last season.

Goff's fantasy Opportunity Ranking places him 10th against his peers. It would be higher, except the Rams have one of the best fantasy RBs in the league to share TDs with.

**Running Back:**

Todd Gurley is equally dangerous in the running and passing game. McVay rewards Gurley's dynamic playmaking ability with a high snap percentage and as many touches as they can give him. He ranks #1 in our fantasy Opportunity Ranking among RB1s.

**Wide Receiver:**

The Rams were aggressive in acquiring WR, Sammy Watkins from Buffalo prior to the 2017 season, but he ended up 4th on the team in total targets. While he only caught 39 passes, he did find the end zone 8 times.

The Rams have to be very optimistic in the output of WR, Robert Woods. He had one of the higher catch rates for a wide receiver at 65.9% and caught 5 touchdown passes. It took a few games for him to build momentum, but he was a difference maker on the field in the middle and end of the season.

Cooper Kupp quietly put up an impressive rookie season. He led the team with 94 targets, and his 62 receptions trailed only Todd Gurley for most on the team.

**Tight End:**

The McVay offense craves a standout at the tight end position, but there were no takers last year. Tyler Higbee led all rams TEs in targets with 45, but he finished the year with only 25 receptions and 1 TD. Look for McVay to get more out of this position in 2018, be it from Tyler Higbee or Gerald Everett.

## 2018 Offseason Analysis

### Transactions

| Key Losses | | | Key Additions | | |
|---|---|---|---|---|---|
| Pos | Player | New Team | Pos | Player | Old Team |
| WR | Tavon Austin | Dallas | WR | Brandin Cooks | New England |
| SS | Maruice Alexander | Seattle | CB | Marcus Peters | Kansas City |
| TE | Derek Carrier | Oakland | DT | Ndamukong Suh | Miami |
| FS | Cody Davis | Jacksonville | CB | Aqib Talib | Denver |
| CB | Trumaine Johnson | NY Jets | ILB | Ramik Wilson | Kansas City |
| LB | Alec Ogletree | NY Giants | | | |
| LB | Robert Quinn | Miami | | | |
| WR | Sammie Watkins | Kansas City | | | |

### Draft Summary

| Round | Overall | Position | Player | College |
|---|---|---|---|---|
| 3 | 89 | OT | Joseph Noteboom | TCU |
| 4 | 111 | C | Brian Allen | Michigan St |
| 4 | 135 | DE | John Franklin-Myers | Stephen F. Austin |
| 5 | 147 | ILB | Micah Kiser | Virginia |
| 5 | 23 | Edge | Ogbonnia Okoronkwo | Oklahoma |
| 6 | 176 | RB | John Kelly | Tennessee |
| 6 | 192 | G | Jamil Demby | Maine |
| 6 | 195 | Dt | Sebastian Joseph | Rutgers |
| 6 | 205 | Edge | Trevon Young | Louisville |
| 7 | 231 | LB | Travin Howard | TCU |
| 7 | 244 | DE | Justin Lalwer | SMU |

### Coaching Changes
Sean McVay lost two key offensive coaches last season to other teams (Matt LeFleur and Greg Olsen). Offensive coordinator duties will now be split between Aaron Kromer and Shane Waldron. Both worked

on the Rams offense last year as offensive line and tight end coaches.  The play calling will remain with McVay, so I don't anticipate much of a change.

## 2018 Fantasy Outlook

### Projected Position Rankings

| Position | Player | PPR Rank vs Position | PPR Overall rank | Standard Rank vs Position | Standard Overall Rank |
|---|---|---|---|---|---|
| Quarterback | Jared Goff | 13 | 83 | 13 | 87 |
| Running Back 1 | Todd Gurley II | 1 | 1 | 1 | 1 |
| Running Back 2 | Malcolm Brown | 31 | 245 | 31 | 243 |
| Wide Receiver 1 | Cooper Kupp | 21 | 94 | 21 | 81 |
| Wide Receiver 2 | Brandin Cooks | 22 | 75 | 18 | 54 |
| Wide Receiver 3 | Robert Woods | 21 | 223 | 22 | 142 |
| Tight End 1 | Tyler Higbee | 27 | 231 | 27 | 229 |
| Kicker | Greg Zuerlein | 1st Against Kickers | | | |
| Defense/ST | Rams | 3rd Against Defense/ST | | | |

**Position Commentary:**

**Quarterback:**

Jared Goff's output should improve slightly in his second season with Sean McVay.  His fantasy Opportunity Rank sits at 13 thanks to Todd Gurley's influence at running back, but remember that Goff was exceptionally efficient last year with a 4:1 TD to INT ratio.  I'll be improving his final ranking as a result. He is a season-long start.

**Running Back:**

Todd Gurley plays nearly every down and is ranked #1 in our fantasy Opportunity Rankings.  He is the top overall player on our board.  No matter where you are picking, if you see his name on the board, pick him.

**Wide Receiver:**

Robert Woods returns to the offense this year and I expect his fantasy output to increase in 2018.  Fantasy football GMs might not be as high on him because he only caught 56 passes for 781 yards in 2017. However, he only started 11 games and it took a while for him to make an impact in the offense.  I expect him to finish over 80 catches and 1,100 yards in 2018, if he can remain healthy.

Brandin Cooks was brought to LA in the offseason and should bring more impact than Sammy Watkins was able to provide.  Watkins put up an underwhelming stat line of 70 targets and only 39 receptions. The Rams have a heavier commitment to the running game and involve Gurley in the passing game, but I still think Cooks will have over 100 targets, if healthy.

Last year's rookie darling, Cooper Kupp, made an immediate impact. He had 94 targets, 62 receptions and 869 yards. Many publications will have him as a sleeper, so I will include him in our section as well, begrudgingly. In reality, he's better than a sleeper; he should be a noteworthy player in 2018. Because the Rams don't have a playmaking tight end, they will use Kupp on a lot of intermediate routes. He will produce for you.

**Tight End:**

McVay would prefer more output from the tight end position than the combination of Tyler Higbee and Gerald Everett gave last year. McVay will give extra targets to Kupp to fill this vacancy. I suggest passing on all Rams tight ends. Their primary value will come on positive matchup weeks, so check back in with The Functional Sportsaholic for our weekly rankings.

**Kicker:**

Greg Zeurlein leads our fantasy Opportunity Rankings for kickers. Draft him and love him all year.

**Defense/Special Teams:**

This unit signed Ndamukon Suh and traded for Aqib Talib in the offseason. Defensive coordinator Wade Phillips will have this unit dialed in. I have them ranked third in our defensive potential rankings. They are a season-long starter thanks primarily to their sack totals. Talib should help give a boost in turnovers as well.

**Sleeper Watch**

*Popular Sleeper: Cooper Kupp, WR*

*94 targets, 62 receptions, 869 yards and 5 TDs in his rookie season. He's a better version of Jamison Crowder.*

*Deep Sleepers: N/A*

*Hibernators: N/A*

# San Francisco 49ers

## 2017 Fantasy Opportunity Summary (Offensive Positions):

| Position | Player | PPR Rank vs Position | PPR Overall Rank |
|---|---|---|---|
| Quarterback | Jimmy Garoppolo / CJ. Beathard / Brian Hoyer | 20 | 20 |
| Running Back | Carlos Hyde | 11 | 13 |
| Running Back 2 | Matt Breida | 21 | 21 |
| Wide Receiver 1 | Pierre Garcon | 24 | 25 |
| Wide Receiver 2 | Marquise Goodwin | 28 | 25 |
| Wide Receiver 3 | Trent Taylor | 27 | 24 |
| Tight End | George Kittle | 18 | 18 |

**Fantasy Opportunity Analysis by Position (Offense Only):**
**Quarterback:**

San Francisco found their quarterback. Jimmy Garoppolo made an immediate impact and won all five of his starts. This short amount of work led to a lengthy extension. In his brief time, Garoppolo's completion percentage was north of 67%. His TD to INT ratio (7:5) must be cleaned up, but he has an entire offense in Kyle Shanahan's system to work on that.

**Running Back:**

Carlos Hyde didn't fit the typical Shanahan-system running style, but he was very productive. He finished the season 11th/13th in PPR/non-PPR fantasy opportunity against RB1s. That placed him toward the end of the RB1 category. Because the 49ers start was rough, not many people noticed that Hyde quietly put up close to 1,300 all-purpose yards and 8 TDs.

RB2 Matt Breida was never a threat to assume control of the backfield, but he did receive 141 touches last year and took 2 rushing TDs away from Hyde. Breida won't be on anybody's radar in fantasy land, but he'll be a worthy matchup play in Daily Fantasy.

**Wide Receiver:**

Pierre Garcon was the clear number 1 wide receiver before injury cut his season short. Had he played a full 16 games, he was on track for 134 targets, 80 receptions, 1,000 yards and 8 TDs. That's also based on his output with C.J. Beathard and Brian Hoyer at QB. Those numbers would have out-paced Mike Evans.

One of my favorite players in 2017 was WR Marquise Goodwin. He took over as WR1 after Garcon's injury and caught 56 passes for 962 yards and 2 TDs. When Garoppolo took over, Goodwin consistently put up high yardage numbers. I had him in my last flex spot and played him weekly in my daily fantasy lineups. He'll continue to be under the radar to start 2018.

**Tight End:**

The McVay system is heavily influenced by his time with Kyle Shanahan in Washington. Like McVay, Kyle Shanahan wants production from the TE spot. George Kittle received the lion's share of targets with 63. He caught close to 70% of his targets for over 500 yards and 2 touchdowns. With improved play at quarterback in 2018, Kittle has real sleeper/deep sleeper potential.

## 2018 Offseason Analysis

### Transactions

| Key Losses | | | Key Additions | | |
|---|---|---|---|---|---|
| Pos | Player | New Team | Pos | Player | Old Team |
| OG | Trent Brown | New England | DE | Jeremiah Attaochu | LA Chargers |
| DE | Tank Carradine | Oakland | OG | Jonathan Cooper | Dallas |
| OG | Brandon Fusco | San Francisco | P | Jeff Locke | Detroit |
| DB | Leon Hall | Oakland | RB | Jerick McKinnon | Minnesota |
| RB | Carlos Hyde | Cleveland | C | Weston Richlburg | NY Giants |
| C | Daniel Kilgore | Miami | CB | Richard Sherman | Seattle |
| DE | Aaron Lynch | Chicago | | | |
| TE | Logan Paulsen | Atlanta | | | |
| SS | Eric Reid | NA | | | |

### Draft Summary

| Round | Overall | Position | Player | College |
|---|---|---|---|---|
| 1 | 9 | OT | Mike McGlinchey | Notre Dame |
| 2 | 44 | WR | Dante Pettis | Washington |
| 3 | 70 | OLB | Fred Warner | BYU |
| 3 | 95 | S | Tavarius Moore | Southern Miss |
| 4 | 128 | DE | Kentavius Street | N.C. State |
| 5 | 142 | CB | D.J. Reed | Kansas St. |
| 6 | 184 | S | Marcell Harris | Florida |
| 7 | 223 | DT | Julian Taylor | Temple |
| 7 | 240 | WR | Richie James | Middle Tennessee |

### Coaching Changes
There were no changes at the head coach or coordinator levels. Expect an improved offensive performance with new quarterback Jimmy Garoppollo having had a full offseason to learn from head coach Kyle Shanahan.

## 2018 Fantasy Outlook

**Projected Position Rankings**

| Position | Player | PPR Rank vs Position | PPR Overall rank | Standard Rank vs Position | Standard Overall Rank |
|----------|--------|----------------------|------------------|---------------------------|------------------------|
| Quarterback | Jimmy Garoppolo | 19 | 89 | 19 | 93 |
| Running Back 1 | Jerick McKinnon | 23 | 53 | 23 | 45 |
| Running Back 2 | Matt Breida | 25 | 222 | 23 | 196 |
| Wide Receiver 1 | Pierre Garcon | 6 | 24 | 7 | 74 |
| Wide Receiver 2 | Marquise Goodwin | 23 | 116 | 23 | 113 |
| Wide Receiver 3 | Trent Taylor | 31 | 242 | 32 | 244 |
| Tight End 1 | George Kittle | 24 | 133 | 25 | 137 |
| Kicker | Robbie Gould | 6th Against Kickers | | | |
| Defense/ST | 49ers | 25th Against Defense/ST | | | |

**Position Commentary:**

**Quarterback:**

When Jimmy Garoppolo took over, this entire offense changed. They were efficient, and they moved the ball. With an entire offseason under his belt and a healthy Pierre Garcon returning to lineup as WR1, I expect Jimmy G. to ascend to starting QB status this season. The 49ers Opportunity Ranking is based on Garoppolo's 4 starts between weeks 13 and 16 and still lies at #19. Shanahan's commitment to the run is one reason, but the efficiency has yet to be properly factored in. As I said, I think he's a legitimate starter, but I think he'll be hyped to the point of being overvalued in fantasy drafts. Be patient because there are a lot of strong QBs out there.

**Running Back:**

Carlos Hyde is out, and Jerrick McKinnon is in. In McKinnon, the 49ers obtain a productive back with receiving skills. If he's in line to get the bulk share of the carries, he will be a standout player. I have San Francisco's RB1 spot valued at 23rd overall because the RB2 will take a lot of carries. Still, McKinnon could easily throw up 1,000 yards and 8-10 TDs.

You'll want to keep an eye out for Joe Williams. He was hand-picked by Kyle Shanahan himself in the 2017 draft, but didn't play a snap last year after being placed on IR. Remember, the Shanahan system will pluck RBs out of obscurity and make them stars from time to time. You won't see his name in many publications, but given Shanahan's love for him last season, it wouldn't be a shock for him to win the starting RB role during the season or perhaps even in training camp. He gives you boom-or-bust potential, and I'll be stashing him late in my fantasy drafts.

**Wide Receiver:**

Pierre Garcon was on track to have another stellar year until injury cut his season short. He offers the similar fantasy Opportunity Rank as Tampa's more famous WR Mike Evans. Trust me, if you have a choice between drafting Mike Evans in the 2nd round or grabbing Garcon in round 6 or 7, take the latter.

WR Marquise Goodwin played exceptionally well in Garcon's absence and had quick chemistry with Jimmy Garoppolo. As a WR2, I have him ranked in the middle of the pack in fantasy opportunity. Garoppolo's efficiency will improve his overall rating. I think he'll be worth a roster spot and could play in your flex rotation.

Rookie Dante Pettis will get playing time. I don't think he's draftable, but pay attention to his production in preseason and early in the season. He's worth a waiver watch.

**Tight End:**

The Shanahan system wants a dependable tight end. George Kittle put up decent numbers through the entire year. He didn't entirely gel with Jimmy Garoppolo late in the year but an offseason of familiarity could change that. The 49ers had ample opportunity to add TE depth in the offseason and didn't add anyone of significance. Kittle's 63 targets in his rookie campaign and 43 catches can be built on. He's a great sleeper or deep sleeper this season.

**Kicker:**

Thanks to San Francisco's improved offense this season, San Francisco's kicker ranks 6th in fantasy opportunity. You can wait until the last round, but Robbie Gould will be a solid play for you.

**Defense/Special Teams:**

San Francisco continues to add talent to the defense, but don't draft them.

**Sleeper Watch**

*Popular Sleeper: Greg Kittle, TE*

*The Shanahan system likes TEs and Kittle produced well in 2017 in spite of QB turmoil. A full year of Garoppolo at QB should give him a nice boost.*

*Deep Sleepers: NA*

*Hibernator: Joe Williams, RB*

*Nobody's talking about him after he missed his rookie season, but Kyle Shanahan was very high on Williams last season. It would not shock me if he wins the starting job early in 2018.*

# Seattle Seahawks

## 2017 Fantasy Opportunity Summary (Offensive Positions):

| Position | Player | PPR Rank vs Position | PPR Overall Rank |
|---|---|---|---|
| Quarterback | Russell Wilson | 1 | 1 |
| Running Back | Eddie Lacy / Chris Carson / Thomas Rawls | 31 | 32 |
| Running Back 2 | Mike Davis / J.D. McKissic | 29 | 29 |
| Wide Receiver 1 | Doug Baldwin | 26 | 28 |
| Wide Receiver 2 | Paul Richardson | 13 | 10 |
| Wide Receiver 3 | Tylrer Lockett | 5 | 5 |
| Tight End | Jimmy Graham | 6 | 4 |

**Fantasy Opportunity Analysis by Position (Offense Only):**
**Quarterback:**

Russell Wilson finished first in our 2017 fantasy Opportunity Rankings among his peers for three reasons:

1) As well-respected as Wilson is, he's still underappreciated.  He's an elite quarterback.

2) He is effective running the ball.  He had 95 carries for 586 yards and 3 touchdowns.  The running output alone made him the number 1 fantasy running back on his team.  He also would have scored the most points at running back for Arizona, Tampa Bay, Green Bay and Detroit.

3) Seattle was so bad elsewhere, he was singularly responsible for putting up points.

**Running Back:**

Russel Wilson led Seattle in rushing attempts with 95.  Not a single running back on this roster carried the ball more than 70 times.  This was the worst position group in the league last season.

**Wide Receiver:**

Frankly, I was surprised to see how low Doug Baldwin ranked in fantasy opportunities against his peers.  After taking another look at the numbers, it does make sense.  Baldwin only received 116 targets, which is low for a WR1.  Interestingly, he caught 61.9% of his targets, making him productive when thrown to.  Jimmy Graham's red zone presence hurt his overall output in 2017.

Paul Richardson and Tyler Locket also came on strong, receiving 80 and 71 targets between them.  The passing attack in Seattle was strong.  If they could have cobbled a running game together, they would have been a tough opponent in the playoffs.

**Tight End:**

He wasn't the heralded Jimmy Graham of Saints fame, but he was still productive. He received the 2nd-most targets on the team (96) and led the team in TD receptions. I had Graham on my primary squad last year, and he rewarded me week in and week out.

## 2018 Offseason Analysis

### Transactions

| Key Losses | | | Key Additions | | |
|---|---|---|---|---|---|
| Pos | Player | New Team | Pos | Player | Old Team |
| DE | Michael Bennett | Philadelphia | SS | Maurice Alexander | LA Rams |
| TE | Jimmy Graham | Green Bay | WR | Jaron Brown | Arizona |
| RB | Thomas Rawls | NY Jets | TE | Ed Dickson | Carolina |
| DT | Sheldon Richardson | Minnesota | OG | D.J. Fluker | NY Giants |
| WR | Paul Richardson | Washington | K | Sebastian Janikowski | Oakland |
| CB | DeShawn Snead | Detroit | WR | Marcus Johnson | Philadelphia |
| CB | Richard Sherman | San Francisco | DT | Tom Johnson | Minnesota |
| OT | Matt Tobin | New England | OLB | Barkevious Mingo | Indianapolis |
| TE | Luke Wilson | Detroit | CB | C.J. Smith | Seattle |

### Draft Summary

| Round | Overall | Position | Player | College |
|---|---|---|---|---|
| 1 | 27 | RB | Rashaad Penny | San Diego St |
| 3 | 79 | DE | Rasheem Green | USC |
| 4 | 120 | TE | Will Dissly | Washington |
| 5 | 141 | OLB | Shaquem Griffin | UCF |
| 5 | 146 | S | Tre Flowers | Oklahoma St |
| 5 | 149 | P | Michael Dickson | Texas |
| 5 | 168 | OT | Jamarco Jones | Ohio St |
| 6 | 186 | Edge | Jake Martin | Temple |
| 7 | 220 | QB | Alex McGough | Florida International |

### Coaching Changes

Seattle's offense has sputtered recently. Their inability to run has made them one-dimensional. Russell Wilson has to single-handedly will them to victory, and that hasn't been a recipe for success as of late.

Brian Schottenheimer was brought on to coach the offense. I find this a bit of a curious hire. His two stints as offensive coordinator came in 2012-2014 with the St. Louis Rams and 2006-2011 with the New

York Jets.  Though those Jets teams made a couple of deep playoff runs, nobody would credit the offense with leading that team.  The silver lining for Seahawks fans is that in Schottenheimer's one season with a "good" quarterback (Brett Favre on the 2008 Jets), they were a top-10 offense.  He's also been able to consistently find a way to run the ball with success.

Ken Norton, ex-Raiders defensive coordinator will take over the same position with the Seahawks.  Norton was on the Seahawks staff between 2010 and 2014 and has familiarity with Pete Carrol's system.  The personnel is shifting, and this season might be a work in progress, but look for this unit to improve on its 2017 campaign overall.

## 2018 Fantasy Outlook

### Projected Position Rankings

| Position | Player | PPR Rank vs Position | PPR Overall rank | Standard Rank vs Position | Standard Overall Rank |
|---|---|---|---|---|---|
| Quarterback | Russell Wilson | 3 | 36 | 3 | 41 |
| Running Back 1 | Rashaad Penny | 17 | 43 | 17 | 64 |
| Running Back 2 | Chris Carson | 20 | 163 | 21 | 169 |
| Wide Receiver 1 | Doug Baldwin | 16 | 66 | 17 | 73 |
| Wide Receiver 2 | Tyler Lockett | 15 | 78 | 13 | 82 |
| Wide Receiver 3 | Brandon Marshall | 4 | 158 | 4 | 157 |
| Tight End 1 | Ed Dickson | 25 | 212 | 24 | 202 |
| Kicker | Sebastian Janikowski | 18th Against Kickers | | | |
| Defense/ST | Seahawks | 6th Against Defense/ST | | | |

### Position Commentary:

### Quarterback:

Russell Wilson makes this offense go.  He's accurate and had a 3:1 TD to INT ratio last year.  He also added 586 yards and 3 TDs in the running game.  Seattle is hoping additions at RB will help spread the workload, but the offensive line didn't see a great deal of turnover.  I expect more rushing issues in Seattle and thus, Wilson will remain in the top-tier of QBs.  He's ranked 3rd in QB opportunity and should be among the first QBs drafted in your league.

### Running Back:

You're going to hear a lot of hype around first round pick Rashaad Penny.  Yes, he should easily win the starting RB job, but who is blocking for him?  Is he worth a draft pick?  Absolutely, but don't pick assuming he will give you the production that Marshawn Lynch gave Seattle a few years ago.

It's hard to project stats. New OC Brian Schottenheimer has had success running the ball in his previous stints. I have Penny ranked in the middle of RB1 in terms of fantasy potential. He's a mid-round pick. Do not draft him in the first 2-3 rounds. Stick with consistent RBs and WRs, as well as standout TEs and QBs.

## Wide Receiver:

Paul Richardson left for the Washington Redskins, and he'll be taking his 80 targets with him. I expect the bulk of those to be distributed between Doug Baldwin and Tyler Lockett. Baldwin will produce for you, but he only had 116 targets last year. The passes were much more closely divided among the WRs last season. I have Baldwin's fantasy Opportunity Rank at 20th/21st in PPR/non-PPR leagues. His draft ranking will be higher due to Wilson's ability to escape the pocket and deliver an accurate ball.

Tyler Locket will ride a wave of hype this offseason. He has great playmaking ability and thanks to the departure of Richardson and Graham, should see his 71 targets from last year increase to somewhere in the 95-105 range. He's worth a roster spot, but be patient with him.

The addition of Brandon Marshall is intriguing, and he should be on everyone's radar. Jimmy Graham was a trusted receiver in the red zone last season and those targets could go to big-bodied Brandon. What does he have left in the tank? We will see.

## Tight End:

Jimmy Graham's exit is going to hurt this offense. If replacing 96 targets at the TE spot wasn't hard enough, the Seahawks also have to replace his 10 TDs. I like Ed Dickson and he'll definitely see targets, but I don't like him enough to draft. You can use him as a spot-starter or Daily Fantasy bargain player when the matchups are just right.

## Kicker:

Seattle doesn't score well enough to make Blair Walsh draft-worthy.

## Defense/Special Teams:

The legion of boom is aging and injury prone, but they are infusing the team with younger talent. Seattle still looks to be a top-10 fantasy player. They will be stable for you, but don't draft them early thinking they are a cut above the rest of the D/ST groups in the league. Remember, they lost three key contributors from last season in CB Richard Sherman, DT Sheldon Richardson and DE Michael Bennett.

## Sleeper Watch

### Popular Sleeper: Tyler Lockett, WR

*With Richardson gone, he should have more opportunities in the passing game.*

### Deep Sleeper: Jaron Brown, WR

*He played well in Arizona. He should have a chance to replace Paul Richardson's numbers.*

### Hibernators: N/A

# RANKINGS

## POINTS PER RECEPTION

# Points Per Reception Rankings

**Strategy Guide & Tier Rankings -**

## Overview

The mistake most people make in Fantasy Drafts is a reliance on a position or hoping to get a specific player or a certain amount of a specific position. In reality, it makes more sense to arrange your draft board like NFL teams arrange their college prospect draft boards.

I've analyzed every player's schedule as well as their strength of competition. As part of this analysis, we've come up with projected points and competitive advantage in relation to other players. We then ranked players into tier levels based on the competitive advantage they will offer throughout the season. This is important as your fantasy draft moves on and you're choosing between a starting quarterback or a flex running back. The correct thing to do when faced with this situation is take the player who will provide the most point advantage over your competition. This is where our Opportunity Rankings, Play Calling analysis and scouting reports come into play.

*Note: If you purchased this book and would like updated rankings throughout the offseason, please contact me at functionalsportsaholic@gmail.com or via Twitter @TFS_Sean*

### Step 1: Draft As Many Tier 1 and Tier 2 Players As Possible

Simply put, no matter who is on the board or how many players at these positions you have, do not draft a lower-tier player until all of these players are off the board.

### Tier 1

| QB | RB | WR | TE | DST | K |
|----|----|----|----|-----|---|
| NA | Todd Gurley | DeAndre Hopkins | NA | NA | NA |
| | Le'Veon Bell | Antonio Brown | | | |
| | Kareem Hunt | | | | |

### Tier 2

| QB | RB | WR | TE | DST | K |
|----|----|----|----|-----|---|
| Deshaun Watson | Ezekiel Elliott | A.J. Green | Rob Gronkowski | NA | NA |
| | Alvin Kamara | Odell Beckham | Zach Ertz | | |
| | Melvin Gordon | Michael Thomas | | | |
| | Leonard Fournette | | | | |

## Step 2: Start Considering Other Positions

The first two tiers will likely be exhausted by the end of the 2nd round. There are 23 players in Tier 3. There are many famous names in lower tiers, so do not be surprised if this list will take you into rounds 5 or 6.

Your goal by the end of round 6 to have a combination of 4 RB/WRs (but you should have 1 starter at both positions) and the best TE OR QB. If you end up with 5 RBs/WRs, don't sweat it. There are sleeper candidates later.

As a reminder, the inclusion of either Doug Martin or Marshawn Lynch in this tier is contingent on one of them winning the starting RB job. This will be important to monitor in training camp. If they will be splitting carries, remove them from this tier and include them at the bottom of tier 5.

| Tier 3 | | | | | |
| --- | --- | --- | --- | --- | --- |
| QB | RB | WR | TE | DST | K |
| Carson Wentz | Mark Ingram | Keenan Allen | Greg Olsen | NA | NA |
| Russell Wilson | Saqon Barkley | Julio Jones | Travis Kelce | | |
| Cam Newton | LeSean McCoy | Pierre Garcon | | | |
| Aaron Rodgers | Christian McCaffrey | Tyreek Hill | | | |
| | Chris Thompson | Alshon Jeffery | | | |
| | Devonta Freeman | Devante Adams | | | |
| | David Johnson | Stefon Diggs | | | |
| | Jordan Howard | | | | |
| | Dalvin Cook | | | | |
| | Doug Martin | | | | |

*NOTE: I LOVE the potential of Chris Thompson and the leading Raiders back. Based on average draft position, I think you'll be able to get one or both after round 5.*

### Step 3: Pick Viable Starters Where You're Weak

By now, you should be well into the middle rounds of the draft. Depending on how your league has drafted, you might have a very strong bench of RB/WR options or you might have starters at all positions, but lack depth. Tiers 4 and 5 are built to ensure that you have a viable starter at every position (except Kicker and Defense/Special Teams) including all Flex positions.

| Tier 4 | | | | | |
| --- | --- | --- | --- | --- | --- |
| QB | RB | WR | TE | DST | K |
| Alex Smith | Jerick McKinnon | T.Y. Hilton | Jimmy Graham | NA | NA |
| Dak Prescott | Dion Lewis | Larry Fitzgerald | Tyler Eiffert | | |
| Andrew Luck | Rashaad Penny | Amari Cooper | Delanie Walker | | |
| Tom Brady | Jamaal Williams | Rishard Matthews | Jordan Reed | | |
| | Lamar Miller | Danny Amendola | | | |
| | Kenyan Drake | Will Fuller V | | | |
| | | Golden Tate | | | |
| | | Sterling Shepard | | | |

## Tier 5

| QB | RB | WR | TE | DST | K |
|---|---|---|---|---|---|
| Andy Dalton | Royce Freeman | Marqise Lee | Trey Burton | NA | NA |
| Jared Goff | Duke Johnson Jr. | Mike Evans | Charles Clay | | |
| Matthew Stafford | | Adam Thielen | | | |
| Ben Roethlisberger | | Josh Gordon | | | |
| Philip Rivers | | Demaryius Thomas | | | |
| Kirk Cousins | | Doug Baldwin | | | |
| Drew Brees | | Robbie Anderson | | | |
| Jimmy Garoppolo | | Mike Jones Jr | | | |
| Eli Manning | | Devin Funchess | | | |
| | | Nelson Agholor | | | |
| | | Jarvis Landry | | | |
| | | Brandin Cooks | | | |
| | | JuJu smith-Schuster | | | |
| | | Tyler Lockett | | | |
| | | Jordy Nelson | | | |

**Step 4: Find Potential**

At this point, you should have starters at all positions and depth at each spot on your roster (except Kicker and Defense / Special Team). Now is that time to find players that have potential to make your starting lineup as the season progresses. Having more viable starting talent on your roster will allow you to be aggressive with trades throughout the season.

You'll notice that I've started to include my top-rated kickers and defense / special teams groups. Draft guides will typically recommend that you wait until the last round for a kicker and as late as the second-to-last round to draft your defense. For the most part I agree, however, remember what we talked about with competitive advantage?

In 2017, I had a roster that was dealing with injuries. I also had K, Greg Zuerlein and DST, Jaguars. These two positions scored well enough for me to win a few key games. I would not have made the playoffs if it weren't for the competitive advantage they represented. Each week, I could count on an advantage of 8-10 points from these two spots.

Because most players will draft their K and DST positions last, I suggest you start earlier. If your draft lasts 20 rounds, rather than waiting until rounds 19 and 20, draft your defense in round 17 and your kicker in round 18. Some will laugh at you, but you'll be fortifying the last two spots on your roster. Then in rounds 19 and 20 when everyone is picking their kickers, you'll be able to find compelling players in Tiers 6 and 7 that could develop into starters by the end of the season.

## Tier 6

| QB | RB | WR | TE | DST | K |
|---|---|---|---|---|---|
| Jameis Wintson | Elijah McGuire | Austin Hurns | Geoff Swaim | NA | NA |
| Blake Bortles | C.J. Anderson | Cooper Cupp | Cameron Brate | | |
| Patrick Mahomes | Javorius Allen | Randall Cobb | Evan Engram | | |
| Matt Ryan | Bilal Powel | Julian Edelman | Jack Doyle | | |
| Josh McCown | Sony Michel | Keelan Cole | | | |
| | Alex Collins | | | | |
| | James White | | | | |
| | Nick Chubb / Carlos Hyde | | | | |

## Tier 7

| QB | RB | WR | TE | DST | K |
|---|---|---|---|---|---|
| NA | Giovani Bernard | Mohamed Sanu | Virgil Green | Jaguars | Greg Zuerlein |
| | Joe Mixon | J.J. Nelson | Jared Cook | Ravens | Harrison Butker |
| | LaGarrette Blount / Kerryon Johnson | Corey Coleman | Kyle Rudolph | Rams | Stephen Gostkowski |
| | Ronald Jones | Marquise Goodwin | George Kittle | Steelers | Jake Elliott |
| | Tarik Cohen | Sammy Watkins | | | |
| | Tevin Coleman | Corey Davis | | | |
| | Nyheim Hines | DeVante Parker | | | |
| | Marlon Mack | Brandon LaFell | | | |
| | Derrick Henry | Kelvin Benjamin | | | |
| | D'Onta Foreman | Kenny Stills | | | |
| | Jay Ajayi | Michael Crabtree | | | |
| | Derrius Guice | Tedd Ginn Jr | | | |
| | | Donte Moncrief | | | |
| | | Martavis Bryant | | | |
| | | Geronimo Allison / J'Mon Moore | | | |

## Step 5: Complete Your Draft, Trade and Play the Waiver Wire

You might find yourself in the last two rounds without a kicker or defense. Tier 8 ranks the best of the last of what I determined to be "draftable". If the defenses and kickers are gone and your league allows you to move forward without selecting a kicker, I would suggest you draft another young talented RB or WR and see what the future holds. If you must draft all positions to fill your roster, I have the rest ranked in the kickers and defense/special teams section.

### Tier 8

| QB | RB | WR | TE | DST | K |
|---|---|---|---|---|---|
| Marcus Mariota | Latavious Murray | Emmanuel Sanders | Hayden Hurst | Chargers | Will Lutz |
| | Peyton Barber | D.J. Moore | | Seahawks | Robbie Gould |
| | Chris Carson | Jordan Matthews | | Bears | Justin Tucker |
| | | DeSean Jackson | | Eagles | Chris Boswell |
| | | Ryan Grant | | Panthers | Matt Prater |
| | | Jamison Crowder | | | Kai Forbath |
| | | Allen Robinson | | | Matt Bryant |
| | | Jamison Crowder | | | Phil Dawson |
| | | Paul Richardson Jr | | | |

## Overall Rankings

| | | | | Projected | | |
|---|---|---|---|---|---|---|
| Rank | Team | Pos | Player | Points | Tier | Note |
| 1 | LA Rams | RB | Todd Gurley | 387.5 | 1 | |
| 2 | Pittsburgh | RB | Le'Veon Bell | 342.6 | 1 | |
| 3 | Houston | WR | DeAndre Hopkins | 329.2 | 1 | |
| 4 | Kansas City | RB | Kareem Hunt | 329.0 | 1 | |
| 5 | Pittsburgh | WR | Antonio Brown | 320.1 | 1 | |
| 6 | Dallas | RB | Ezekiel Elliott | 302.3 | 2 | |
| 7 | New Orleans | RB | Alvin Kamara | 293.9 | 2 | Higher because of Ingram's suspension. |
| 8 | LA Chargers | RB | Melvin Gordon | 278.5 | 2 | |
| 9 | Jacksonville | RB | Leonard Fournette | 257.5 | 2 | I like his dominance of snaps. Upgrading ranking. |
| 10 | Cincinnati | WR | A.J. Green | 259.3 | 2 | |
| 11 | NY Giants | WR | Odell Beckham | 201.1 | 2 | |
| 12 | New Orleans | WR | Michael Thomas | 255.5 | 2 | |
| 13 | New England | TE | Rob Gronkowski | 241.2 | 2 | |
| 14 | Houston | QB | Deshaun Watson | 497.6 | 2 | |
| 15 | Philadelphia | TE | Zach Ertz | 227.3 | 2 | |
| 16 | Washington | RB | Chris Thompson | 295.4 | 2 | ADP is so much lower that I will move him down the board. Make sure you draft him. |
| 17 | Oakland | RB | Doug Martin | 275.0 | 3 | He's a risky play at #8, so moving him down. |
| 18 | New Orleans | RB | Mark Ingram | 266.4 | 3 | Moving down due to suspension. |
| 19 | NY Giants | RB | Saquon Barkley | 249.1 | 3 | |
| 20 | LA Chargers | WR | Keenan Allen | 241.1 | 3 | |
| 21 | Buffalo | RB | LeSean McCoy | 238.1 | 3 | |
| 22 | Carolina | RB | Christian McCaffrey | 235.3 | 3 | |
| 23 | Atlanta | WR | Julio Jones | 211.2 | 3 | |
| 24 | San Francisco | WR | Pierre Garcon | 220.8 | 3 | undervalued |
| 25 | Kansas City | WR | Tyreek Hill | 220.2 | 3 | |
| 26 | Philadelphia | WR | Alshon Jeffery | 217.3 | 3 | |
| 27 | Green Bay | WR | Devante Adams | 216.9 | 3 | |
| 28 | Atlanta | RB | Devonta Freeman | 216.1 | 3 | |
| 29 | Arizona | RB | David Johnson | 216.1 | 3 | |
| 30 | Minnesota | WR | Stefon Diggs | 215.1 | 3 | |
| 31 | Chicago | RB | Jordan Howard | 212.9 | 3 | |
| 32 | Minnesota | RB | Dalvin Cook | 208.6 | 3 | He was so explosive in a short time. Upgrading. |

| | | | | | | |
|---|---|---|---|---|---|---|
| 33 | Carolina | TE | Greg Olsen | 202.7 | 3 | |
| 34 | Kansas City | TE | Travis Kelce | 191.7 | 3 | |
| 35 | Philadelphia | QB | Carson Wentz | 431.6 | 3 | |
| 36 | Seattle | QB | Russell Wilson | 396.8 | 3 | |
| 37 | Carolina | QB | Cam Newton | 395.3 | 3 | |
| 38 | Green Bay | QB | Aaron Rodgers | 370.5 | 3 | |
| 39 | Indianapolis | WR | T.Y. Hilton | 190.1 | 4 | |
| 40 | Arizona | WR | Larry Fitzgerald | 211.2 | 4 | |
| 41 | Oakland | WR | Amari Cooper | 170.9 | 4 | |
| 42 | Tennessee | RB | Dion Lewis | 229.8 | 4 | Downgrade due to splitting of carries. |
| 43 | Seattle | RB | Rashaad Penny | 197.8 | 4 | Upgrading past questionable RB2s. |
| 44 | Green Bay | RB | Ty Montgomery | 226.5 | 4 | |
| 45 | Tennessee | WR | Rishard Matthews | 222.6 | 4 | |
| 46 | Houston | RB | Lamar Miller | 220.1 | 4 | |
| 47 | Miami | WR | Danny Amendola | 217.5 | 4 | |
| 48 | Houston | WR | Will Fuller V | 208.9 | 4 | |
| 49 | Detroit | WR | Golden Tate | 195.8 | 4 | |
| 50 | Miami | RB | Kenyan Drake | 208.2 | 4 | |
| 51 | Cincinnati | TE | Tyler Eiffert | 188.7 | 4 | |
| 52 | Tennessee | TE | Delanie Walker | 185.1 | 4 | |
| 53 | San Francisco | RB | Jerick McKinnon | 176.1 | 4 | Will give a boost based on Shanahan's running scheme. |
| 54 | Washington | TE | Jordan Reed | 123.6 | 4 | |
| 55 | Green Bay | TE | Jimmy Graham | 108.0 | 4 | |
| 56 | Washington | QB | Alex Smith | 394.7 | 4 | |
| 57 | Dallas | QB | Dak Prescott | 381.6 | 4 | |
| 58 | Indianapolis | QB | Andrew Luck | 363.7 | 4 | |
| 59 | New England | QB | Tom Brady | 343.1 | 4 | |
| 60 | NY Giants | WR | Sterling Shepard | 131.4 | 4 | |
| 61 | Jacksonville | WR | Marqise Lee | 207.1 | 5 | |
| 62 | Tampa Bay | WR | Mike Evans | 206.7 | 5 | |
| 63 | Minnesota | WR | Adam Thielen | 201.0 | 5 | |
| 64 | Cleveland | WR | Josh Gordon | 200.1 | 5 | |
| 65 | Denver | WR | Demaryius Thomas | 199.7 | 5 | |
| 66 | Seattle | WR | Doug Baldwin | 199.1 | 5 | |
| 67 | New England | WR | Julian Edelman | 198.8 | 5 | |
| 68 | NY Jets | WR | Robbie Anderson | 196.9 | 5 | |
| 69 | Detroit | WR | Mike Jones Jr | 212.3 | 5 | |
| 70 | Carolina | WR | Devin Funchess | 196.7 | 5 | |
| 71 | Philadelphia | WR | Nelson Agholor | 189.6 | 5 | |
| 72 | Cleveland | WR | Jarvis Landry | 186.7 | 5 | |
| 73 | Denver | RB | Royce Freeman | 184.4 | 5 | Upgrading based purely on potential. |
| 74 | Cleveland | RB | Duke Johnson Jr. | 182.8 | 5 | |
| 75 | LA Rams | WR | Brandin Cooks | 170.4 | 5 | |
| 76 | Chicago | TE | Trey Burton | 168.8 | 5 | |

| 77 | Pittsburgh | WR | JuJu smith-Schuster | 168.1 | 5 | |
|---|---|---|---|---|---|---|
| 78 | Seattle | WR | Tyler Lockett | 164.5 | 5 | |
| 79 | Oakland | WR | Jordy Nelson | 140.9 | 5 | |
| 80 | Jacksonville | WR | Keelan Cole | 163.6 | 5 | |
| 81 | Buffalo | TE | Charles Clay | 161.7 | 5 | |
| 82 | Cincinnati | QB | Andy Dalton | 349.2 | 5 | |
| 83 | LA Rams | QB | Jared Goff | 325.4 | 5 | |
| 84 | Detroit | QB | Matthew Stafford | 322.6 | 5 | |
| 85 | Pittsburgh | QB | Ben Roethlisberger | 322.2 | 5 | |
| 86 | LA Chargers | QB | Philip Rivers | 307.2 | 5 | |
| 87 | Minnesota | QB | Kirk Cousins | 302.2 | 5 | |
| 88 | New Orleans | QB | Drew Brees | 298.7 | 5 | |
| 89 | San Francisco | QB | Jimmy Garoppolo | 296.8 | 5 | |
| 90 | NY Giants | QB | Eli Manning | 275.4 | 5 | |
| 91 | NY Jets | RB | Bilal Powel | 198.4 | 6 | |
| 92 | Carolina | RB | C.J. Anderson | 197.9 | 6 | |
| 93 | Dallas | WR | Austin Hurns | 191.9 | 6 | |
| 94 | LA Rams | WR | Cooper Kupp | 187.9 | 6 | |
| 95 | Baltimore | RB | Javorius Allen | 185.8 | 6 | |
| 96 | Green Bay | WR | Randall Cobb | 183.9 | 6 | |
| 97 | NY Jets | RB | Elijah McGuire / Isiah Crowell | 181.8 | 6 | |
| 98 | New England | RB | Sony Michel | 177.7 | 6 | |
| 99 | Baltimore | RB | Alex Collins | 166.7 | 6 | |
| 100 | Dallas | TE | Geoff Swaim | 152.6 | 6 | |
| 101 | New England | RB | James White | 149.6 | 6 | |
| 102 | Tampa Bay | TE | Cameron Brate | 147.7 | 6 | |
| 103 | NY Giants | TE | Evan Engram | 147.6 | 6 | |
| 104 | Indianapolis | TE | Jack Doyle | 147.1 | 6 | |
| 105 | Cleveland | RB | Nick Chubb / Carlos Hyde | 136.9 | 6 | Slight boost in Haley's scheme. Beware Duke Johnson Jr. |
| 106 | Tampa Bay | QB | Jameis Wintson | 358.5 | 6 | |
| 107 | Jacksonville | QB | Blake Bortles | 332.2 | 6 | |
| 108 | Kansas City | QB | Patrick Mahomes | 283.3 | 6 | |
| 109 | Atlanta | QB | Matt Ryan | 276.2 | 6 | |
| 110 | NY Jets | QB | Josh McCown | 275.3 | 6 | |
| 111 | Atlanta | WR | Mohamed Sanu | 169.3 | 7 | |
| 112 | Arizona | WR | J.J. Nelson | 169.3 | 7 | |
| 113 | Cincinnati | RB | Giovani Bernard | 162.5 | 7 | |
| 114 | Cleveland | WR | Corey Coleman | 158.2 | 7 | |
| 115 | Cincinnati | RB | Joe Mixon | 156.4 | 7 | |
| 116 | San Francisco | WR | Marquise Goodwin | 154.9 | 7 | |
| 117 | Kansas City | WR | Sammy Watkins | 152.5 | 7 | |
| 118 | Tennessee | WR | Corey Davis | 152.3 | 7 | |

| | | | | | | |
|---|---|---|---|---|---|---|
| 119 | Detroit | RB | LeGarrette Blount or Kerryon Johnson | 152.1 | 7 | Likely to split carries between the two. Johnson will start to take over towrads the end of the season. |
| 120 | Miami | WR | DeVante Parker | 151.4 | 7 | |
| 121 | Cincinnati | WR | Brandon LaFell | 150.9 | 7 | |
| 122 | Buffalo | WR | Kelvin Benjamin | 150.1 | 7 | |
| 123 | Miami | WR | Kenny Stills | 148.5 | 7 | |
| 124 | Tampa Bay | RB | Ronald Jones | 146.6 | 7 | |
| 125 | Baltimore | WR | Michael Crabtree | 146.4 | 7 | |
| 126 | LA Chargers | TE | Virgil Green | 145.5 | 7 | |
| 127 | Chicago | RB | Tarik Cohen | 133.5 | 7 | |
| 128 | Atlanta | RB | Tevin Coleman | 133.3 | 7 | |
| 129 | Oakland | TE | Jared Cook | 131.2 | 7 | |
| 130 | Minnesota | TE | Kyle Rudolph | 129.5 | 7 | |
| 131 | New Orleans | WR | Tedd Ginn Jr | 128.6 | 7 | |
| 132 | Indianapolis | RB | Nyheim Hines | 122.2 | 7 | I like his chances to take over RB1 duties by the end of the year. |
| 133 | San Francisco | TE | George Kittle | 108.5 | 7 | |
| 134 | Indianapolis | RB | Marlon Mack | 107.5 | 7 | |
| 135 | Jacksonville | WR | Donte Moncrief | 106.0 | 7 | |
| 136 | Oakland | WR | Martavis Bryant | 103.6 | 7 | |
| 137 | Tennessee | RB | Derrick Henry | 89.0 | 7 | |
| 138 | Houston | RB | D'Onta Foreman | 79.3 | 7 | |
| 139 | Green Bay | RB | Aaron Jones | 38.9 | 7 | |
| 140 | Green Bay | WR | Geronimo Allison or J'Mon Moore | 248.1 | 7 | |
| 141 | Jacksonville | DST | Jaguars | | 7 | |
| 142 | Baltimore | DST | Ravens | | 7 | |
| 143 | LA Rams | DST | Rams | | 7 | |
| 144 | Pittsburgh | DST | Steelers | | 7 | |
| 145 | Philadelphia | RB | Jay Ajayi | 131.2 | 7 | |
| 146 | Washington | RB | Derrius Guice | 82.8 | 7 | |
| 147 | LA Rams | K | Greg Zuerlein | | 7 | |
| 148 | Kansas City | K | Harrison Butker | | 7 | |
| 149 | New England | K | Stephen Gostkowski | | 7 | |
| 150 | Philadelphia | K | Jake Elliott | | 7 | |
| 151 | Tennessee | QB | Marcus Mariota | 312.8 | | |
| 152 | Denver | WR | Emmanuel Sanders | 138.0 | 8 | |
| 153 | Carolina | WR | D.J. Moore | 143.7 | 8 | |
| 154 | New England | WR | Jordan Matthews | 136.0 | 8 | |
| 155 | Tampa Bay | WR | DeSean Jackson | 135.9 | 8 | |
| 156 | Indianapolis | WR | Ryan Grant | 144.4 | 8 | |
| 157 | Washington | WR | Jamison Crowder | 131.0 | 8 | |
| 158 | Seattle | WR | Brandon Marshall | 119.2 | 8 | |
| 159 | Chicago | WR | Allen Robinson | 122.1 | 8 | |

| 160 | Washington | WR | Paul Richardson Jr. | 116.6 | 8 | |
|---|---|---|---|---|---|---|
| 161 | Minnesota | RB | Latavius Murray | 141.6 | 8 | |
| 162 | Tampa Bay | RB | Peyton Barber | 46.5 | 8 | |
| 163 | Seattle | RB | Chris Carson | 98.9 | 8 | |
| 164 | Tennessee | WR | Tajae' Sharpe | 94.9 | 8 | |
| 165 | LA Chargers | DST | Chargers | | 8 | |
| 166 | Seattle | DST | Seahawks | | 8 | |
| 167 | Chicago | DST | Bears | | 8 | |
| 168 | Philadelphia | DST | Eagles | | 8 | |
| 169 | Carolina | DST | Panthers | | 8 | |
| 170 | Baltimore | TE | Hayden Hurst | 122.5 | 8 | |
| 171 | New Orleans | K | Will Lutz | | 8 | |
| 172 | San Francisco | K | Robbie Gould | | 8 | |
| 173 | Baltimore | K | Justin Tucker | | 8 | |
| 174 | Pittsburgh | K | Chris Boswell | | 8 | |
| 175 | Detroit | K | Matt Prater | | 8 | |
| 176 | Minnesota | K | Kai Forbath | | 8 | |
| 177 | Atlanta | K | Matt Bryant | | 8 | |
| 178 | Arizona | K | Phil Dawson | | 8 | |
| 179 | Detroit | RB | Theo Riddick | 107.1 | | |
| 180 | Denver | RB | Devontae Booker | 98.0 | | |
| 181 | Miami | RB | Frank Gore | 77.2 | | |
| 182 | Miami | QB | Ryan Tannehill | 308.6 | | |
| 183 | Denver | QB | Case Keenum | 300.5 | | |
| 184 | Cleveland | QB | Tyrod Taylor | 282.6 | | |
| 185 | Arizona | QB | Sam Bradford | 276.2 | | |
| 186 | Buffalo | QB | AJ McCaroon | 274.4 | | |
| 187 | Oakland | QB | Derek Carr | 274.0 | | |
| 188 | Chicago | QB | Mitch Trubiksky | 229.7 | | |
| 189 | Baltimore | QB | Joe Flacco | 214.0 | | |
| 190 | NY Jets | WR | Quincy Enunwa | 158.2 | | |
| 191 | Arizona | RB | Elijah Penny | 133.3 | | |
| 192 | Dallas | WR | Terrance Williams | 132.8 | | |
| 193 | Detroit | TE | Levine Toilolo | 126.8 | | |
| 194 | LA Chargers | WR | Tyrell Williams | 120.5 | | |
| 195 | Buffalo | WR | Jeremy Kerley | 118.5 | | |
| 196 | NY Jets | TE | Eric Tomlinson | 116.4 | | |
| 197 | Philadelphia | RB | Corey Clement | 116.2 | | |
| 198 | Kansas City | RB | Damien Williams | 111.2 | | |
| 199 | Philadelphia | WR | Mike Wallace | 109.9 | | |
| 200 | Tampa Bay | WR | Adam Humphries | 108.9 | | |
| 201 | LA Chargers | WR | Travis Benjamin | 108.2 | | |
| 202 | Atlanta | TE | Austin Hooper | 107.4 | | |
| 203 | Arizona | TE | Jermaine Gresham | 107.4 | | |
| 204 | LA Chargers | RB | Austin Ekeler | 106.8 | | |
| 205 | Denver | WR | Courtland Sutton | 105.9 | | |
| 206 | NY Giants | RB | Jonathan Stewart | 105.8 | | |
| 207 | New England | WR | Chris Hogan | 105.4 | | |

| 208 | Jacksonville | RB | T.J. Yeldon | 105.1 | | |
|---|---|---|---|---|---|---|
| 209 | Indianapolis | WR | Chester Rogers | 104.4 | | |
| 210 | Pittsburgh | TE | Jesse James | 102.8 | | |
| 211 | Baltimore | WR | John Brown | 102.8 | | |
| 212 | Seattle | TE | Ed Dickson | 100.6 | | |
| 213 | Pittsburgh | WR | James Washington | 98.8 | | |
| 214 | NY Giants | WR | Cody Latimer | 98.1 | | |
| 215 | Detroit | WR | TJ Jones | 97.4 | | |
| 216 | Chicago | WR | Kevin White | 94.4 | | |
| 217 | Cleveland | TE | David Njoku | 94.3 | | |
| 218 | Buffalo | WR | Zay Jones | 92.0 | | |
| 219 | Houston | TE | Ryan Griffen | 88.9 | | |
| 220 | Chicago | WR | Dontrelle Inman | 88.7 | | |
| 221 | Dallas | WR | Tavon Austin | 87.7 | | |
| 222 | San Francisco | RB | Matt Breida | 87.3 | | |
| 223 | LA Rams | WR | Robert Woods | 86.1 | | |
| 224 | Washington | WR | Josh Doctson | 85.9 | | |
| 225 | Atlanta | WR | Calvin Ridley | 84.3 | | |
| 226 | Arizona | WR | Christian Kirk | 84.3 | | |
| 227 | New Orleans | WR | Brandon Coleman | 82.8 | | |
| 228 | Kansas City | WR | Demarcus Robinson | 74.8 | | |
| 229 | Jacksonville | TE | Austin Sefarian-Jenkins | 74.6 | | |
| 230 | New Orleans | TE | Benjamin Watson | 70.4 | | |
| 231 | LA Rams | TE | Tyler Higbee | 69.9 | | |
| 232 | Miami | TE | Mike Gescki | 69.9 | | |
| 233 | NY Jets | WR | Jermaine Kerase | 68.8 | | |
| 234 | Oakland | RB | DeAndre Washington | 66.2 | | |
| 235 | Cincinnati | WR | Tyler Boyd | 63.5 | | |
| 236 | Minnesota | WR | Laquon Treadwell | 61.6 | | |
| 237 | Baltimore | WR | Willie Snead IV | 58.2 | | |
| 238 | Houston | WR | Bruce Ellington | 51.1 | | |
| 239 | Carolina | WR | Torrey Smith | 49.2 | | |
| 240 | Buffalo | RB | Chris Ivory | 46.2 | | |
| 241 | Denver | TE | Jeff Heuerman | 43.9 | | |
| 242 | San Francisco | WR | Trent Taylor | 43.3 | | |
| 243 | Pittsburgh | RB | Stevan Ridley | 17.5 | | |
| 244 | Dallas | RB | Rod Smith | 47.5 | | |
| 245 | LA Rams | RB | Malcolm Brown | 29.6 | | |

## Quarterbacks

| PPR Quarterback Rankings | | | | |
|---|---|---|---|---|
| Rank | Team | Player | Projected Points | Tier |

| | | | | |
|---|---|---|---|---|
| 1 | Houston | Deshaun Watson | 497.6 | 2 |
| 2 | Philadelphia | Carson Wentz | 431.6 | 3 |
| 3 | Seattle | Russell Wilson | 396.8 | 3 |
| 4 | Carolina | Cam Newton | 395.3 | 3 |
| 5 | Green Bay | Aaron Rodgers | 370.5 | 3 |
| 6 | Washington | Alex Smith | 394.7 | 4 |
| 7 | Dallas | Dak Prescott | 381.6 | 4 |
| 8 | Indianapolis | Andrew Luck | 363.7 | 4 |
| 9 | New England | Tom Brady | 343.1 | 4 |
| 10 | Cincinnati | Andy Dalton | 349.2 | 5 |
| 11 | LA Rams | Jared Goff | 325.4 | 5 |
| 12 | Detroit | Matthew Stafford | 322.6 | 5 |
| 13 | Pittsburgh | Ben Roethlisberger | 322.2 | 5 |
| 14 | LA Chargers | Philip Rivers | 307.2 | 5 |
| 15 | Minnesota | Kirk Cousins | 302.2 | 5 |
| 16 | New Orleans | Drew Brees | 298.7 | 5 |
| 17 | San Francisco | Jimmy Garoppolo | 296.8 | 5 |
| 18 | NY Giants | Eli Manning | 275.4 | 5 |
| 19 | Tampa Bay | Jameis Wintson | 358.5 | 6 |
| 20 | Jacksonville | Blake Bortles | 332.2 | 6 |
| 21 | Kansas City | Patrick Mahomes | 283.3 | 6 |
| 22 | Atlanta | Matt Ryan | 276.2 | 6 |
| 23 | NY Jets | Josh McCown | 275.3 | 6 |
| 24 | Tennessee | Marcus Mariota | 312.8 | |
| 25 | Miami | Ryan Tannehill | 308.6 | |
| 26 | Denver | Case Keenum | 300.5 | |
| 27 | Cleveland | Tyrod Taylor | 282.6 | |
| 28 | Arizona | Sam Bradford | 276.2 | |
| 29 | Buffalo | AJ McCaroon | 274.4 | |
| 30 | Oakland | Derek Carr | 274.0 | |
| 31 | Chicago | Mitch Trubiksky | 229.7 | |
| 32 | Baltimore | Joe Flacco | 214.0 | |

**Running Backs**

## PPR Running Back Rankings

| Rank | Team | Player | Projected Points | Tier | Note |
|---|---|---|---|---|---|
| 1 | LA Rams | Todd Gurley | 387.5 | 1 | |
| 2 | Pittsburgh | Le'Veon Bell | 342.6 | 1 | |
| 3 | Kansas City | Kareem Hunt | 329.0 | 1 | |

| | | | | | |
|---|---|---|---|---|---|
| 4 | Dallas | Ezekiel Elliott | 302.3 | 2 | |
| 5 | New Orleans | Alvin Kamara | 293.9 | 2 | Boosted due to Ingram's suspenstion. |
| 6 | LA Chargers | Melvin Gordon | 278.5 | 2 | |
| 7 | Jacksonville | Leonard Fournette | 257.5 | 2 | I like his dominance of snaps. Upgrading ranking. |
| 8 | New Orleans | Mark Ingram | 266.4 | 3 | Moving down due to suspension. |
| 9 | NY Giants | Saqon Barkley | 249.1 | 3 | |
| 10 | Buffalo | LeSean McCoy | 238.1 | 3 | |
| 11 | Carolina | Christian McCaffrey | 235.3 | 3 | |
| 12 | Washington | Christian Thompson | 295.4 | 3 | ADP is so much lower that I will move him down the board.  Make sure you draft him. |
| 13 | Atlanta | Devonta Freeman | 216.1 | 3 | |
| 14 | Arizona | David Johnson | 216.1 | 3 | |
| 15 | Chicago | Jordan Howard | 212.9 | 3 | |
| 16 | Minnesota | Dalvin Cook | 208.6 | 3 | He was so explosive in a short time. Upgrading. |
| 17 | Oakland | Doug Martin | 275.0 | 3 | He's a risky play at #8, so moving him down. |
| 18 | San Francisco | Jerick McKinnon | 176.1 | 4 | Will give a boost based on Shanahan's running scheme. |
| 19 | Tennessee | Dion Lewis | 229.8 | 4 | Downgraded due to the Titans desire to split carries. |
| 20 | Seattle | Rashaad Penny | 197.8 | 4 | I've upgraded due to his potential to win carries. |
| 21 | Green Bay | Aaron Jones | 38.9 | 7 | |
| 22 | Houston | Lamar Miller | 220.1 | 4 | |

| | | | | | |
|---|---|---|---|---|---|
| 23 | Miami | Kenyan Drake | 208.2 | 4 | |
| 24 | Philadelphia | Jay Ajayi | 131.2 | 5 | |
| 25 | Denver | Royce Freeman | 184.4 | 5 | Upgrading based purely on potential. |
| 26 | Cleveland | Duke Johnson Jr. | 182.8 | 5 | |
| 27 | NY Jets | Bilal Powel | 198.4 | 6 | |
| 28 | Carolina | C.J. Anderson | 197.9 | 6 | |
| 29 | Baltimore | Javorius Allen | 185.8 | 6 | |
| 30 | NY Jets | Elijah McGuire / Isiah Crowell | 181.8 | 6 | |
| 31 | New England | Sony Michel | 177.7 | 6 | |
| 32 | Baltimore | Alex Collins | 166.7 | 6 | |
| 33 | New England | James White | 149.6 | 6 | |
| 34 | Cleveland | Nick Chubb / Carlos Hyde | 136.9 | 6 | Slight boost in Haley's scheme. Beware Duke Johnson Jr. |
| 35 | Cincinnati | Giovani Bernard | 162.5 | 7 | |
| 36 | Cincinnati | Joe Mixon | 156.4 | 7 | |
| 37 | Detroit | LaGarrette Blount/Kerryon Johnson | 152.1 | 7 | Likely to split carries between the two. Johnson will start to take over towrads the end of the season. |
| 38 | Tampa Bay | Ronald Jones | 146.6 | 7 | |
| 39 | Chicago | Tarik Cohen | 133.5 | 7 | |
| 40 | Atlanta | Tevin Coleman | 133.3 | 7 | |
| 41 | Indianapolis | Nyheim Hines | 122.2 | 7 | I like his chances to take over RB1 duties by the end of the year. |
| 42 | Indianapolis | Marlon Mack | 107.5 | 7 | |
| 43 | Tennessee | Derrick Henry | 89.0 | 7 | |
| 44 | Houston | D'Onta Foreman | 79.3 | 7 | |
| 45 | Washington | Derrius Guice | 82.8 | 7 | |
| 46 | Minnesota | Latavius Murray | 141.6 | 8 | |
| 47 | Tampa Bay | Peyton Barber | 46.5 | 8 | |
| 48 | Seattle | Chris Carson | 98.9 | 8 | |
| 49 | Detroit | Theo Riddick | 107.1 | | |

| 50 | Denver | Devontae Booker | 98.0 | | |
|---|---|---|---|---|---|
| 51 | Miami | Frank Gore | 77.2 | | |
| 52 | Philadelphia | Corey Clement | 116.2 | | |
| 53 | Kansas City | Damien Williams | 111.2 | | |
| 54 | LA Chargers | Austin Ekeler | 106.8 | | |
| 55 | Arizona | Elijah Penny | 133.3 | | |
| 56 | NY Giants | Jonathan Stewart | 105.8 | | |
| 57 | Jacksonville | T.J. Yeldon | 105.1 | | |
| 58 | San Francisco | Matt Breida | 87.3 | | |
| 59 | Oakland | DeAndre Washington | 66.2 | | |
| 60 | Dallas | Rod Smith | 47.5 | | |
| 61 | Buffalo | Chris Ivory | 46.2 | | |
| 62 | LA Rams | Malcolm Brown | 29.6 | | |
| 63 | Pittsburgh | Stevan Ridley | 17.5 | | |

**Wide Receivers**

| Rank | Team | Player | Projected Points | Tier | Note |
|------|------|--------|------------------|------|------|
| \multicolumn{6}{c}{**PPR Wide Reiver Rankings**} |
| 1 | Houston | DeAndre Hopkins | 329.2 | 1 | |
| 2 | Pittsburgh | Antonio Brown | 320.1 | 1 | |
| 3 | Cincinnati | A.J. Green | 259.3 | 2 | |
| 4 | NY Giants | Odell Beckham | 201.1 | 2 | |
| 5 | New Orleans | Michael Thomas | 255.5 | 2 | |
| 6 | LA Chargers | Keenan Allen | 241.1 | 3 | |
| 7 | Atlanta | Julio Jones | 211.2 | 3 | |
| 8 | San Francisco | Pierre Garcon | 220.8 | 3 | undervalued |
| 9 | Kansas City | Tyreek Hill | 220.2 | 3 | |
| 10 | Philadelphia | Alshon Jeffery | 217.3 | 3 | |
| 11 | Green Bay | Devante Adams | 216.9 | 3 | |
| 12 | Minnesota | Stefon Diggs | 215.1 | 3 | |
| 13 | Indianapolis | T.Y. Hilton | 190.1 | 4 | |
| 14 | Arizona | Larry Fitzgerald | 211.2 | 4 | |
| 15 | Oakland | Amari Cooper | 170.9 | 4 | |
| 16 | Tennessee | Rishard Matthews | 222.6 | 4 | |
| 17 | Miami | Danny Amendola | 217.5 | 4 | |
| 18 | Houston | Will Fuller V | 208.9 | 4 | |
| 19 | Detroit | Golden Tate | 195.8 | 4 | |
| 20 | NY Giants | Sterling Shepard | 131.4 | 4 | |
| 21 | Jacksonville | Marqise Lee | 207.1 | 5 | |
| 22 | Tampa Bay | Mike Evans | 206.7 | 5 | |
| 23 | Minnesota | Adam Thielen | 201.0 | 5 | |
| 24 | Cleveland | Josh Gordon | 200.1 | 5 | |
| 25 | Denver | Demaryius Thomas | 199.7 | 5 | |
| 26 | Seattle | Doug Baldwin | 199.1 | 5 | |
| 27 | NY Jets | Robbie Anderson | 196.9 | 5 | |
| 28 | Detroit | Mike Jones Jr | 212.3 | 5 | |
| 29 | Carolina | Devin Funchess | 196.7 | 5 | |
| 30 | Philadelphia | Nelson Agholor | 189.6 | 5 | |
| 31 | Cleveland | Jarvis Landry | 186.7 | 5 | |
| 32 | LA Rams | Brandin Cooks | 170.4 | 5 | |
| 33 | Pittsburgh | JuJu smith-Schuster | 168.1 | 5 | |
| 34 | Seattle | Tyler Lockett | 164.5 | 5 | |
| 35 | Oakland | Jordy Nelson | 140.9 | 5 | |

| | | | | | |
|---|---|---|---|---|---|
| 36 | New England | Julian Edelman | 198.8 | 6 | |
| 37 | Dallas | Austin Hurns | 191.9 | 6 | |
| 38 | LA Rams | Cooper Kupp | 187.9 | 6 | |
| 39 | Green Bay | Randall Cobb | 183.9 | 6 | |
| 40 | Jacksonville | Keelan Cole | 163.6 | 7 | |
| 41 | Atlanta | Mohamed Sanu | 169.3 | 7 | |
| 42 | Arizona | J.J. Nelson | 169.3 | 7 | |
| 43 | Cleveland | Corey Coleman | 158.2 | 7 | |
| 44 | San Francisco | Marquise Goodwin | 154.9 | 7 | |
| 45 | Kansas City | Sammy Watkins | 152.5 | 7 | |
| 46 | Tennessee | Corey Davis | 152.3 | 7 | |
| 47 | Miami | DeVante Parker | 151.4 | 7 | |
| 48 | Cincinnati | Brandon LaFell | 150.9 | 7 | |
| 49 | Buffalo | Kelvin Benjamin | 150.1 | 7 | |
| 50 | Miami | Kenny Stills | 148.5 | 7 | |
| 51 | Baltimore | Michael Crabtree | 146.4 | 7 | |
| 52 | New Orleans | Tedd Ginn Jr | 128.6 | 7 | |
| 53 | Jacksonville | Donte Moncrief | 106.0 | 7 | |
| 54 | Oakland | Martavis Bryant | 103.6 | 7 | |
| 55 | Green Bay | Geronimo Allison / J'Mon Moore | 150.0 | 7 | Check training camp to see who is winning more targets. |
| 56 | Denver | Emmanuel Sanders | 138.0 | 8 | |
| 57 | Carolina | D.J. Moore | 143.7 | 8 | |
| 58 | New England | Jordan Matthews | 136.0 | 8 | |
| 59 | Tampa Bay | DeSean Jackson | 135.9 | 8 | |
| 60 | Indianapolis | Ryan Grant | 144.4 | 8 | |
| 61 | Washington | Jamison Crowder | 131.0 | 8 | |
| 62 | Seattle | Brandon Marshall | 119.2 | 8 | |
| 63 | Chicago | Allen Robinson | 122.1 | 8 | |
| 64 | Washington | Paul Richardson Jr. | 116.6 | 8 | |
| 65 | Tennessee | Tajae' Sharpe | 94.9 | 8 | |
| 66 | NY Jets | Quincy Enunwa | 158.2 | | |
| 67 | Dallas | Terrance Williams | 132.8 | | |
| 68 | LA Chargers | Tyrell Williams | 120.5 | | |

| 69 | Buffalo | Jeremy Kerley | 118.5 | | |
|----|---------|---------------|-------|---|---|
| 70 | Philadelphia | Mike Wallace | 109.9 | | |
| 71 | Tampa Bay | Adam Humphries | 108.9 | | |
| 72 | LA Chargers | Travis Benjamin | 108.2 | | |
| 73 | Denver | Courtland Sutton | 105.9 | | |
| 74 | New England | Chris Hogan | 105.4 | | |
| 75 | Indianapolis | Chester Rogers | 104.4 | | |
| 76 | Baltimore | John Brown | 102.8 | | |
| 77 | Pittsburgh | James Washington | 98.8 | | |
| 78 | NY Giants | Cody Latimer | 98.1 | | |
| 79 | Detroit | TJ Jones | 97.4 | | |
| 80 | Chicago | Kevin White | 94.4 | | |
| 81 | Buffalo | Zay Jones | 92.0 | | |
| 82 | Chicago | Dontrelle Inman | 88.7 | | |
| 83 | Dallas | Tavon Austin | 87.7 | | |
| 84 | LA Rams | Robert Woods | 86.1 | | |
| 85 | Washington | Josh Doctson | 85.9 | | |
| 86 | Atlanta | Calvin Ridley | 84.3 | | |
| 87 | Arizona | Christian Kirk | 84.3 | | |
| 88 | New Orleans | Brandon Coleman | 82.8 | | |
| 89 | Kansas City | Demarcus Robinson | 74.8 | | |
| 90 | NY Jets | Jermaine Kerase | 68.8 | | |
| 91 | Cincinnati | Tyler Boyd | 63.5 | | |
| 92 | Minnesota | Laquon Treadwell | 61.6 | | |
| 93 | Baltimore | Willie Snead IV | 58.2 | | |
| 94 | Houston | Bruce Ellington | 51.1 | | |
| 95 | Carolina | Torrey Smith | 49.2 | | |
| 96 | San Francisco | Trent Taylor | 43.3 | | |

## Tight Ends

| Rank | Rank | Team | Player | Projected Points | Tier |
|------|------|------|--------|------------------|------|
| **PPR Tight End Rankings** | | | | | |
| 1 | New England | TE1 | Rob Gronkowski | 241.2 | 2 |
| 2 | Philadelphia | TE1 | Zach Ertz | 227.3 | 2 |
| 3 | Carolina | TE1 | Greg Olsen | 202.7 | 3 |
| 4 | Kansas City | TE1 | Travis Kelce | 191.7 | 3 |
| 5 | Cincinnati | TE1 | Tyler Eiffert | 188.7 | 4 |
| 6 | Tennessee | TE1 | Delanie Walker | 185.1 | 4 |
| 7 | Washington | TE1 | Jordan Reed | 123.6 | 4 |
| 8 | Green Bay | TE1 | Jimmy Graham | 108.0 | 4 |
| 9 | Chicago | TE1 | Trey Burton | 168.8 | 5 |
| 10 | Buffalo | TE1 | Charles Clay | 161.7 | 5 |
| 11 | Dallas | TE1 | Geoff Swaim | 152.6 | 6 |
| 12 | Tampa Bay | TE1 | Cameron Brate | 147.7 | 6 |
| 13 | NY Giants | TE1 | Evan Engram | 147.6 | 6 |
| 14 | Indianapolis | TE1 | Jack Doyle | 147.1 | 6 |
| 15 | LA Chargers | TE1 | Virgil Green | 145.5 | 7 |
| 16 | Oakland | TE1 | Jared Cook | 131.2 | 7 |
| 17 | Minnesota | TE1 | Kyle Rudolph | 129.5 | 7 |
| 18 | San Francisco | TE1 | George Kittle | 108.5 | 7 |
| 19 | Baltimore | TE1 | Hayden Hurst | 122.5 | 8 |
| 20 | Detroit | TE1 | Levine Toilolo | 126.8 | |
| 21 | NY Jets | TE1 | Eric Tomlinson | 116.4 | |
| 22 | Atlanta | TE1 | Austin Hooper | 107.4 | |
| 23 | Arizona | TE1 | Jermaine Gresham | 107.4 | |
| 24 | Pittsburgh | TE1 | Jesse James | 102.8 | |
| 25 | Seattle | TE1 | Ed Dickson | 100.6 | |
| 26 | Cleveland | TE1 | David Njoku | 94.3 | |
| 27 | Houston | TE1 | Ryan Griffen | 88.9 | |
| 28 | Jacksonville | TE1 | Austin Sefarian-Jenkins | 74.6 | |
| 29 | New Orleans | TE1 | Benjamin Watson | 70.4 | |
| 30 | LA Rams | TE1 | Tyler Higbee | 69.9 | |
| 31 | Miami | TE1 | Mike Gescki | 69.9 | |
| 32 | Denver | TE1 | Jeff Heuerman | 43.9 | |

**Kickers**

## Kicker Rankings

| Rank | Team | Player | Tier |
|---|---|---|---|
| 1 | LA Rams | Greg Zuerlein | 7 |
| 2 | Kansas City | Harrison Butker | 7 |
| 3 | New England | Stephen Gostkowski | 7 |
| 4 | Philadelphia | Jake Elliott | 7 |
| 5 | New Orleans | Will Lutz | 8 |
| 6 | San Francisco | Robbie Gould | 8 |
| 7 | Baltimore | Justin Tucker | 8 |
| 8 | Pittsburgh | Chris Boswell | 8 |
| 9 | Detroit | Matt Prater | 8 |
| 10 | Minnesota | Kai Forbath | 8 |
| 11 | Atlanta | Matt Bryant | 8 |
| 12 | Arizona | Phil Dawson | 8 |
| 13 | Tennessee | Ryan Succop | |
| 14 | Jacksonville | Josh Lambo | |
| 15 | Carolina | Graham Gano | |
| 16 | Tampa Bay | Chandler Catanzaro | |
| 17 | LA Chargers | Caleb Sturgis | |
| 18 | Seattle | Sebastian Janikowski | |
| 19 | Dallas | Dan Bailey | |
| 20 | Indianapolis | Adam Vinatieri | |
| 21 | Denver | Brandon McManus | |
| 22 | Washington | Dustin Hopkins | |
| 23 | Buffalo | Steven Hauschka | |
| 24 | NY Jets | Cairo Santos | |
| 25 | Houston | Ka'imi Fairbairn | |
| 26 | NY Giants | Aldrick Rosas | |
| 27 | Oakland | Giorgio Tavecchio | |
| 28 | Miami | Jason Sanders | |
| 29 | Chicago | Cody Parkey | |
| 30 | Green Bay | Mason Crosby | |
| 31 | Cincinnati | Randy Bullock | |
| 32 | Cleveland | Zane Gonzalez | |

**Defense / Special Teams**

| Rank | Team | Player | Tier |
|---|---|---|---|
| | **Kicker Rankings** | | |
| 1 | Jacksonville | Jaguars | 7 |
| 2 | Baltimore | Ravens | 7 |
| 3 | LA Rams | Rams | 7 |
| 4 | Pittsburgh | Steelers | 7 |
| 5 | LA Chargers | Chargers | 8 |
| 6 | Seattle | Seahawks | 8 |
| 7 | Chicago | Bears | 8 |
| 8 | Philadelphia | Eagles | 8 |
| 9 | Carolina | Panthers | 8 |
| 10 | Tennessee | Titans | |
| 11 | Washington | Redskins | |
| 12 | Detroit | Lions | |
| 13 | New Orleans | Saints | |
| 14 | Arizona | Cardinals | |
| 15 | Dallas | Cowboys | |
| 16 | Minnesota | Vikings | |
| 17 | Cincinnati | Bengals | |
| 18 | Denver | Broncos | |
| 19 | Atlanta | Falcons | |
| 20 | Green Bay | Packers | |
| 21 | New England | Patriots | |
| 22 | Buffalo | Bills | |
| 23 | Kansas City | Chiefs | |
| 24 | Cleveland | Browns | |
| 25 | San Francisco | 49ers | |
| 26 | NY Jets | Jets | |
| 27 | Miami | Dolphins | |
| 28 | Houston | Texans | |
| 29 | Oakland | Raiders | |
| 30 | NY Giants | Giants | |
| 31 | Indianapolis | Colts | |
| 32 | Tampa Bay | Buccaneers | |

RANKINGS
STANDARD (NON-PPR)

# Standard (Non-Points Per Reception) Rankings
## Strategy Guide & Tier Rankings

### Overview

The mistake most people make in Fantasy Drafts is a reliance on a position or hoping to get a specific player or a certain amount of a specific position. In reality, it makes more sense to arrange your draft board like NFL teams arrange their college prospect draft boards.

I've analyzed every player's schedule as well as their strength of competition. As part of this analysis, I've come up with projected points and competitive advantage in relation to other players. I then ranked players into tier levels based on the competitive advantage they will offer throughout the season. This is important as your fantasy draft moves on and you're choosing between a starting quarterback or a flex running back. The correct thing to do when faced with this situation is take the player who will provide the most point advantage over your competition. This is where our Opportunity Rankings, Play Calling analysis and scouting reports come into play.

**Note: If you purchased this book and would like updated rankings throughout the offseason, please contact me at functionalsportsaholic@gmail.com or via Twitter @TFS_Sean.**

### Step 1: Draft As Many Tier 1 and Tier 2 Players As Possible

Simply put, no matter who is on the board or how many players at these positions you have, do not draft a lower-tier player until all of these players are off the board.

| Tier 1 | | | | | |
|---|---|---|---|---|---|
| **QB** | **RB** | **WR** | **TE** | **DST** | **K** |
| NA | Todd Gurley | DeAndre Hopkins | NA | NA | NA |
| | Kareem Hunt | Antonio Brown | | | |
| | Ezekiel Elliott | | | | |
| | Le'Veon Bell | | | | |

| Tier 2 | | | | | |
|---|---|---|---|---|---|
| **QB** | **RB** | **WR** | **TE** | **DST** | **K** |
| Deshaun Watson | Melvin Gordon | Odell Beckham | NA | NA | NA |
| | Leonard Fournette | A.J. Green | | | |
| | Alvin Kamara | Julio Jones | | | |
| | Saqon Barkley | Michael Thomas | | | |
| | Jordan Howard | Alshon Jeffery | | | |
| | | Keenan Allen | | | |
| | | Devante Adams | | | |

## Step 2: Start Considering Other Positions

The first two tiers will likely be exhausted by the end of the 2nd round.   There are 23 players in Tier 3. There are many famous names in lower tiers, so do not be surprised if this list will take you into rounds 5 or 6.

Your goal by the end of round 6 to have a combination of 4 RB/WRs (but you should have 1 starter at both positions) and the best TE OR QB.   If you end up with 5 RBs/WRs, don't sweat it.  There are sleeper candidates later.

As a reminder, the inclusion of either Doug Martin or Marshawn Lynch in this tier is contingent on one of them winning the starting RB job.  This will be important to monitor in training camp.  If they will be splitting carries, remove them from this tier and include them at the bottom of tier 5.

| QB | RB | WR | TE | DST | K |
|---|---|---|---|---|---|
| | | **Tier 3** | | | |
| Carson Wentz | Dalvin Cook | Will Fuller V | Rob Gronkowski | NA | NA |
| Russell Wilson | LeSean McCoy | T.Y. Hilton | Zach Ertz | | |
| Cam Newton | Chris Thompson | Larry Fitzgerald | Travis Kelce | | |
| Aaron Rodgers | Mark Ingram | Amari Cooper | | | |
| | Devonta Freeman | Rishard Matthews | | | |
| | Doug Martin / Marshawn Lynch | Mike Jones Jr | | | |
| | Christian McCaffrey | Tyreek Hill | | | |
| | | Julian Edelman | | | |
| | | Mike Evans | | | |
| | | Adam Thielen | | | |
| | | Stefon Diggs | | | |

*NOTE: I LOVE the potential of Chris Thompson and the leading Raiders back.  Based on average draft position, I think you'll be able to get one or both after round 5.*

## Step 3: Pick Viable Starters Where You're Weak

By now, you should be well into the middle rounds of the draft.  Depending on how your league has drafted, you might have a very strong bench of RB/WR options or you might have starters at all positions, but lack depth.  Tiers 4 and 5 are built to ensure that you have a viable starter at every position (except Kicker and Defense/Special Teams) including all Flex positions.

## Tier 4

| QB | RB | WR | TE | DST | K |
|---|---|---|---|---|---|
| Alex Smith | David Johnson | Nelson Agholor | Delanie Walker | NA | NA |
| Dak Prescott | Jerick McKinnon | Marqise Lee | Jimmy Graham | | |
| Andrew Luck | Jamaal Williams | Robbie Anderson | | | |
| Tom Brady | Kenyan Drake | Devin Funchess | | | |
| | Lamar Miller | Brandin Cooks | | | |
| | Royce Freeman | Danny Amendola | | | |
| | | Josh Gordon | | | |

## Tier 5

| QB | RB | WR | TE | DST | K |
|---|---|---|---|---|---|
| Andy Dalton | Dion Lewis | Sterling Shepard | Greg Olsen | NA | NA |
| Jared Goff | Rashaad Penny | JuJu smith-Schuster | Jordan Reed | | |
| Matthew Stafford | Bilal Powel | Golden Tate | Tyler Eiffert | | |
| Ben Roethlisberger | Sony Michel | Doug Baldwin | Jack Doyle | | |
| Philip Rivers | Joe Mixon | Pierre Garcon | Trey Burton | | |
| Kirk Cousins | | Jarvis Landry | | | |
| Drew Brees | | Randall Cobb | | | |
| Jimmy Garoppolo | | Demaryius Thomas | | | |
| Eli Manning | | Austin Hurns | | | |
| | | Jordy Nelson | | | |
| | | Cooper Kupp | | | |
| | | Tyler Lockett | | | |
| | | Keelan Cole | | | |

### Step 4: Find Potential

At this point, you should have starters at all positions and depth at each spot on your roster (except Kicker and Defense / Special Team).  Now is that time to find players that have potential to make your starting lineup as the season progresses.  Having more viable starting talent on your roster will allow you to be aggressive with trades throughout the season.

You'll notice that I've started to include my top-rated kickers and defense / special teams groups.  Draft guides will typically recommend that you wait until the last round for a kicker and as late as the second-to-last round to draft your defense.  For the most part I agree, however, remember what we talked about with competitive advantage?

In 2017, I had a roster that was dealing with injuries.  I also had K, Greg Zuerlein and DST, Jaguars.  These two positions scored well enough for me to win a few key games.  I would not have made the playoffs if it weren't for the competitive advantage they represented. Each week, I could count on an advantage of 8-10 points from these two spots.

Because most players will draft their K and DST positions last, I suggest you start earlier. If your draft lasts 20 rounds, rather than waiting until rounds 19 and 20, draft your defense in round 17 and your kicker in round 18. Some will laugh at you, but you'll be fortifying the last two spots on your roster. Then in rounds 19 and 20 when everyone is picking their kickers, you'll be able to find compelling players in Tiers 6 and 7 that could develop into starters by the end of the season.

## Tier 6

| QB | RB | WR | TE | DST | K |
|----|----|----|----|-----|---|
| Jameis Wintson | C.J. Anderson | Corey Coleman | Charles Clay | NA | NA |
| Blake Bortles | Elijah McGuire | Kelvin Benjamin | Kyle Rudolph | | |
| Patrick Mahomes | James White | Mohamed Sanu | Virgil Green | | |
| Matt Ryan | Ronald Jones | Corey Davis | | | |
| Josh McCown | LaGarrette Blount/Kerryon Johnson | Quincy Enunwa | | | |
| | Jay Ajayi | Kenny Stills | | | |
| | Duke Johnson Jr. | Marquise Goodwin | | | |
| | Giovani Bernard | DeVante Parker | | | |
| | Nick Chubb / Carlos Hyde | Sammy Watkins | | | |
| | Tevin Coleman | DeSean Jackson | | | |
| | | Brandon LaFell | | | |

## Tier 7

| QB | RB | WR | TE | DST | K |
|----|----|----|----|-----|---|
| NA | Alex Collins | Ryan Grant | Cameron Brate | Jaguars | Greg Zuerlein |
| | Nyheim Hines | Tedd Ginn Jr | Evan Engram | Ravens | Harrison Butker |
| | Tarik Cohen | Martavis Bryant | Jared Cook | Rams | Stephen Gostkowski |
| | D'Onta Foreman | Tajae' Sharpe | George Kittle | Steelers | Jake Elliott |
| | Marlon Mack | Calvin Ridley | | | |
| | Derrick Henry | Robert Woods | | | |
| | Derrius Guice | Michael Crabtree | | | |
| | Javorius Allen | Geronimo Allison / J'Mon Moore | | | |
| | Ty Montgomery | | | | |

## Step 5: Complete Your Draft, Trade and Play the Waiver Wire

You might find yourself in the last two rounds without a kicker or defense.  Tier 8 ranks the best of the last of what I determined to be "draftable".  If the defenses and kickers are gone and your league allows you to move forward without selecting a kicker, I would suggest you draft another young talented RB or WR and see what the future holds.  If you must draft all positions to fill your roster, I have the rest ranked in the kickers and defense/special teams section.

| Tier 8 | | | | | |
| --- | --- | --- | --- | --- | --- |
| **QB** | **RB** | **WR** | **TE** | **DST** | **K** |
| Marcus Mariota | Latavious Murray | D.J. Moore | Hayden Hurst | Chargers | Will Lutz |
| | Petyon Barber | Emmanuel Sanders | | Seahawks | Robbie Gould |
| | Chris Carson | Jordan Matthews | | Bears | Justin Tucker |
| | | Jamison Crowder | | Eagles | Chris Boswell |
| | | Allen Robinson | | Panthers | Matt Prater |
| | | Paul Richardson Jr. | | | Kai Forbath |
| | | | | | Matt Bryant |
| | | | | | Phil Dawson |

## Overall Rankings

| Rank | Team | Pos | Player | Projected Points | Tier |
|------|------|-----|--------|------------------|------|
| | | **Non-PPR RB Rankings** | | | |
| 1 | LA Rams | RB | Todd Gurley | 321.5 | 1 |
| 2 | Kansas City | RB | Kareem Hunt | 268.0 | 1 |
| 3 | Dallas | RB | Ezekiel Elliott | 265.3 | 1 |
| 4 | Pittsburgh | RB | Le'Veon Bell | 257.9 | 1 |
| 5 | Houston | WR | DeAndre Hopkins | 229.7 | 1 |
| 6 | Pittsburgh | WR | Antonio Brown | 212.8 | 1 |
| 7 | LA Chargers | RB | Melvin Gordon | 224.8 | 2 |
| 8 | Jacksonville | RB | Leonard Fournette | 223.1 | 2 |
| 9 | New Orleans | RB | Alvin Kamara | 215.0 | 2 |
| 10 | NY Giants | RB | Saqon Barkley | 201.9 | 2 |
| 11 | NY Giants | WR | Odell Beckham | 116.0 | 2 |
| 12 | Chicago | RB | Jordan Howard | 190.2 | 2 |
| 13 | Cincinnati | WR | A.J. Green | 179.7 | 2 |
| 14 | Atlanta | WR | Julio Jones | 134.8 | 2 |
| 15 | New Orleans | WR | Michael Thomas | 153.5 | 2 |
| 16 | Philadelphia | WR | Alshon Jeffery | 156.5 | 2 |
| 17 | LA Chargers | WR | Keenan Allen | 150.2 | 2 |
| 18 | Green Bay | WR | Devante Adams | 147.5 | 2 |
| 19 | Houston | QB | Deshaun Watson | 497.6 | 2 |
| 20 | Minnesota | RB | Dalvin Cook | 178.8 | 3 |
| 21 | Buffalo | RB | LeSean McCoy | 188.2 | 3 |
| 22 | New England | TE | Rob Gronkowski | 167.5 | 3 |
| 23 | Philadelphia | TE | Zach Ertz | 154.0 | 3 |
| 24 | Washington | RB | Chris Thompson | 229.4 | 3 |
| 25 | New Orleans | RB | Mark Ingram | 214.5 | 3 |
| 26 | Atlanta | RB | Devonta Freeman | 181.7 | 3 |
| 27 | Oakland | RB | Doug Martin | 228.4 | 3 |
| 28 | Houston | WR | Will Fuller V | 166.1 | 3 |
| 29 | Carolina | RB | Christian McCaffrey | 156.7 | 3 |
| 30 | Indianapolis | WR | T.Y. Hilton | 131.8 | 3 |
| 31 | Arizona | WR | Larry Fitzgerald | 107.9 | 3 |
| 32 | Oakland | WR | Amari Cooper | 108.6 | 3 |
| 33 | Tennessee | WR | Rishard Matthews | 146.9 | 3 |
| 34 | Detroit | WR | Mike Jones Jr | 154.1 | 3 |
| 35 | Kansas City | WR | Tyreek Hill | 142.6 | 3 |
| 36 | Tampa Bay | WR | Mike Evans | 136.6 | 3 |

| 37 | Minnesota | WR | Adam Thielen | 135.7 | 3 |
|---|---|---|---|---|---|
| 38 | Minnesota | WR | Stefon Diggs | 133.4 | 3 |
| 39 | Kansas City | TE | Travis Kelce | 124.9 | 3 |
| 40 | Philadelphia | QB | Carson Wentz | 431.6 | 3 |
| 41 | Seattle | QB | Russell Wilson | 396.8 | 3 |
| 42 | Carolina | QB | Cam Newton | 395.3 | 3 |
| 43 | Green Bay | QB | Aaron Rodgers | 370.5 | 3 |
| 44 | Arizona | RB | David Johnson | 149.3 | 4 |
| 45 | San Francisco | RB | Jerick McKinnon | 145.2 | 4 |
| 46 | Green Bay | RB | Ty Montgomery | 186.9 | 4 |
| 47 | Miami | RB | Kenyan Drake | 181.4 | 4 |
| 48 | Houston | RB | Lamar Miller | 180.5 | 4 |
| 49 | Denver | RB | Royce Freeman | 150.0 | 4 |
| 50 | Philadelphia | WR | Nelson Agholor | 135.3 | 4 |
| 51 | Jacksonville | WR | Marqise Lee | 135.0 | 4 |
| 52 | NY Jets | WR | Robbie Anderson | 134.6 | 4 |
| 53 | Carolina | WR | Devin Funchess | 133.6 | 4 |
| 54 | LA Rams | WR | Brandin Cooks | 129.3 | 4 |
| 55 | Miami | WR | Danny Amendola | 128.9 | 4 |
| 56 | Cleveland | WR | Josh Gordon | 126.4 | 4 |
| 57 | Tennessee | TE | Delanie Walker | 124.4 | 4 |
| 58 | Washington | QB | Alex Smith | 394.7 | 4 |
| 59 | Dallas | QB | Dak Prescott | 381.6 | 4 |
| 60 | Indianapolis | QB | Andrew Luck | 363.7 | 4 |
| 61 | New England | QB | Tom Brady | 343.1 | 4 |
| 62 | NY Giants | WR | Sterling Shepard | 80.5 | 5 |
| 63 | Tennessee | RB | Dion Lewis | 176.8 | 5 |
| 64 | Seattle | RB | Rashaad Penny | 163.3 | 5 |
| 65 | Pittsburgh | WR | JuJu smith-Schuster | 110.4 | 5 |
| 66 | NY Jets | RB | Bilal Powel | 153.9 | 5 |
| 67 | New England | RB | Sony Michel | 148.2 | 5 |
| 68 | Cincinnati | RB | Joe Mixon | 142.4 | 5 |
| 69 | Carolina | TE | Greg Olsen | 127.5 | 5 |
| 70 | Washington | TE | Jordan Reed | 56.1 | 5 |
| 71 | Cincinnati | TE | Tyler Eiffert | 137.9 | 5 |
| 72 | Detroit | WR | Golden Tate | 111.2 | 5 |
| 73 | Seattle | WR | Doug Baldwin | 125.1 | 5 |
| 74 | San Francisco | WR | Pierre Garcon | 124.8 | 5 |
| 75 | Cleveland | WR | Jarvis Landry | 124.5 | 5 |
| 76 | Green Bay | WR | Randall Cobb | 103.8 | 5 |

| 77 | Denver | WR | Demaryius Thomas | 118.1 | 5 |
|---|---|---|---|---|---|
| 78 | New England | WR | Julian Edelman | 140.4 | 3 |
| 79 | Dallas | WR | Austin Hurns | 122.8 | 5 |
| 80 | Oakland | WR | Jordy Nelson | 94.5 | 5 |
| 81 | LA Rams | WR | Cooper Kupp | 119.7 | 5 |
| 82 | Seattle | WR | Tyler Lockett | 115.9 | 5 |
| 83 | Indianapolis | TE | Jack Doyle | 92.8 | 5 |
| 84 | Green Bay | TE | Jimmy Graham | 53.3 | 5 |
| 85 | Chicago | TE | Trey Burton | 108.0 | 5 |
| 86 | Cincinnati | QB | Andy Dalton | 349.2 | 5 |
| 87 | LA Rams | QB | Jared Goff | 325.4 | 5 |
| 88 | Detroit | QB | Matthew Stafford | 322.6 | 5 |
| 89 | Pittsburgh | QB | Ben Roethlisberger | 322.2 | 5 |
| 90 | LA Chargers | QB | Philip Rivers | 307.2 | 5 |
| 91 | Minnesota | QB | Kirk Cousins | 302.2 | 5 |
| 92 | New Orleans | QB | Drew Brees | 298.7 | 5 |
| 93 | San Francisco | QB | Jimmy Garoppolo | 296.8 | 5 |
| 94 | NY Giants | QB | Eli Manning | 275.4 | 5 |
| 95 | Jacksonville | WR | Keelan Cole | 112.7 | 6 |
| 96 | Cleveland | WR | Corey Coleman | 93.3 | 6 |
| 97 | Buffalo | WR | Kelvin Benjamin | 93.1 | 6 |
| 98 | Carolina | RB | C.J. Anderson | 153.3 | 6 |
| 99 | NY Jets | RB | Elijah McGuire / Isiah Crowell | 152.4 | 6 |
| 100 | New England | RB | James White | 122.7 | 6 |
| 101 | Tampa Bay | RB | Ronald Jones | 122.3 | 6 |
| 102 | Detroit | RB | LaGarrette Blount/Kerryon Johnson | 122.2 | 6 |
| 103 | Philadelphia | RB | Jay Ajayi | 121.4 | 6 |
| 104 | Cleveland | RB | Duke Johnson Jr. | 118.3 | 6 |
| 105 | Cincinnati | RB | Giovani Bernard | 117.8 | 6 |
| 106 | Cleveland | RB | Nick Chubb / Carlos Hyde | 109.4 | 6 |
| 107 | Buffalo | TE | Charles Clay | 106.7 | 6 |
| 108 | Atlanta | WR | Mohamed Sanu | 106.4 | 6 |
| 109 | Tennessee | WR | Corey Davis | 103.0 | 6 |
| 110 | Atlanta | RB | Tevin Coleman | 101.1 | 6 |
| 111 | NY Jets | WR | Quincy Enunwa | 98.5 | 6 |
| 112 | Miami | WR | Kenny Stills | 97.0 | 6 |
| 113 | San Francisco | WR | Marquise Goodwin | 96.8 | 6 |
| 114 | Miami | WR | DeVante Parker | 95.7 | 6 |
| 115 | Kansas City | WR | Sammy Watkins | 93.3 | 6 |
| 116 | Tampa Bay | WR | DeSean Jackson | 91.5 | 6 |

| 117 | Cincinnati | WR | Brandon LaFell | 90.5 | 6 |
|---|---|---|---|---|---|
| 118 | Minnesota | TE | Kyle Rudolph | 89.1 | 6 |
| 119 | LA Chargers | TE | Virgil Green | 88.6 | 6 |
| 120 | Tampa Bay | QB | Jameis Wintson | 358.5 | 6 |
| 121 | Jacksonville | QB | Blake Bortles | 332.2 | 6 |
| 122 | Kansas City | QB | Patrick Mahomes | 283.3 | 6 |
| 123 | Atlanta | QB | Matt Ryan | 276.2 | 6 |
| 124 | NY Jets | QB | Josh McCown | 275.3 | 6 |
| 125 | Tampa Bay | TE | Cameron Brate | 97.0 | 7 |
| 126 | Baltimore | RB | Alex Collins | 93.0 | 7 |
| 127 | Indianapolis | RB | Nyheim Hines | 90.6 | 7 |
| 128 | Indianapolis | WR | Ryan Grant | 86.0 | 7 |
| 129 | Chicago | RB | Tarik Cohen | 85.8 | 7 |
| 130 | NY Giants | TE | Evan Engram | 84.3 | 7 |
| 131 | Oakland | TE | Jared Cook | 79.7 | 7 |
| 132 | New Orleans | WR | Tedd Ginn Jr | 77.2 | 7 |
| 133 | Houston | RB | D'Onta Foreman | 77.1 | 7 |
| 134 | Indianapolis | RB | Marlon Mack | 76.5 | 7 |
| 135 | Tennessee | RB | Derrick Henry | 72.3 | 7 |
| 136 | Washington | RB | Derrius Guice | 69.4 | 7 |
| 137 | San Francisco | TE | George Kittle | 67.0 | 7 |
| 138 | Oakland | WR | Martavis Bryant | 64.8 | 7 |
| 139 | Tennessee | WR | Tajae' Sharpe | 55.9 | 7 |
| 140 | Baltimore | RB | Javorius Allen | 54.3 | 7 |
| 141 | Atlanta | WR | Calvin Ridley | 53.6 | 7 |
| 142 | LA Rams | WR | Robert Woods | 47.9 | 7 |
| 143 | Green Bay | RB | Aaron Jones | 32.8 | 7 |
| 144 | Baltimore | WR | Michael Crabtree | 30.4 | 7 |
| 145 | Jacksonville | DST | Jaguars | | 7 |
| 146 | Baltimore | DST | Ravens | | 7 |
| 147 | LA Rams | DST | Rams | | 7 |
| 148 | Pittsburgh | DST | Steelers | | 7 |
| 149 | LA Rams | K | Greg Zuerlein | | 7 |
| 150 | Kansas City | K | Harrison Butker | | 7 |
| 151 | New England | K | Stephen Gostkowski | | 7 |
| 152 | Philadelphia | K | Jake Elliott | | 7 |
| 153 | Carolina | WR | D.J. Moore | 88.0 | 8 |
| 154 | Denver | WR | Emmanuel Sanders | 79.3 | 8 |
| 155 | New England | WR | Jordan Matthews | 77.3 | 8 |
| 156 | Washington | WR | Jamison Crowder | 67.2 | 8 |
| 157 | Seattle | WR | Brandon Marshall | 73.2 | |

| 158 | Chicago | WR | Allen Robinson | 65.9 | 8 |
|---|---|---|---|---|---|
| 159 | Washington | WR | Paul Richardson Jr. | 87.3 | 8 |
| 160 | Tennessee | QB | Marcus Mariota | 312.8 | 8 |
| 161 | LA Chargers | DST | Chargers | | 8 |
| 162 | Seattle | DST | Seahawks | | 8 |
| 163 | Chicago | DST | Bears | | 8 |
| 164 | Philadelphia | DST | Eagles | | 8 |
| 165 | Carolina | DST | Panthers | | 8 |
| 166 | Baltimore | TE | Hayden Hurst | 68.1 | 8 |
| 167 | Minnesota | RB | Latavius Murray | 93.3 | 8 |
| 168 | Tampa Bay | RB | Peyton Barber | 23.9 | 8 |
| 169 | Seattle | RB | Chris Carson | 71.9 | 8 |
| 170 | New Orleans | K | Will Lutz | | 8 |
| 171 | San Francisco | K | Robbie Gould | | 8 |
| 172 | Baltimore | K | Justin Tucker | | 8 |
| 173 | Pittsburgh | K | Chris Boswell | | 8 |
| 174 | Detroit | K | Matt Prater | | 8 |
| 175 | Minnesota | K | Kai Forbath | | 8 |
| 176 | Atlanta | K | Matt Bryant | | 8 |
| 177 | Arizona | K | Phil Dawson | | 8 |
| 178 | Detroit | RB | Theo Riddick | 69.6 | |
| 179 | Miami | RB | Frank Gore | 55.4 | |
| 180 | Denver | RB | Devontae Booker | 67.1 | |
| 181 | Miami | QB | Ryan Tannehill | 308.6 | |
| 182 | Denver | QB | Case Keenum | 300.5 | |
| 183 | Arizona | QB | Sam Bradford | 295.1 | |
| 184 | Cleveland | QB | Tyrod Taylor | 282.6 | |
| 185 | Buffalo | QB | AJ McCaroon | 274.4 | |
| 186 | Oakland | QB | Derek Carr | 274.0 | |
| 187 | Chicago | QB | Mitch Trubiksky | 229.7 | |
| 188 | Green Bay | WR | Geronimo Allison / J'Mon Moore | 174.8 | |
| 189 | Baltimore | QB | Joe Flacco | 136.3 | |
| 190 | Philadelphia | RB | Corey Clement | 98.7 | |
| 191 | Kansas City | RB | Damien Williams | 96.7 | |
| 192 | Dallas | TE | Geoff Swaim | 86.5 | |
| 193 | LA Chargers | RB | Austin Ekeler | 83.1 | |
| 194 | Arizona | WR | J.J. Nelson | 82.2 | |
| 195 | LA Chargers | WR | Tyrell Williams | 81.9 | |
| 196 | San Francisco | RB | Matt Breida | 78.1 | |
| 197 | Jacksonville | RB | T.J. Yeldon | 77.5 | |

| 198 | Detroit | TE | Levine Toilolo | 76.1 | |
|-----|---------|-----|---------------|------|---|
| 199 | Dallas | WR | Terrance Williams | 73.5 | |
| 200 | Philadelphia | WR | Mike Wallace | 70.3 | |
| 201 | Arizona | WR | Christian Kirk | 70.1 | |
| 202 | Seattle | TE | Ed Dickson | 70.1 | |
| 203 | New England | WR | Chris Hogan | 69.0 | |
| 204 | Buffalo | WR | Jeremy Kerley | 68.2 | |
| 205 | Baltimore | WR | John Brown | 68.1 | |
| 206 | Denver | WR | Courtland Sutton | 67.5 | |
| 207 | Arizona | RB | Elijah Penny | 67.0 | |
| 208 | Jacksonville | WR | Donte Moncrief | 65.1 | |
| 209 | Chicago | WR | Kevin White | 64.8 | |
| 210 | Atlanta | TE | Austin Hooper | 64.6 | |
| 211 | NY Giants | RB | Jonathan Stewart | 64.3 | |
| 212 | Indianapolis | WR | Chester Rogers | 62.9 | |
| 213 | Detroit | WR | TJ Jones | 62.0 | |
| 214 | Buffalo | WR | Zay Jones | 60.4 | |
| 215 | NY Jets | TE | Eric Tomlinson | 60.2 | |
| 216 | Pittsburgh | WR | James Washington | 60.2 | |
| 217 | Cleveland | TE | David Njoku | 60.0 | |
| 218 | NY Giants | WR | Cody Latimer | 59.4 | |
| 219 | LA Chargers | WR | Travis Benjamin | 58.6 | |
| 220 | New Orleans | WR | Brandon Coleman | 58.2 | |
| 221 | Pittsburgh | TE | Jesse James | 57.6 | |
| 222 | Jacksonville | TE | Austin Sefarian-Jenkins | 55.2 | |
| 223 | Houston | TE | Ryan Griffen | 54.7 | |
| 224 | Chicago | WR | Dontrelle Inman | 52.8 | |
| 225 | Tampa Bay | WR | Adam Humphries | 52.3 | |
| 226 | Miami | TE | Mike Gescki | 46.0 | |
| 227 | Dallas | WR | Tavon Austin | 45.8 | |
| 228 | Kansas City | WR | Demarcus Robinson | 42.5 | |
| 229 | LA Rams | TE | Tyler Higbee | 41.7 | |
| 230 | Dallas | RB | Rod Smith | 41.5 | |
| 231 | Oakland | RB | DeAndre Washington | 41.4 | |
| 232 | New Orleans | TE | Benjamin Watson | 41.1 | |
| 233 | Washington | WR | Josh Doctson | 40.0 | |
| 234 | Buffalo | RB | Chris Ivory | 38.4 | |
| 235 | NY Jets | WR | Jermaine Kerase | 37.9 | |
| 236 | Minnesota | WR | Laquon Treadwell | 35.2 | |
| 237 | Cincinnati | WR | Tyler Boyd | 34.1 | |
| 238 | Baltimore | WR | Willie Snead IV | 30.4 | |

| 239 | Carolina | WR | Torrey Smith | 29.5 | |
|-----|----------|-----|-----------------|------|--|
| 240 | Houston | WR | Bruce Ellington | 28.7 | |
| 241 | Denver | TE | Jeff Heuerman | 26.5 | |
| 242 | Arizona | TE | Jermaine Gresham | 25.5 | |
| 243 | LA Rams | RB | Malcolm Brown | 24.2 | |
| 244 | San Francisco | WR | Trent Taylor | 22.9 | |
| 245 | Pittsburgh | RB | Stevan Ridley | 17.1 | |

# Quarterbacks

| Non-PPR QB Rankings | | | | |
|---|---|---|---|---|
| Rank | Team | Player | Projected Points | Tier |
| 1 | Houston | Deshaun Watson | 497.6 | 2 |
| 2 | Philadelphia | Carson Wentz | 431.6 | 3 |
| 3 | Seattle | Russell Wilson | 396.8 | 3 |
| 4 | Carolina | Cam Newton | 395.3 | 3 |
| 5 | Green Bay | Aaron Rodgers | 370.5 | 3 |
| 6 | Washington | Alex Smith | 394.7 | 4 |
| 7 | Dallas | Dak Prescott | 381.6 | 4 |
| 8 | Indianapolis | Andrew Luck | 363.7 | 4 |
| 9 | New England | Tom Brady | 343.1 | 4 |
| 10 | Cincinnati | Andy Dalton | 349.2 | 5 |
| 11 | LA Rams | Jared Goff | 325.4 | 5 |
| 12 | Detroit | Matthew Stafford | 322.6 | 5 |
| 13 | Pittsburgh | Ben Roethlisberger | 322.2 | 5 |
| 14 | LA Chargers | Philip Rivers | 307.2 | 5 |
| 15 | Minnesota | Kirk Cousins | 302.2 | 5 |
| 16 | New Orleans | Drew Brees | 298.7 | 5 |
| 17 | San Francisco | Jimmy Garoppolo | 296.8 | 5 |
| 18 | NY Giants | Eli Manning | 275.4 | 5 |
| 19 | Tampa Bay | Jameis Wintson | 358.5 | 6 |
| 20 | Jacksonville | Blake Bortles | 332.2 | 6 |
| 21 | Kansas City | Patrick Mahomes | 283.3 | 6 |
| 22 | Atlanta | Matt Ryan | 276.2 | 6 |
| 23 | NY Jets | Josh McCown | 275.3 | 6 |
| 24 | Tennessee | Marcus Mariota | 312.8 | |
| 25 | Miami | Ryan Tannehill | 308.6 | |
| 26 | Denver | Case Keenum | 300.5 | |
| 27 | Arizona | Sam Bradford | 295.1 | |
| 28 | Cleveland | Tyrod Taylor | 282.6 | |
| 29 | Buffalo | AJ McCaroon | 274.4 | |
| 30 | Oakland | Derek Carr | 274 | |
| 31 | Chicago | Mitch Trubiksky | 229.7 | |
| 32 | Baltimore | Joe Flacco | 136.3 | |

# Running Backs

## Non-PPR RB Rankings

| Rank | Team | Player | Projected Points | Tier |
|------|------|--------|------------------|------|
| 1 | LA Rams | Todd Gurley | 321.5 | 1 |
| 2 | Kansas City | Kareem Hunt | 268 | 1 |
| 3 | Dallas | Ezekiel Elliott | 265.3 | 1 |
| 4 | Pittsburgh | Le'Veon Bell | 257.9 | 1 |
| 5 | LA Chargers | Melvin Gordon | 224.8 | 2 |
| 6 | Jacksonville | Leonard Fournette | 223.1 | 2 |
| 7 | New Orleans | Alvin Kamara | 215 | 2 |
| 8 | NY Giants | Saqon Barkley | 201.9 | 2 |
| 9 | Chicago | Jordan Howard | 190.2 | 2 |
| 10 | Minnesota | Dalvin Cook | 178.8 | 3 |
| 11 | Buffalo | LeSean McCoy | 188.2 | 3 |
| 12 | Washington | Chris Thompson | 229.4 | 3 |
| 13 | New Orleans | Mark Ingram | 214.5 | 3 |
| 14 | Atlanta | Devonta Freeman | 181.7 | 3 |
| 15 | Oakland | Doug Martin | 228.4 | 3 |
| 16 | Carolina | Christian McCaffrey | 156.7 | 3 |
| 17 | Arizona | David Johnson | 149.3 | 4 |
| 18 | San Francisco | Jerick McKinnon | 145.2 | 4 |
| 19 | Green Bay | Ty Montgomery | 186.9 | 4 |
| 20 | Miami | Kenyan Drake | 181.4 | 4 |
| 21 | Houston | Lamar Miller | 180.5 | 4 |
| 22 | Denver | Royce Freeman | 150 | 4 |
| 23 | Tennessee | Dion Lewis | 176.8 | 5 |
| 24 | Seattle | Rashaad Penny | 163.3 | 5 |
| 25 | NY Jets | Bilal Powel | 153.9 | 5 |
| 26 | New England | Sony Michel | 148.2 | 5 |
| 27 | Cincinnati | Joe Mixon | 142.4 | 5 |
| 28 | Carolina | C.J. Anderson | 153.3 | 6 |
| 29 | NY Jets | Elijah McGuire/Isaiah Crowell | 152.4 | 6 |
| 30 | New England | James White | 122.7 | 6 |
| 31 | Tampa Bay | Ronald Jones | 122.3 | 6 |
| 32 | Detroit | LaGarrette Blount/Kerryon Johnson | 122.2 | 6 |
| 33 | Philadelphia | Jay Ajayi | 121.4 | 6 |
| 34 | Cleveland | Duke Johnson Jr. | 118.3 | 6 |

| 35 | Cincinnati | Giovani Bernard | 117.8 | 6 |
|----|------------|-----------------|-------|---|
| 36 | Cleveland | Nick Chubb / Carlos Hyde | 109.4 | 6 |
| 37 | Atlanta | Tevin Coleman | 101.1 | 6 |
| 38 | Baltimore | Alex Collins | 93 | 7 |
| 39 | Indianapolis | Nyheim Hines | 90.6 | 7 |
| 40 | Chicago | Tarik Cohen | 85.8 | 7 |
| 41 | Houston | D'Onta Foreman | 77.1 | 7 |
| 42 | Indianapolis | Marlon Mack | 76.5 | 7 |
| 43 | Tennessee | Derrick Henry | 72.3 | 7 |
| 44 | Washington | Derrius Guice | 69.4 | 7 |
| 45 | Baltimore | Javorius Allen | 54.3 | 7 |
| 46 | Green Bay | Aaron Jones | 32.8 | 7 |
| 47 | Seattle | Chris Carson | 71.9 | 8 |
| 48 | Minnesota | Latavius Murray | 93.3 | 8 |
| 49 | Detroit | Theo Riddick | 69.6 | |
| 50 | Miami | Frank Gore | 55.4 | |
| 51 | Denver | Devontae Booker | 67.1 | |
| 52 | Philadelphia | Corey Clement | 98.7 | |
| 53 | Kansas City | Damien Williams | 96.7 | |
| 54 | LA Chargers | Austin Ekeler | 83.1 | |
| 55 | San Francisco | Matt Breida | 78.1 | |
| 56 | Jacksonville | T.J. Yeldon | 77.5 | |
| 57 | Arizona | Elijah Penny | 67 | |
| 58 | NY Giants | Jonathan Stewart | 64.3 | |
| 59 | Dallas | Rod Smith | 41.5 | |
| 60 | Oakland | DeAndre Washington | 41.4 | |
| 61 | Buffalo | Chris Ivory | 38.4 | |
| 62 | LA Rams | Malcolm Brown | 24.2 | |
| 63 | Tampa Bay | Peyton Barber | 23.9 | |
| 64 | Pittsburgh | Stevan Ridley | 17.1 | |

## Wide Receivers

| Non-PPR WR Rankings | | | | |
|---|---|---|---|---|
| Rank | Team | Player | Projected Points | Tier |
| 1 | Houston | DeAndre Hopkins | 229.7 | 1 |
| 2 | Pittsburgh | Antonio Brown | 212.8 | 1 |
| 3 | NY Giants | Odell Beckham | 116 | 2 |
| 4 | Cincinnati | A.J. Green | 179.7 | 2 |

| 5 | Atlanta | Julio Jones | 134.8 | 2 |
|---|---|---|---|---|
| 6 | New Orleans | Michael Thomas | 153.5 | 2 |
| 7 | Philadelphia | Alshon Jeffery | 156.5 | 2 |
| 8 | LA Chargers | Keenan Allen | 150.2 | 2 |
| 9 | Green Bay | Devante Adams | 147.5 | 2 |
| 10 | Houston | Will Fuller V | 166.1 | 3 |
| 11 | Indianapolis | T.Y. Hilton | 131.8 | 3 |
| 12 | Arizona | Larry Fitzgerald | 107.9 | 3 |
| 13 | Oakland | Amari Cooper | 108.6 | 3 |
| 14 | Tennessee | Rishard Matthews | 146.9 | 3 |
| 15 | Detroit | Mike Jones Jr | 154.1 | 3 |
| 16 | Kansas City | Tyreek Hill | 142.6 | 3 |
| 17 | Tampa Bay | Mike Evans | 136.6 | 3 |
| 18 | Minnesota | Adam Thielen | 135.7 | 3 |
| 19 | Minnesota | Stefon Diggs | 133.4 | 3 |
| 20 | Philadelphia | Nelson Agholor | 135.3 | 4 |
| 21 | Jacksonville | Marqise Lee | 135 | 4 |
| 22 | NY Jets | Robbie Anderson | 134.6 | 4 |
| 23 | Carolina | Devin Funchess | 133.6 | 4 |
| 24 | LA Rams | Brandin Cooks | 129.3 | 4 |
| 25 | Miami | Danny Amendola | 128.9 | 4 |
| 26 | Cleveland | Josh Gordon | 126.4 | 4 |
| 27 | NY Giants | Sterling Shepard | 80.5 | 5 |
| 28 | Pittsburgh | JuJu smith-Schuster | 110.4 | 5 |
| 29 | Detroit | Golden Tate | 111.2 | 5 |
| 30 | Seattle | Doug Baldwin | 125.1 | 5 |
| 31 | San Francisco | Pierre Garcon | 124.8 | 5 |
| 32 | Cleveland | Jarvis Landry | 124.5 | 5 |
| 33 | Green Bay | Randall Cobb | 103.8 | 5 |
| 34 | Denver | Demaryius Thomas | 118.1 | 5 |
| 35 | New England | Julian Edelman | 140.4 | 5 |
| 36 | Dallas | Austin Hurns | 122.8 | 5 |
| 37 | Oakland | Jordy Nelson | 94.5 | 5 |
| 38 | LA Rams | Cooper Kupp | 119.7 | 5 |
| 39 | Seattle | Tyler Lockett | 115.9 | 5 |
| 40 | Jacksonville | Keelan Cole | 112.7 | 6 |
| 41 | Cleveland | Corey Coleman | 93.3 | 6 |
| 42 | Buffalo | Kelvin Benjamin | 93.1 | 6 |
| 43 | Atlanta | Mohamed Sanu | 106.4 | 6 |
| 44 | Tennessee | Corey Davis | 103 | 6 |
| 45 | NY Jets | Quincy Enunwa | 98.5 | 6 |

| | | | | |
|---|---|---|---|---|
| 46 | Miami | Kenny Stills | 97 | 6 |
| 47 | San Francisco | Marquise Goodwin | 96.8 | 6 |
| 48 | Miami | DeVante Parker | 95.7 | 6 |
| 49 | Kansas City | Sammy Watkins | 93.3 | 6 |
| 50 | Tampa Bay | DeSean Jackson | 91.5 | 6 |
| 51 | Cincinnati | Brandon LaFell | 90.5 | 6 |
| 52 | Indianapolis | Ryan Grant | 86 | 7 |
| 53 | New Orleans | Tedd Ginn Jr | 77.2 | 7 |
| 54 | Oakland | Martavis Bryant | 64.8 | 7 |
| 55 | Tennessee | Tajae' Sharpe | 55.9 | 7 |
| 56 | Atlanta | Calvin Ridley | 53.6 | 7 |
| 57 | LA Rams | Robert Woods | 47.9 | 7 |
| 58 | Baltimore | Michael Crabtree | 30.4 | 7 |
| 59 | Green Bay | Geronimo Allison / J'Mon Moore | 174.8 | 7 |
| 60 | Carolina | D.J. Moore | 88 | 8 |
| 61 | Denver | Emmanuel Sanders | 79.3 | 8 |
| 62 | New England | Jordan Matthews | 77.3 | 8 |
| 63 | Washington | Jamison Crowder | 67.2 | 8 |
| 64 | Seattle | Brandon Marshall | 73.2 | 8 |
| 65 | Chicago | Allen Robinson | 65.9 | 8 |
| 66 | Washington | Paul Richardson Jr. | 87.3 | 8 |
| 67 | Arizona | J.J. Nelson | 82.2 | |
| 68 | LA Chargers | Tyrell Williams | 81.9 | |
| 69 | Dallas | Terrance Williams | 73.5 | |
| 70 | Philadelphia | Mike Wallace | 70.3 | |
| 71 | Arizona | Christian Kirk | 70.1 | |
| 72 | New England | Chris Hogan | 69 | |
| 73 | Buffalo | Jeremy Kerley | 68.2 | |
| 74 | Baltimore | John Brown | 68.1 | |
| 75 | Denver | Courtland Sutton | 67.5 | |
| 76 | Jacksonville | Donte Moncrief | 65.1 | |
| 77 | Chicago | Kevin White | 64.8 | |
| 78 | Indianapolis | Chester Rogers | 62.9 | |
| 79 | Detroit | TJ Jones | 62 | |
| 80 | Buffalo | Zay Jones | 60.4 | |
| 81 | Pittsburgh | James Washington | 60.2 | |
| 82 | NY Giants | Cody Latimer | 59.4 | |
| 83 | LA Chargers | Travis Benjamin | 58.6 | |
| 84 | New Orleans | Brandon Coleman | 58.2 | |
| 85 | Chicago | Dontrelle Inman | 52.8 | |

| 86 | Tampa Bay | Adam Humphries | 52.3 | |
| 87 | Dallas | Tavon Austin | 45.8 | |
| 88 | Kansas City | Demarcus Robinson | 42.5 | |
| 89 | Washington | Josh Doctson | 40 | |
| 90 | NY Jets | Jermaine Kerase | 37.9 | |
| 91 | Minnesota | Laquon Treadwell | 35.2 | |
| 92 | Cincinnati | Tyler Boyd | 34.1 | |
| 93 | Baltimore | Willie Snead IV | 30.4 | |
| 94 | Carolina | Torrey Smith | 29.5 | |
| 95 | Houston | Bruce Ellington | 28.7 | |
| 96 | San Francisco | Trent Taylor | 22.9 | |

## Tight Ends

| Non-PPR TE Rankings | | | | |
|---|---|---|---|---|
| **Rank** | **Team** | **Player** | **Projected Points** | **Tier** |
| 1 | New England | Rob Gronkowski | 167.5 | 3 |
| 2 | Philadelphia | Zach Ertz | 154 | 3 |
| 3 | Kansas City | Travis Kelce | 124.9 | 3 |
| 4 | Tennessee | Delanie Walker | 124.4 | 4 |
| 5 | Carolina | Greg Olsen | 127.5 | 5 |
| 6 | Washington | Jordan Reed | 56.1 | 5 |
| 7 | Cincinnati | Tyler Eiffert | 137.9 | 5 |
| 8 | Indianapolis | Jack Doyle | 92.8 | 5 |
| 27 | Green Bay | Jimmy Graham | 53.3 | 5 |
| 9 | Chicago | Trey Burton | 108 | 5 |
| 10 | Buffalo | Charles Clay | 106.7 | 6 |
| 11 | Minnesota | Kyle Rudolph | 89.1 | 6 |
| 12 | LA Chargers | Virgil Green | 88.6 | 6 |
| 13 | Tampa Bay | Cameron Brate | 97 | 7 |
| 14 | NY Giants | Evan Engram | 84.3 | 7 |
| 15 | Oakland | Jared Cook | 79.7 | 7 |
| 16 | San Francisco | George Kittle | 67 | 7 |
| 20 | Baltimore | Hayden Hurst | 68.1 | 8 |
| 17 | Dallas | Geoff Swaim | 86.5 | |
| 18 | Detroit | Levine Toilolo | 76.1 | |
| 19 | Seattle | Ed Dickson | 70.1 | |
| 21 | Atlanta | Austin Hooper | 64.6 | |
| 22 | NY Jets | Eric Tomlinson | 60.2 | |

| 23 | Cleveland | David Njoku | 60 | |
|----|-----------|-------------|------|--|
| 24 | Pittsburgh | Jesse James | 57.6 | |
| 25 | Jacksonville | Austin Sefarian-Jenkins | 55.2 | |
| 26 | Houston | Ryan Griffen | 54.7 | |
| 28 | Miami | Mike Gescki | 46 | |
| 29 | LA Rams | Tyler Higbee | 41.7 | |
| 30 | New Orleans | Benjamin Watson | 41.1 | |
| 31 | Denver | Jeff Heuerman | 26.5 | |
| 32 | Arizona | Jermaine Gresham | 25.5 | |

# Kickers

## Kicker Rankings

| Rank | Team | Player | Tier |
|---|---|---|---|
| 1 | LA Rams | Greg Zuerlein | 7 |
| 2 | Kansas City | Harrison Butker | 7 |
| 3 | New England | Stephen Gostkowski | 7 |
| 4 | Philadelphia | Jake Elliott | 7 |
| 5 | New Orleans | Will Lutz | 8 |
| 6 | San Francisco | Robbie Gould | 8 |
| 7 | Baltimore | Justin Tucker | 8 |
| 8 | Pittsburgh | Chris Boswell | 8 |
| 9 | Detroit | Matt Prater | 8 |
| 10 | Minnesota | Kai Forbath | 8 |
| 11 | Atlanta | Matt Bryant | 8 |
| 12 | Arizona | Phil Dawson | 8 |
| 13 | Tennessee | Ryan Succop | |
| 14 | Jacksonville | Josh Lambo | |
| 15 | Carolina | Graham Gano | |
| 16 | Tampa Bay | Chandler Catanzaro | |
| 17 | LA Chargers | Caleb Sturgis | |
| 18 | Seattle | Sebastian Janikowski | |
| 19 | Dallas | Dan Bailey | |
| 20 | Indianapolis | Adam Vinatieri | |
| 21 | Denver | Brandon McManus | |
| 22 | Washington | Dustin Hopkins | |
| 23 | Buffalo | Steven Hauschka | |
| 24 | NY Jets | Cairo Santos | |
| 25 | Houston | Ka'imi Fairbairn | |
| 26 | NY Giants | Aldrick Rosas | |
| 27 | Oakland | Giorgio Tavecchio | |
| 28 | Miami | Jason Sanders | |
| 29 | Chicago | Cody Parkey | |
| 30 | Green Bay | Mason Crosby | |
| 31 | Cincinnati | Randy Bullock | |
| 32 | Cleveland | Zane Gonzalez | |

# Defense / Special Teams

| Rank | Team | Player | Tier |
|------|------|--------|------|
| | **DST Rankings** | | |
| 1 | Jacksonville | Jaguars | 7 |
| 2 | Baltimore | Ravens | 7 |
| 3 | LA Rams | Rams | 7 |
| 4 | Pittsburgh | Steelers | 7 |
| 5 | LA Chargers | Chargers | 8 |
| 6 | Seattle | Seahawks | 8 |
| 7 | Chicago | Bears | 8 |
| 8 | Philadelphia | Eagles | 8 |
| 9 | Carolina | Panthers | 8 |
| 10 | Tennessee | Titans | |
| 11 | Washington | Redskins | |
| 12 | Detroit | Lions | |
| 13 | New Orleans | Saints | |
| 14 | Arizona | Cardinals | |
| 15 | Dallas | Cowboys | |
| 16 | Minnesota | Vikings | |
| 17 | Cincinnati | Bengals | |
| 18 | Denver | Broncos | |
| 19 | Atlanta | Falcons | |
| 20 | Green Bay | Packers | |
| 21 | New England | Patriots | |
| 22 | Buffalo | Bills | |
| 23 | Kansas City | Chiefs | |
| 24 | Cleveland | Browns | |
| 25 | San Francisco | 49ers | |
| 26 | NY Jets | Jets | |
| 27 | Miami | Dolphins | |
| 28 | Houston | Texans | |
| 29 | Oakland | Raiders | |
| 30 | NY Giants | Giants | |
| 31 | Indianapolis | Colts | |
| 32 | Tampa Bay | Buccaneers | |

# RANKINGS
## ROOKIES

## Rookie Rankings

| Rank | Pos | Team | Player | Player |
|------|-----|------|--------|--------|
| 1 | RB | NY Giants | Saquon Barkley | I anticipate heavy usage from Pat Shurmur |
| 2 | RB | Seattle | Rashaad Penny | He'll have opportunities, but where's the blocking? |
| 3 | RB | Washington | Derrius Guice | He should immeidately dominate first and second down carries |
| 4 | RB | Denver | Royce Freeman | I like his chances to lead the backfield in carries this season |
| 5 | RB | Tampa Bay | Ronald Jones | I hate him in Koetter's system, but I think Koetter gets fired this season |
| 6 | RB | New England | Sony Michel | He's had a few balls drop from Brady.  If he can't catch, he'll be a situational player |
| 7 | RB | Cleveland | Nick Chubb / Carlos Hyde | He will give too many touches away to Duke Johnson Jr |
| 8 | WR | Carolina | D.J. Moore | I haven't been high on Panthers receivers, but Norv Turner's scheme should help |
| 9 | WR | Atlanta | Calvin Ridley | He's talented, but there are too many people in front of him for now |
| 10 | RB | Indianapolis | Nyheim Hines | It'll take a while, but he could beat Mack out for carries |
| 11 | WR | Pittsburgh | James Washington | He should fill Bryant's void |
| 12 | TE | Baltimore | Hayden Hurst | The Ravens have been looking for an answer at TE for a few years |
| 13 | WR | Green Bay | J'Mon Moore | If he wins the 3rd WR job, he will be in line for a lot of catches and TDs |
| 14 | WR | Denver | Courtland Sutton | Has D. Thomas and E. Sanders ahead of him this season |
| 15 | WR | New Orleans | Tre'Quan Smith | Produced well in college, but he's a young player on a talented offense |
| 16 | WR | Arizona | Christian Kirk | I'm not worried about his talent so much as who is throwing for Arz |

| | | | | |
|---|---|---|---|---|
| 17 | RB | Detroit | Kerryon Johnson | He'll eventually start, but Blount, Reddick and Abdullah could make it hard |
| 18 | WR | Chicago | Anthony Miller | Heavy production in college, but Trubiski is still young. Lots of potential. |
| 19 | WR | Dallas | Michael Gallup | Dez took the lion's share of targets with him. Plenty of opportunity. |
| 20 | QB | NY Jets | Sam Darnold | I think he'll be the first rookie to start a game and the Jets offense is underrated |
| 21 | QB | Cleveland | Baker Mayfield | He can scramble, is accurate and has a great team of pass catchers |
| 22 | TE | Miami | Mike Gesicki | Talented, but the Dolphins haven't used the TE position much |
| 23 | QB | Arizona | Josh Rosen | My favorite QB of the draft, but don't love that he went to a defensive HC |
| 24 | WR | San Francisco | Dante Pettis | If he can crack the lineup, Shanahan's scheme will give him points |
| 25 | TE | Philadelphia | Dallas Goedert | Very talented, but Zach Ertz will get the bulk of the targets for years to come |
| 26 | RB | Atlanta | Ito Smith | I don't think Tevin Coleman will sign his next contract with Atlanta, so Smith could eventually score |
| 27 | WR | Jacksonville | D.J. Chark | The Jags aren't afraid to play a talented rookie early |
| 28 | QB | Baltimore | Lamar Jackson | He won't play in 2018, but will score points when he gets into the lineup |
| 29 | RB | Dallas | Bo Scarbrough | The Cowboys will eventually need a RB to spell Elliott |
| 30 | WR | Green Bay | Marquez Valdes-Scantling | Any GB receiver who plays will score. Is he good enough? Time will tell. |
| 31 | RB | Indianapolis | Jordan Wilkins | Can he beat Hines for carries? If so, he will shoot up my board |

ADDITIONAL
INFORMATION

# Undervalued Players and Sleepers

| Team | Type | Pos | Player |
|------|------|-----|--------|
| Miami | Undervalued | WR | Danny Amendola |
| New England | Undervalued | RB | James White |
| NY Jets | Undervalued | WR | Robbie Anderson |
| Houston | Undervalued | WR | Will Fuller |
| Tennessee | Undervalued | WR | Rishard Matthews |
| Oakland | Undervalued | RB | Doug Martin / Marshawn Lynch |
| Buffalo | Sleeper | TE | Charles Clay |
| New England | Sleeper | WR | Jordan Matthews |
| NY Jets | Sleeper | RB | Elijah McGuire |
| Houston | Sleeper | RB | D'Onta Foreman |
| Dallas | Sleeper | WR | Tavon Austin |
| Washington | Sleeper | WR | Paul Richardson |
| Philadelphia | Sleeper | TE | Trey Burton |
| Atlanta | Sleeper | WR | Calvin Ridley |
| Carolina | Sleeper | WR | D.J. Moore |
| New Orleans | Sleeper | TE | Ben Watson |
| LA Rams | Sleeper | WR | Cooper Kupp |
| San Francisco | Sleeper | TE | George Kittle |
| Seattle | Sleeper | WR | Tyler Lockett |
| Buffalo | Deep Sleeper | WR | Zay Jones |
| Baltimore | Deep Sleeper | WR | John Brown |
| Cleveland | Deep Sleeper | TE | David Njoku |
| Pittsburgh | Deep Sleeper | WR | James Washington |
| Indianapolis | Deep Sleeper | WR | Ryant Grant |
| Jacksonville | Deep Sleeper | WR | Keelan Cole |
| Dallas | Deep Sleeper | WR | Michael Gallup |
| Detroit | Deep Sleeper | WR | Kenny Golladay |
| Detroit | Deep Sleeper | WR | T.J. Jones |
| Green Bay | Deep Sleeper | WR | Geronimo Allison |
| Atlanta | Deep Sleeper | TE | Austin Hooper |
| Arizona | Deep Sleeper | WR | J.J. Nelson |
| Arizona | Deep Sleeper | WR | Christian Kirk |
| Seattle | Deep Sleeper | WR | Jaron Brown |
| NY Jets | Hibernator | WR | Quincy Enunwa |

| Baltimore | Hibernator | WR | Chris Moore |
|---|---|---|---|
| Cincinnati | Hibernator | WR | John Ross |
| Indianapolis | Hibernator | RB | Nyheim Hines |
| Jacksonville | Hibernator | WR | D.J. Clark |
| Tennessee | Hibernator | WR | Tajae Sharpe |
| Denver | Hibernator | TE | Jeff Heuerman |
| Denver | Hibernator | WR | Courtland Sutton |
| Dallas | Hibernator | TE | Geoff Swaim |
| Chicago | Hibernator | WR | Kevin White |
| Green Bay | Hibernator | RB | Jamaal Williams |
| Green Bay | Hibernator | WR | J'mon Moore |
| Carolina | Hibernator | RB/WR | Curtis Samuel |
| New Orleans | Hibernator | WR | Tre-quan Smith |
| San Francisco | Hibernator | WR | Joe Williams |

# Overall Draft Tracker

| Round | Team 1 | Team 2 | Team 3 | Team 4 | Team 5 | Team 6 | Team 7 | Team 8 | Team 9 | Team 10 | Team 11 | Team 12 |
|---|---|---|---|---|---|---|---|---|---|---|---|---|
| 1 | 1 | 2 | 3 | 4 | 5 | 6 | 7 | 8 | 9 | 10 | 11 | 12 |
| 2 | 24 | 23 | 22 | 21 | 20 | 19 | 18 | 17 | 16 | 15 | 14 | 13 |
| 3 | 25 | 26 | 27 | 28 | 29 | 30 | 31 | 32 | 33 | 34 | 35 | 36 |
| 4 | 48 | 47 | 46 | 45 | 44 | 43 | 42 | 41 | 40 | 39 | 38 | 37 |
| 5 | 49 | 50 | 51 | 52 | 53 | 54 | 55 | 56 | 57 | 58 | 59 | 60 |
| 6 | 72 | 71 | 70 | 69 | 68 | 67 | 66 | 65 | 64 | 63 | 62 | 61 |
| 7 | 73 | 74 | 75 | 76 | 77 | 78 | 79 | 80 | 81 | 82 | 83 | 84 |
| 8 | 96 | 95 | 94 | 93 | 92 | 91 | 90 | 89 | 88 | 87 | 86 | 85 |
| 9 | 97 | 98 | 99 | 100 | 101 | 102 | 103 | 104 | 105 | 106 | 107 | 108 |
| 10 | 120 | 119 | 118 | 117 | 116 | 115 | 114 | 113 | 112 | 111 | 110 | 109 |
| 11 | 121 | 122 | 123 | 124 | 125 | 126 | 127 | 128 | 129 | 130 | 131 | 132 |
| 12 | 144 | 143 | 142 | 141 | 140 | 139 | 138 | 137 | 136 | 135 | 134 | 133 |
| 13 | 145 | 146 | 147 | 148 | 149 | 150 | 151 | 152 | 153 | 154 | 155 | 156 |
| 14 | 168 | 167 | 166 | 165 | 164 | 163 | 162 | 161 | 160 | 159 | 158 | 157 |
| 15 | 169 | 170 | 171 | 172 | 173 | 174 | 175 | 176 | 177 | 178 | 179 | 180 |
| 16 | 192 | 191 | 190 | 189 | 188 | 187 | 186 | 185 | 184 | 183 | 182 | 181 |
| 17 | 193 | 194 | 195 | 196 | 197 | 198 | 199 | 200 | 201 | 202 | 203 | 204 |
| 18 | 216 | 215 | 214 | 213 | 212 | 211 | 210 | 209 | 208 | 207 | 206 | 205 |
| 19 | 217 | 218 | 219 | 220 | 221 | 222 | 223 | 224 | 225 | 226 | 227 | 228 |
| 20 | 240 | 239 | 238 | 237 | 236 | 235 | 234 | 233 | 232 | 231 | 230 | 229 |

# Team Draft Worksheets

| Team: | | | | | | | |
|---|---|---|---|---|---|---|---|
| QB1 | RB1 | | WR1 | | TE1 | K | |
| QB2 | RB2 | | WR2 | | TE2 | | DST |
| | RB3 | | WR3 | | | | |
| | RB4 | | WR4 | | | | |

# Team:

| | QB1 | QB2 | | | RB1 | RB2 | RB3 | RB4 | | | WR1 | WR2 | WR3 | WR4 | | | TE1 | TE2 | | | K | | | DST | |
|---|---|---|---|---|---|---|---|---|---|---|---|---|---|---|---|---|---|---|---|---|---|---|---|---|---|
| | | | | | | | | | | | | | | | | | | | | | | | | | |

# Team:

| | | | | | | | | |
|---|---|---|---|---|---|---|---|---|
| QB1 | RB1 | | WR1 | | TE1 | | K | | DST | |
| QB2 | RB2 | | WR2 | | TE2 | | | |
| | RB3 | | WR3 | | | | |
| | RB4 | | WR4 | | | | |
| | | | | | | | |
| | | | | | | | |

# Team:

| | QB1 | RB1 | WR1 | TE1 | K | DST |
|---|---|---|---|---|---|---|
| | QB2 | RB2 | WR2 | TE2 | | |
| | | RB3 | WR3 | | | |
| | | RB4 | WR4 | | | |
| | | | | | | |
| | | | | | | |

# Team:

| | | | | | | | | |
|---|---|---|---|---|---|---|---|---|
| QB1 | RB1 | WR1 | TE1 | K | | DST | | |
| QB2 | RB2 | WR2 | TE2 | | | | | |
| | RB3 | WR3 | | | | | | |
| | RB4 | WR4 | | | | | | |
| | | | | | | | | |

# Team:

| QB1 | RB1 | WR1 | TE1 | K | DST |
|-----|-----|-----|-----|---|-----|
| QB2 | RB2 | WR2 | TE2 | | |
| | RB3 | WR3 | | | |
| | RB4 | WR4 | | | |

# Team:

| | | | | | | | | | | |
|---|---|---|---|---|---|---|---|---|---|---|
| QB1 | RB1 | WR1 | TE1 | | K | | | DST | | |
| QB2 | RB2 | WR2 | TE2 | | | | | | | |
| | RB3 | WR3 | | | | | | | | |
| | RB4 | WR4 | | | | | | | | |
| | | | | | | | | | | |
| | | | | | | | | | | |

# Team:

| QB1 | RB1 | WR1 | TE1 | K | DST |
| --- | --- | --- | --- | --- | --- |
| QB2 | RB2 | WR2 | TE2 | | |
| | RB3 | WR3 | | | |
| | RB4 | WR4 | | | |

# Team:

| QB1 | RB1 | WR1 | | TE1 | | K | | DST | |
|-----|-----|-----|---|-----|---|---|---|-----|---|
| QB2 | RB2 | WR2 | | TE2 | | | | | |
| | RB3 | WR3 | | | | | | | |
| | RB4 | WR4 | | | | | | | |
| | | | | | | | | | |
| | | | | | | | | | |

# Team:

| | | | | | | | | | |
|---|---|---|---|---|---|---|---|---|---|
| QB1 | RB1 | WR1 | | TE1 | | K | | DST | |
| QB2 | RB2 | WR2 | | TE2 | | | | | |
| | RB3 | WR3 | | | | | | | |
| | RB4 | WR4 | | | | | | | |
| | | | | | | | | | |

# Team:

| | QB1 | RB1 | WR1 | | TE1 | | K | | DST | |
|---|---|---|---|---|---|---|---|---|---|---|
| | QB2 | RB2 | WR2 | | TE2 | | | | | |
| | | RB3 | WR3 | | | | | | | |
| | | RB4 | WR4 | | | | | | | |
| | | | | | | | | | | |

# Team:

| | | | | | | | | | | |
|---|---|---|---|---|---|---|---|---|---|---|
| QB1 | RB1 | WR1 | | TE1 | | K | | DST | | |
| QB2 | RB2 | WR2 | | TE2 | | | | | | |
| | RB3 | WR3 | | | | | | | | |
| | RB4 | WR4 | | | | | | | | |
| | | | | | | | | | | |

# Appendix 1: Offensive Opportunity Ranking - PPR

| Team | QB | RB1 | RB2 | WR1 | WR2 | WR3 | TE1 |
|------|----|----|----|----|----|----|----|
| Buffalo | 23 | 6 | 26 | 32 | 29 | 24 | 16 |
| Miami | 25 | 15 | 13 | 8 | 7 | 2 | 23 |
| New England | 22 | 28 | 9 | 16 | 6 | 23 | 17 |
| NY Jets | 6 | 20 | 10 | 19 | 15 | 3 | 3 |
| Baltimore | 32 | 21 | 6 | 29 | 25 | 25 | 15 |
| Cincinnati | 29 | 17 | 14 | 10 | 21 | 29 | 21 |
| Cleveland | 18 | 27 | 4 | 30 | 30 | 28 | 24 |
| Pittsburgh | 9 | 2 | 32 | 1 | 4 | 9 | 22 |
| Houston | 7 | 14 | 24 | 2 | 12 | 22 | 26 |
| Indianapolis | 30 | 22 | 16 | 25 | 31 | 31 | 5 |
| Jacksonville | 15 | 7 | 2 | 20 | 10 | 6 | 30 |
| Tennessee | 28 | 16 | 15 | 28 | 24 | 12 | 4 |
| Denver | 26 | 18 | 17 | 17 | 17 | 10 | 32 |
| Kansas City | 3 | 3 | 27 | 5 | 27 | 26 | 1 |
| LA Chargers | 14 | 5 | 19 | 3 | 22 | 4 | 10 |
| Oakland | 21 | 19 | 25 | 22 | 5 | 15 | 13 |
| Dallas | 13 | 8 | 23 | 21 | 26 | 20 | 9 |
| Ny Giants | 27 | 26 | 18 | 15 | 19 | 13 | 7 |
| Philadelphia | 2 | 25 | 20 | 18 | 3 | 11 | 2 |
| Washington | 4 | 30 | 5 | 27 | 20 | 8 | 11 |
| Chicago | 31 | 13 | 11 | 31 | 32 | 16 | 25 |
| Detroit | 11 | 23 | 12 | 14 | 1 | 14 | 12 |
| Green Bay | 12 | 10 | 30 | 11 | 8 | 1 | 27 |
| Minnesota | 16 | 9 | 8 | 9 | 2 | 32 | 8 |
| Atlanta | 19 | 12 | 7 | 7 | 9 | 19 | 19 |
| Carolina | 5 | 32 | 3 | 23 | 14 | 30 | 20 |
| New Orleans | 17 | 4 | 1 | 6 | 18 | 21 | 31 |
| Tampa Bay | 8 | 29 | 28 | 12 | 16 | 7 | 14 |
| Arizona | 24 | 24 | 22 | 4 | 23 | 18 | 28 |
| LA Rams | 10 | 1 | 31 | 13 | 10 | 17 | 29 |
| San Francisco | 20 | 11 | 21 | 24 | 28 | 27 | 18 |
| Seattle | 1 | 31 | 29 | 26 | 13 | 5 | 6 |

# Appendix 2: Offensive Opportunity Ranking – Non-PPR

| Team | QB | RB1 | RB2 | WR1 | WR2 | WR3 | TE1 |
|------|-----|-----|-----|-----|-----|-----|-----|
| Buffalo | 23 | 9 | 24 | 32 | 26 | 23 | 20 |
| Miami | 25 | 16 | 25 | 14 | 7 | 3 | 23 |
| New England | 6 | 17 | 10 | 12 | 19 | 2 | 1 |
| NY Jets | 22 | 26 | 9 | 13 | 8 | 25 | 22 |
| Baltimore | 32 | 19 | 7 | 30 | 28 | 27 | 15 |
| Cincinnati | 29 | 23 | 13 | 6 | 23 | 30 | 16 |
| Cleveland | 18 | 31 | 6 | 29 | 32 | 29 | 21 |
| Pittsburgh | 9 | 2 | 32 | 2 | 4 | 6 | 24 |
| Houston | 7 | 14 | 20 | 1 | 9 | 22 | 26 |
| Indianapolis | 30 | 21 | 17 | 19 | 30 | 31 | 8 |
| Jacksonville | 15 | 6 | 1 | 18 | 11 | 7 | 27 |
| Tennessee | 28 | 20 | 11 | 26 | 27 | 15 | 5 |
| Denver | 26 | 18 | 18 | 22 | 17 | 4 | 32 |
| Kansas City | 3 | 3 | 27 | 3 | 24 | 26 | 2 |
| LA Chargers | 14 | 5 | 16 | 4 | 18 | 9 | 9 |
| Oakland | 21 | 15 | 26 | 21 | 6 | 1/ | 1e |
| Dallas | 13 | 4 | 19 | 20 | 29 | 21 | 10 |
| NY Giants | 27 | 30 | 22 | 24 | 22 | 13 | 7 |
| Philadelphia | 2 | 22 | 15 | 11 | 3 | 10 | 3 |
| Washington | 4 | 29 | 4 | 27 | 15 | 8 | 14 |
| Chicago | 31 | 12 | 12 | 31 | 31 | 11 | 25 |
| Detroit | 11 | 24 | 14 | 23 | 1 | 14 | 11 |
| Green Bay | 12 | 10 | 28 | 7 | 13 | 1 | 31 |
| Minnesota | 16 | 8 | 8 | 10 | 2 | 32 | 6 |
| Atlanta | 19 | 11 | 5 | 5 | 12 | 20 | 19 |
| Carolina | 5 | 28 | 3 | 17 | 16 | 28 | 17 |
| New Orleans | 17 | 7 | 2 | 9 | 20 | 16 | 30 |
| Tampa Bay | 8 | 27 | 30 | 15 | 14 | 19 | 12 |
| Arizona | 24 | 25 | 23 | 8 | 21 | 12 | 29 |
| LA Rams | 10 | 1 | 31 | 16 | 5 | 18 | 28 |
| San Francisco | 20 | 13 | 21 | 25 | 25 | 24 | 18 |
| Seattle | 1 | 32 | 29 | 28 | 10 | 5 | 4 |

# Appendix 3: Defensive Rankings vs Position - PPR

| Team | QB | RB1 | RB2 | WR1 | WR2 | WR3 | TE1 |
|------|-----|-----|-----|-----|-----|-----|-----|
| Buffalo | 3 | 17 | 29 | 24 | 10 | 2 | 18 |
| Miami | 19 | 20 | 22 | 14 | 7 | 5 | 29 |
| New England | 29 | 12 | 15 | 27 | 21 | 9 | 26 |
| NY Jets | 30 | 28 | 6 | 21 | 27 | 32 | 15 |
| Baltimore | 2 | 26 | 7 | 19 | 9 | 6 | 24 |
| Cincinnati | 11 | 30 | 27 | 6 | 6 | 20 | 16 |
| Cleveland | 25 | 14 | 11 | 26 | 1 | 8 | 32 |
| Pittsburgh | 6 | 23 | 8 | 15 | 12 | 3 | 11 |
| Houston | 32 | 8 | 4 | 31 | 8 | 25 | 21 |
| Indianapolis | 23 | 15 | 17 | 7 | 22 | 13 | 6 |
| Jacksonville | 4 | 3 | 24 | 5 | 3 | 1 | 2 |
| Tennessee | 27 | 27 | 32 | 29 | 26 | 15 | 25 |
| Denver | 16 | 4 | 5 | 2 | 5 | 10 | 30 |
| Kansas City | 20 | 7 | 20 | 22 | 32 | 23 | 3 |
| LA Chargers | 5 | 22 | 2 | 11 | 4 | 14 | 14 |
| Oakland | 9 | 19 | 26 | 3 | 17 | 18 | 28 |
| Dallas | 24 | 9 | 19 | 30 | 19 | 26 | 23 |
| Ny Giants | 31 | 18 | 9 | 28 | 14 | 21 | 31 |
| Philadelphia | 18 | 2 | 21 | 20 | 24 | 30 | 13 |
| Washington | 15 | 25 | 10 | 9 | 15 | 11 | 27 |
| Chicago | 7 | 10 | 16 | 13 | 20 | 27 | 22 |
| Detroit | 12 | 24 | 28 | 8 | 28 | 24 | 19 |
| Green Bay | 26 | 31 | 18 | 25 | 31 | 16 | 7 |
| Minnesota | 1 | 5 | 3 | 1 | 16 | 28 | 12 |
| Atlanta | 17 | 6 | 23 | 23 | 2 | 6 | 20 |
| Carolina | 14 | 1 | 13 | 18 | 25 | 19 | 4 |
| New Orleans | 13 | 13 | 25 | 10 | 29 | 4 | 1 |
| Tampa Bay | 22 | 29 | 31 | 32 | 30 | 29 | 9 |
| LA Rams | 8 | 11 | 30 | 16 | 11 | 22 | 8 |
| San Francisco | 28 | 21 | 14 | 17 | 18 | 12 | 10 |
| Seattle | 10 | 32 | 1 | 12 | 23 | 17 | 5 |

# Appendix 4: Defensive Rankings vs Position – Non-PPR

| Team | QB | RB1 | RB2 | WR1 | WR2 | WR3 | TE1 |
|------|----|----|----|----|----|----|----|
| Buffalo | 3 | 20 | 29 | 21 | 5 | 2 | 17 |
| Miami | 19 | 18 | 21 | 17 | 7 | 11 | 28 |
| New England | 30 | 29 | 4 | 20 | 26 | 32 | 10 |
| NY Jets | 29 | 13 | 23 | 29 | 16 | 10 | 29 |
| Baltimore | 2 | 27 | 8 | 16 | 8 | 6 | 22 |
| Cincinnati | 11 | 25 | 25 | 5 | 10 | 23 | 19 |
| Cleveland | 25 | 11 | 18 | 27 | 2 | 7 | 31 |
| Pittsburgh | 6 | 23 | 9 | 19 | 12 | 3 | 12 |
| Houston | 32 | 8 | 6 | 32 | 11 | 26 | 21 |
| Indianapolis | 23 | 14 | 27 | 9 | 22 | 21 | 9 |
| Jacksonville | 4 | 3 | 26 | 7 | 4 | 1 | 2 |
| Tennessee | 27 | 22 | 32 | 26 | 29 | 18 | 24 |
| Denver | 16 | 4 | 5 | 2 | 9 | 16 | 30 |
| Kansas City | 20 | 12 | 24 | 23 | 32 | 19 | 6 |
| LA Chargers | 5 | 28 | 3 | 11 | 3 | 9 | 15 |
| Oakland | 9 | 17 | 12 | 4 | 14 | 12 | 26 |
| Dallas | 24 | 7 | 14 | 28 | 21 | 28 | 23 |
| Ny Giants | 31 | 21 | 15 | 31 | 17 | 15 | 32 |
| Philadelphia | 18 | 2 | 13 | 18 | 25 | 31 | 7 |
| Washington | 15 | 31 | 10 | 10 | 18 | 4 | 27 |
| Chicago | 7 | 9 | 19 | 12 | 20 | 27 | 20 |
| Detroit | 12 | 19 | 28 | 3 | 23 | 24 | 25 |
| Green Bay | 26 | 26 | 21 | 25 | 31 | 22 | 5 |
| Minnesota | 1 | 6 | 2 | 1 | 15 | 25 | 8 |
| Atlanta | 17 | 5 | 17 | 24 | 1 | 8 | 13 |
| Carolina | 14 | 1 | 16 | 22 | 24 | 20 | 11 |
| New Orleans | 13 | 15 | 20 | 8 | 30 | 5 | 1 |
| Tampa Bay | 22 | 32 | 31 | 30 | 28 | 30 | 4 |
| LA Rams | 8 | 16 | 30 | 15 | 6 | 17 | 14 |
| San Francisco | 28 | 24 | 11 | 14 | 19 | 14 | 18 |
| Seattle | 10 | 30 | 1 | 13 | 27 | 13 | 3 |

Made in the USA
Middletown, DE
10 July 2018